Forever, Erma

*Best-Loved Writing from
America's Favorite Humorist*

Erma Bombeck

MJF BOOKS
NEW YORK

Published by MJF Books
Fine Communications
Two Lincoln Square
60 West 66th Street
New York, NY 10023

Forever, Erma
Library of Congress Catalog Card Number 99-76036
ISBN 1-56731-365-5

Acknowledgments: The publisher gratefully acknowledges the generous permission of the
following individuals to reprint their words from personal letters or memorials: Sister Agnes
Immaculata S.N.D.N., the Most Reverend Thomas J. O'Brien. Marla Adelman, Robert A.
Kelly, Betty Cohen, Lynn Colwell, Phil Donahue, Helen Gurley Brown, Pat McMahon,
Tom Cecil, Marilyn Potts, Aaron Priest, Father Tom Walsh, and Bil Keane.

All colums dated from January 1965 through March 1970 © copyright Newsday, Inc.
Reprinted with permission from Newsday. All rights reserved. **p.248** BENSON © 1996,
United Feature Syndicate. Reprinted by Permission. **p.249** Art Buchwald column, *The
Washington Post*, April 23, 1996 © 1996 Art Buchwald. Reprinted with permission. **p.252**
Liz Carpenter column, *Austin American-Statesman*, April 23, 1996 © 1996 Liz Carpenter.
Reprinted with permission. **p.254** From "You Could Save a Life," *The Catholic Sun*,
editorial, May 2, 1996 © 1996. Reprinted with permission. **p.255** Kevin Cuneo column, *The
Erie (PA) Times*, April 25, 1996 © 1996 The Erie Pa. Times. Reprinted with permission. **p.
258** Pat Murphy column, Tribune (AZ) Newspapers, April 24, 1996 © 1996 Tribune
Newspapers. Reprinted with permission. **p.259** Ellen Goodman column, *The Boston Globe,·*
April 25, 1996 © 1996 Washington Post Writers Group. Reprinted with permission. **p.264**
D.L. Stewart column, *Dayton Daily News*, April 25, 1996 © Dayton Daily News. Reprinted
with permission. **p.265** Mary McCarty column, *Dayton Daily News*, April 25, 1996 ©
Dayton Daily News. Reprinted with permission. **p.267** John Sherffius cartoon, *Ventura
County Star*, April 24, 1996 © by Sherffius. Reprinted with permission. **p.270** Mike Ritter
cartoon, Tribune (AZ) Newspapers, April 23, 1996 © 1996 Mike Ritter. Reprinted with
permission.

Manufactured in the United States of America on acid-free paper
MJF Books and the MJF colophon are trademarks of Fine Creative Media, Inc.

10   9   8   7   6   5   4   3   2   1

Contents

Hello, Young Mothers

All My Children

Home Sweet Home

Dear Old Dad

Food for Thought

The Empty Nest

Special People

Wish You Were Here (Instead of Me)

The Holidays

The Gang's All Here

Of Missing Socks, Promiscuous Hangers and Other Unexplained Phenomena

The Catchall Drawer

Foreword

Erma Bombeck published more than four thousand syndicated columns from 1965 until her death on April 22, 1996. From this extraordinary output of wit and compassion, the daunting task of selecting this collection fell to us. (We had both edited Erma's work.) Every person who knew what we were doing recognized the impossibility of the mission but could not forbear telling us, "Oh, you can't leave out. . . ." Since virtually any of Erma's millions of readers, if solicited for an opinion, would also suggest a column that couldn't be omitted, we hope we've included at least a few of everyone's favorites.

Let us mention that we, at least, benefited from the expert guidance of Erma's longtime secretary, Norma Born—who was able to provide us with a list of the most-requested columns—and to some extent from the guidance of Erma herself. When Erma took a vacation she always picked a group of her favorite columns to be rerun in her absence. We are happy to say that Erma had a strong vote in our selection.

Sitting in Erma's living room, reading her columns and laughing out loud, listening to Norma and Erma's husband, Bill, reminiscing, we would often remark that Erma could have gotten a column (and a few laughs) out of our efforts.

We also discovered long-forgotten gems that gave us some insight into Erma's motivation for writing her column. Back on April 4, 1969, for instance, Erma published the following column:

> A Mrs. "R.N." of Boston has raised a rather interesting question. "Mrs. Bombeck's column is devoted merely to the gripes of a suburban housewife. Her infantile self-absorption is annoying. Why doesn't she direct her writing toward a more constructive topic?"
>
> I'm surely glad you brought up that little thing, Mrs. R.N. You see, on a newspaper, reporters have areas they cover called "beats." Some men cover politics, business, crime,

medicine, government, radio and television, while women cover fashions, food, society.

I cover the utility room beat.

I used to cover obituaries, but it was a pretty thankless job. No one patted you on the back and said "Loved your lead" or sent you a Whitman's Sampler for spelling his name right. So when the utility room beat came up I grabbed it.

Oh, I had big plans. I was going to do columns on "A Mother Looks at Eric Sevareid," "Would a Bake Sale Help Russia with Her U.N. Dues?" "Racist Is a Six-Letter Word (unless it's plural, then it's seven)," "How Political Science Has Made Me a Woman." And I had a dandy line on a series that would blow the lid off a ring of primary teachers who were selling show-and-tell tapes as underground movies.

It never worked out, Mrs. R.N. Somewhere between my typewriter and the editor's office, my "constructive topics" underwent drastic surgery. "I want you to make housewives laugh," said the editor.

"I mean no disrespect, sir, but that's like making me photo editor of *Reader's Digest*."

"That's where the challenge comes in." He smiled. "Why, in a few years you'll rank right up there with those other famous humorists from Ohio, Robert A. Taft and the Wright Brothers."

I've been at the helm of "Mission Impossible" for four years now. It's a challenge. If I am consumed with my self-absorption, it is for a reason.

Long ago it became apparent there were only two people in the world I could take a crack at in print without being sued or severely criticized: Adolf Hitler and me!

Furthermore, I wouldn't trade my beat for anything else on the newspaper. Sometimes as I sift through the grim, the ugly, the shocking, I recoil here between the hot water heater and the detergent and I get my perspective.

Screaming kids, unpaid bills, green leftovers, husbands behind newspapers, basketballs in the bathroom. They're real . . . they're warm . . . they're the only bit of normalcy left in this cockeyed world, and I'm going to cling to it like life itself.

On the occasion of her twenty-fifth anniversary of writing the column, in April 1990, Erma interviewed herself. To the question, "What do you hope your column has accomplished?" she responded:

I like to imagine that after a person has read our waters are polluted, the world is in flames, streets are crime-ridden, drugs are rampant and her horoscope predicts her sign just collided with something that will reduce her to poverty, she'll read how the dryer returns only one sock to me from every two I put in and I tell my kids, "The other one went to live with Jesus," and maybe smile.

The most gratifying comment on her career, however, came at the end of a column written on March 10, 1987:

I always had a dream that when I am asked to give an accounting of my life to a higher court, it will go like this: "So, empty your pockets. What have you got left of your life? Any dreams that were unfulfilled? Any unused talent that we gave you when you were born that you still have left? Any unsaid compliments or bits of love that you haven't spread around?"

And I will answer, "I've nothing to return. I spent everything you gave me. I'm as naked as the day I was born."

Who could have spent it better?

Donna Martin   Alan McDermott

My deeds will be measured not by my youthful appearance,
but by the concern lines on my forehead,
the laugh lines around my mouth,
and the chins from seeing what can be done
for those smaller than me or who have fallen.

April 17, 1996
(from Erma Bombeck's last column)

Hello, Young Mothers

Paint Tint Caper—September 4, 1965

Once . . . just once . . . I'd like to be dressed for an emergency.

I don't mean like my grandmother used to warn: "That is not underwear to be hit by a car in." I mean just to be glued together, so you're not standing in a hospital hallway in a sweatshirt (PROPERTY OF NOTRE DAME ATHLETIC DEPT.) and a pair of bedroom slippers.

In a way, it's almost as if fate were waging a cruel war and you're in the middle of it. Not only are you (a) bleeding to death, (b) grimacing in pain, and (c) worried half out of your skull, you are also plagued with the fear that the nurses in East Wing C are passing the hat to adopt you and your family for Thanksgiving.

Take our Paint Tint Caper, for example. Our small son climbed into bed with us early one morning and smiled broadly. I'm intuitive. I'm a mother. I sensed something was wrong. His teeth were blue. He had bitten into a tube of paint tint. Now if you're visualizing some sweet, tousled-hair boy in his fire-engine pajamas, forget it. This kid looked like he was being raised by werewolves!

In addition to his blue teeth, he was wearing a pair of training pants and his father's old T-shirt, which caught him loosely around the ankles. This was obviously no time to be proud or to explain that I was a few years behind in the laundry. We rode like the wind to the emergency ward of the hospital, where the doctor checked over his blue teeth so calmly I thought there was something wrong with mine because they were white.

"What kind of paint tint?" he asked clinically.

"Sky blue," we said shakily, pointing to the color on his T-shirt.

1

"I can see that," he said irritably. "I mean, what did it contain chemically?"

My husband and I stared at each other. Normally, you understand, we don't let a can of paint into the house until we've committed the chemical contents and their percentages to memory. This one had escaped us somehow.

While they were pumping his stomach, we took a good look at ourselves. My husband was in a pair of thrown-over-the-chair denims and his pajama top. I was wearing yesterday's house dress with no belt, no hose, and a scarf around my uncombed hair. I was clutching a dish towel, my only accessory. We looked like a family of Okies who had just stepped into the corridor long enough to get a tin can of water for our boiling radiator.

There are other stories, other dilemmas, but the characters never change. We're always standing around, unwashed, uncurled, harried, penniless, memory gone, no lipstick, no hose, unmatched shoes, and using the dirtiest cloth in the house to bind our wounds.

Makes you want to plan your next accident, doesn't it?

Birds, Bees and Guppies—January 6, 1966

The sex education of a child is pretty important. None of us wants to blow it.

I have a horror of ending up like the woman in the old joke who was asked by her child where he came from and, after she explained all the technical processes in a well-chosen vocabulary, he looked at her intently and said, "I just wondered. Mike came from Hartford, Connecticut."

I figured I had the problem whipped the day my son took an interest in fish. What better way to explain the beautiful reproduction cycle of life than through the animal kingdom? We bought two pairs of guppies and a small aquarium. That was our first mistake. We should either have bought four males and a small aquarium, four females and a small aquarium or two pairs and a reservoir. I had heard of population explosions before, but this was ridiculous! The breakfast conversation ran something like this:

"What's new at Peyton Place by the Sea?" inquired my husband.

"Mrs. Guppy is e-n-c-e-i-n-t-e again," I'd spell.

"Put a little salt in the water. That'll cure anything," he mumbled.

"Daddy," said my son, "that means she's pregnant."

"Again!" choked Daddy. "Can't we organize an intramural volleyball game in there or something?"

The first aquarium begat a second aquarium with no relief in sight. "Are you getting anything out of your experiences with guppies?" I asked delicately one afternoon.

"Oh, yeah, they're neat," my son exclaimed enthusiastically.

"I mean, now that you've watched the male and the female, do you understand the processes that go into the offspring? Have you noticed the role of the mother in all this?"

"Yeah," he said, bright-eyed. "You oughta see her eat her babies."

We added a third aquarium, which was promptly filled with saltwater and three pairs of seahorses.

"Now, I want you to pay special attention to the female," I instructed. "The chances are it won't take her long to be with child, and perhaps you can even see the birth."

"The female doesn't give birth, Mom," he explained. "The male seahorse gives birth."

I felt myself smiling, perhaps anticipating a trend. "Ridiculous," I said, "females always give birth."

The male began to take on weight. I thought I saw his ankles swell. He became a mother on the twenty-third of the month.

"That's pretty interesting," said my son. "I hope I'm not a mother when I grow up, but if I am, I hope my kids are born on land."

I had blown it. I knew I would.

Good Neighbor Policy—May 16, 1966

Occasionally, I will overhear a woman boast, "Well, I don't neighbor. I'm much too busy to be running in and out, drinking coffee and making small talk with a bunch of women!"

Well, who wouldn't prefer making small talk with a bunch of men! But if I have to compromise, I'll take neighbors. If it hadn't been for neighbors, I'd have flunked my ink blot tests years ago!

When the children were quite small we moved into a new house that was rather isolated. (Rather isolated! These people had never seen a wheel until we unpacked the kids' tricycles.) After three days of explaining to a five-year-old why birds don't get electrocuted when they sit on telephone wires, watching a three-year-old eat egg yolks with his fingers and listening to a three-month-old cry around the clock, I was ready to chuck the whole mess and trade them all for a ride in a shiny new car with a vanilla salesman.

Enter my first neighbor—a woman who spoke in complete, coherent sentences, who ate with a knife and fork and who only cried at weddings. I couldn't help myself. In a dramatic gesture, I bolted the door and threw my body across it to prevent her exit. She understood.

Since then, I've had some winners and some losers. (I had one who would have borrowed my eyeballs if they had fit into a cup and survived the trip across the lawn.) If I were to make a composite of the perfect neighbor, I'd have to list a good neighbor as one who:

1. Doesn't call you up and ask you why your son wants to borrow 30 pounds of cement. Just says "No!" and calls the police.
2. Doesn't whip in and out of your utility room like Doris Day just to tell you your bleach is weak and your laundry second-rate.
3. Doesn't snicker when you unpack eight bags of groceries, then borrow coffee, butter and potatoes for your dinner.
4. Doesn't sulk in your privet hedge when you borrow ice, card tables and silverware for a party to which she hasn't been invited.
5. Doesn't feel she has the right to comment on your relatives just because she hears about them from you four hours out of every day.
6. Doesn't deny she knows you well enough to write a best-selling novel about you but not well enough to walk into your house without knocking.

Yes, sir, you show me a woman who doesn't neighbor—and I'll show you a woman who gets talked about by the ones who do!

Waking Up Momma—July 4, 1966

How I am awakened in the morning usually determines how I feel the rest of the day.

When allowed to wake up in the natural way, I find myself quite civil and reasonable to cope with the routine. When the children do the job for me, I awake surly, uncommunicative and tire easily. (I once fell asleep while I was having my tooth filled.)

It all begins at some small hour in the morning. The children line up at my bedside and stare at me as if I'm a white whale that has been washed onto the beach.

"I think she hears us. Her eyelids fluttered."

"Wait till she turns over, then everybody cough."

"Get him out of here."

"She's pulling the covers over her ears. Start coughing."

I don't know how long it will be before one of them discovers that by taking my pulse they will be able to figure out by its rapid beat if I am faking or not. But it will come.

When they were smaller, they were even less subtle. They would stick their wet fingers in the openings of my face and whisper, "You awake yet?" Or good old Daddy would simply heave a flannel-wrapped bundle at me and say, "Here's Mommy's little boy." (Any mother with half a skull knows that when Daddy's little boy becomes Mommy's little boy, Daddy's little boy is so wet he's treading water!)

The imagination of children never fails to stagger me. Once they put a hamster on my chest, and when I bolted upright (my throat muscles paralyzed with fright) they asked, "Do you have any alcohol for the chemistry set?"

Probably the most unnerving eye-opener was a couple of weeks ago, when my eyes popped open without the slightest provocation. "Those rotten kids have done it again," I grumbled. "How can I sleep with that infernal quiet? The last time it was this quiet they were eating cereal on the front lawn in raggy pajamas." I hurried to find them.

I found them in the kitchen intent on their cereal. No noise. No nonsense. "Go back to bed," they yelled. "We won't want any lunch until nine-thirty or so."

It was going to be another one of those days.

When Last Child Goes to School—September 5, 1966

One of the foremost exponents of modern-day terrorism is the woman who asks, "What are you going to do with yourself when all your children are in school?"

They go on to paint a dismal picture of the lonely mother who plucks a pair of sticky socks off the ceiling and sobs uncontrollably into them, "My baby! My baby!" A woman who wanders through the house, unfulfilled and fighting bravely against the realization that she's being replaced by a 35-cent plate lunch and a woman she'd like to sue for alienation of affection. A disillusioned woman without purpose who must fill her time somehow until the big yellow bus deposits her brood at the curb so she can once again run and fetch!

For many a woman, this will be a rather accurate prediction. She's the woman who didn't have many interests going for her in the first place. When the children came along, it was the answer to her problem. Here was her crutch, her ace in the hole, her reason for not having to go outside the home, invent diversions, meet new friends, put up her hair, read a book or function as a woman. She wore her children like a hair shirt and told everyone how they depended upon her—when it was the other way around.

To most women, however, the school bell will sound as glorious as VE Day. It's over. She's done it. She is back to some semblance of a schedule, some precious time to herself. She wanted children too, but for another reason. They fulfilled a strong desire to love, raise and leave as a legacy another human being. But they didn't fulfill her ambitions, her struggle for individuality or her need to make a contribution to this life, no matter how small.

I have seen women emerge like great beautiful butterflies from a cocoon existence that was limited to naps and peanut butter. I have seen them assume leadership, develop and grow into active citizens, unearth artful talents that surprised everyone—even themselves, revert to skills they had BB (Before Babies), and set about restoring their own personal appearance.

I have also seen them sink into despondency, scrub the kitchen twice a week to pass the time and mechanically mouth the same old routine, "I can't . . . (name anything). I've got the children."

From a woman who has lived through the "last one into school" bit, may I give you a piece of advice. Allow yourself the luxury of that one last look as he waves goodbye from the bus. Pour yourself a cup of coffee and have a good cry for at least five minutes. Then, if you haven't suffered enough, walk slowly through the house and let the quiet pound at your eardrums. If you like, enjoy a round of guilt complex. ("Why was I so rotten to him all summer?")

Now, straighten your shoulders, take a deep breath and look out of your window. There's a big world out there. You earned it! Now, enjoy it!

Surviving Motherhood—September 1966

I have discovered that one of the rich rewards of motherhood is casting maledictions on your children in the event they become parents. It's a unique way of saying, "Just wait, kid . . . you're gonna get yours."

One of my earliest recollections of this tribal custom dates back to my childhood when one day I was nailed in the act of throwing mud balls at Mother's corset flapping on the clothesline.

Enraged, my mother shook her fists at me and yelled, "May all your children have ingrown toenails!" Observing that didn't shake me, she added a bonus. "And may your tears be so salty you spit brine for a week!"

I'm not saying I fully comprehended all this, but from her tone I sensed she wasn't wishing me a happy birthday. I noticed Grandma talked this way too. Sometimes when Mother had had a bad day Grandma would smile, rather pleased with herself, and say, "I told you, Missy, if you made your bed of thorns, you'd have to walk through it in your bare feet."

Or when she really wanted to sink Mother, she'd say, "Didn't I predict that lip of yours would grow so long you'd have to take a tuck in it?"

Throughout childhood, the words of wisdom continued to flow until I felt like I was living with a couple of hollow-eyed gypsies. Words of encouragement, like "May you have a wart on your nose on your wedding day and heartburn on your honeymoon." Or,

"Take care, missy, little girls who sass their mothers live to see their best friends chalk dirty words on their tombstones."

None of this made much sense until I had children of my own. Now, casting curses on my children is a way of life. It's the most comforting way I know to get rid of all my anxieties, hostilities and frustrations.

And the beauty is that the kids don't comprehend a word I'm saying.

I have one that's a real teaser. I just drop my shoulders, let my arms fall limp to my sides and nod my head tiredly. I don't say anything at first until I am sure I have their attention. Then I say, "Wait . . . just wait . . . until you're a mother." (Occasionally, my son, who is very bright for 11, will remind me he's a boy and only the female species bear their young, but he gets the message. I know he does.)

Casting curses isn't the easiest thing in the world. To work up to a pitch you need incentive, like the other day when I found a pile of dirty socks stuffed in the Erector set box.

I yelled at the top of my voice, "I hope you have identical twins . . . two weeks apart! May your patio face southwest. May your father belch loudly at the father-son banquet. May you have a rainbow over your playpen!"

When they get home from school, I'll think of some more.

Costume for the School Play—May 29, 1968

There is nothing that does more for my mornings than to have a child announce hysterically, "Mom! I'm in a play today. I need a costume!"

Some mothers are lucky. They have children who get all the good parts. Their little girls are fairy princesses with magic wands and Sunday dresses. Or their little boys are assigned roles as toy soldiers who can be outfitted from the toy box.

Not my kids. They are always cast as a bad tooth, the Sixteenth Amendment or Mr. Courtesy.

With the bad tooth, we faked it. I wrapped the kid in a white sheet and stuck a raisin in his navel to depict a cavity.

The Sixteenth Amendment was a bit more complicated. It deals, of course, with the power of Congress to lay and collect taxes on incomes. We outfitted her in a baggy suit with the pockets inside out and a blank check across her mouth stamped INSUFFICIENT FUNDS.

Mr. Courtesy was a real challenge. We finally put him in a Superman suit, changed the big red S to a big red C and told him to smile until his face broke.

Last week, one of the kids did it again. "Hey, Mom. I forgot to tell you, but I'm in a play today."

"Don't sweat it," I said calmly. "I'll get a costume. What are you?"

"I'm a participle," he said.

I steadied myself against the stove. "Split or dangling?"

"You're confused," he said. "I only dangle. Dan Freeby is the one who splits. He's an infinitive."

"Wonderful," I said. "Now, what did you have in mind?"

"I don't care. The teachers just want me to modify Mike Ferrett."

"What's he wearing?"

"I don't know. Whatever nouns wear."

"You're right," I said. "You see one noun, you've seen them all. Look, why don't you just wear a clean shirt and your slipover with your Sunday pants?"

"That's dumb," he said. "Who'd know I was a participle?"

"Who'd know you weren't?" I snapped.

"If this will help you," he said, "I look exactly like a gerund."

I promised myself a good stiff belt of vanilla if I lived through this morning.

Outgrowing Naps—August 14, 1968

A group of young mothers huddled around the kiddie pool the other day discussing children's naps.

"I think Lisa has outgrown naps," said one pretty blonde. "She's twenty-two months now and told me she didn't want to rest in the afternoons anymore."

I nearly fell out of my water wings. What is the world coming to when a child under two sets her own schedule?

In my book the question was never to nap or not to nap but

rather how old should a mother be before her naps are discontinued? It seems like only yesterday my son confronted me with the decision.

"Do I have to nap again today?"

"Yes."

"Why?"

"Because I fell asleep while having my teeth filled this morning."

"Were you tired?"

"I wasn't bored."

"Can I mess around while you nap?"

"No!"

"Why?"

"Because you get into things."

"Name me one."

"Putting bubble gum on the nozzle of the garden hose, turning on the water and having it break and flood the living room."

"Name me two."

"Go to sleep."

"Can I have a drink?"

"No."

"Look at my foot! My toenail is turning black."

"Try washing it."

"What happens if I don't take a nap now?"

"You go to bed at five-thirty."

"Why do *I* have to sleep when *you're* tired?"

"For the same reason I put a sweater on you when I am cold."

"I'm the only fifth-grader I know who comes to ball practice with chenille creases on his face."

"That's the thanks a mother gets for sacrificing herself two hours every afternoon to see that her child gets the proper rest."

He sighed and said, "If you snore, should I roll you over on your side?"

Smart-mouth kid.

A Mother's Eye—August 18, 1968

Of all the means of communication known to man, none is quite as effective as the Mother's Eye. Or, as we say, one glance is worth a thousand punches in the mouth. There are a variety, depending upon the situation, but these are a few of the old standards.

THE LOOK OF DEATH: This is used on a child with a busy finger up his nose. (It is similar to the Frozen Stare usually employed to catch a waiter's eye, but is somewhat different.) It's a steady gaze, unflinching and unyielding. The brow is furrowed, the lips are firm with no trace of a smile. The face remains in a hypnotic state until the finger is removed from the nose.

THE DEADPAN GLARE: This is the one most often used at the dinner table for children who fill their glasses to overflowing, eat gravy with their fingers and bulge their cheeks with food. On some occasions, the Deadpan Glare is accompanied by a good swift kick in the thigh under the table.

THE MARTYR'S COUNTENANCE: This is unmistakably the look of pain and is conjured up when a child parades down the church aisle carrying his training pants or demands the $2 you borrowed from him in the middle of a cocktail party. Some people confuse the Martyr's Countenance with the Deadpan Glare. When in doubt, remember that the Martyr's Countenance is accompanied by tears, biting of the lower lip until it bleeds and fainting.

THE DESPERATE SQUINT is a real study in pantomime. The jaw is set firm, the lips curl and the eyes are narrow and menacing. They dart back and forth. It is used when a child is loose at the mouth and asks in a loud voice if it is true Aunt Helen wouldn't know what to do with a man if she found one. If Aunt Helen happens to be in the room at the time these words are uttered, a mother often goes into her Divine Guidance Stare.

THE DIVINE GUIDANCE STARE is a desperate look where her head is tilted upward, her eyes roll back until the whites show and the lips utter what seems to be a Buddhist prayer.

Perhaps the most feared of all looks is a mother's No Look look. This appears to be a blank expression to a child who is jumping on the sofa with his muddy feet or running around at an adult party at

2 A.M., but beware. The most literal translation of the No Look look comes from a youngster who interpreted it as "When the company goes, head for the bed and look small and helpless until it blows over."

No More Oatmeal Kisses—January 29, 1969

A young mother writes: "I know you've written before about the empty-nest syndrome, that lonely period after the children are grown and gone. Right now I'm up to my eyeballs in laundry and muddy boots. The baby is teething; the boys are fighting. My husband just called and said to eat without him, and I fell off my diet. Lay it on me again, will you?"

OK. One of these days, you'll shout, "Why don't you kids grow up and act your age!" And they will. Or, "You guys get outside and find yourselves something to do . . . and don't slam the door!" And they won't.

You'll straighten up the boys' bedroom neat and tidy: bumper stickers discarded, bedspread tucked and smooth, toys displayed on the shelves. Hangers in the closet. Animals caged. And you'll say out loud, "Now I want it to stay this way." And it will.

You'll prepare a perfect dinner with a salad that hasn't been picked to death and a cake with no finger traces in the icing, and you'll say, "Now, there's a meal for company." And you'll eat it alone.

You'll say, "I want complete privacy on the phone. No dancing around. No demolition crews. Silence! Do you hear?" And you'll have it.

No more plastic tablecloths stained with spaghetti. No more bedspreads to protect the sofa from damp bottoms. No more gates to stumble over at the top of the basement steps. No more clothespins under the sofa. No more playpens to arrange a room around.

No more anxious nights under a vaporizer tent. No more sand on the sheets or Popeye movies in the bathroom. No more iron-on patches, rubber bands for ponytails, tight boots or wet knotted shoestrings.

Imagine. A lipstick with a point on it. No baby-sitter for New Year's Eve. Washing only once a week. Seeing a steak that isn't ground. Having your teeth cleaned without a baby on your lap.

No PTA meetings. No car pools. No blaring radios. No one washing her hair at 11 o'clock at night. Having your own roll of Scotch tape.

Think about it. No more Christmas presents out of toothpicks and library paste. No more sloppy oatmeal kisses. No more tooth fairy. No giggles in the dark. No knees to heal, no responsibility.

Only a voice crying, "Why don't you grow up?" and the silence echoing, "I did."

Confirmed Shouter—March 5, 1969

Ever since President Nixon's inaugural plea to "speak quietly enough so that our words can be heard as well as our voices," I've had misgivings about my big mouth.

I've always admired parents who discipline their children in hushed whispers: "Arthur, you are a naughty boy for turning on all the gas jets. Now I want you to drag your little sister out into the fresh air, give her mouth-to-mouth resuscitation and apologize. Don't make Mama have to raise her voice."

I'm a shouter. Once on a vacation when one of the kids turned on the car heater while going through Georgia, my mother told me they felt the vibrations as far north as Port Huron, Michigan.

No one is born a shrew. I used to watch women getting flushed and angry while they chewed out their children and I'd say to myself, "My goodness, that woman is going to have a heart attack. No one should discipline a child in anger." (I was five at the time and being flogged with a yardstick by my mother.)

Having children of my own knocked a hole in that theory. To begin with, there were only 32 hours out of every week when I wasn't angry, and then I was sleeping.

Also, I discovered children never took a "no" seriously unless the dishes rattled when you said it.

And the real clincher came when I discovered I had runners. "Runners" are kids who, when they commit some sin, take off for the fields, trees, basements, neighbors, attics or sewers.

Did you ever try to whisper to someone you couldn't see? I took to shouting.

We once had a neighbor who was born out of her time. She belonged in a hoopskirt eating a basket lunch at Tara.

I lived next to her for four years, and not once did that disgusting old dame raise her voice. Of course you can imagine what that made me sound like. (The Shore Patrol breaking up a floating crap game.)

Anyway, one day the boys were throwing a ball against her house and she appeared like an apparition at the door, gestured to them and said softly, "Boys, would you-all come here for a moment?"

I watched her gesturing, talking and smiling. When she finished the boys disbanded.

I pounced on my son. "What did that mealy-mouthed little frail have to say to you boys?"

"She said if we broke her windows, she'd break our faces!"

From that day forward I forgave her for her quietness. What she lacked in volume she made up for in content. What class!

I should love to follow President Nixon's advice, but when you've got varicose neck veins from years of shouting, it isn't going to be easy. *Will you put down that coffee cup and pay attention? I said it isn't going to be easy!*

Youngest Child Tries to Tell a Joke—May 23, 1969

Our youngest child has been trying to tell a joke at the dinner table for the last three years. The same one.

I feel sorry for the kid. To be on the tail end of a family means anything you come up with has either been told or isn't worth telling. We can always tell when his favorite magazine comes in the mail. He will rush into the kitchen and say, "Why did it take three Boy Scouts to help a little old lady across the street?" and one of the older ones will shout, "Because she didn't want to go, you cluck!"

Personally I wish he'd take the magazine, crumple it and stuff it in every opening in his face, but he never does. He always looks amazed that someone knew the answer and says, "That's right."

Next month, it's the same old deal. "How do you stop an elephant from charging?" His sister, looking bored, will snap, "Let me guess. You take away his credit cards."

"That's right," he says, perplexed.

About three years ago he said, "Have you heard the story about a man who bought a mousetrap and went to the refrigerator for cheese and—"

"Which reminds me," interrupted his father. "Who ate the beer cheese?"

"I didn't eat it," one of the kids said. "I used it for bass bait."

In the months to follow, we were to hear the preamble to the joke dozens of times . . . always with interruptions, never completed.

Finally, one day last week I said, "Tell me your joke about the man with the mousetrap and the cheese for bait."

"Well," he said, perching himself on the stool, "he found out he didn't have any cheese for bait, so he cut a picture from a magazine of a piece of cheese. When he woke up the next morning, know what he found in his trap? A picture of a mouse."

"Tell it at dinner," I urged.

Under protest, the family sat rigid and listened to the story without interruption. By the time he got to his punch line he was hysterical. His eyes were shining with excitement, and I thought he was going to explode as he built for his big finish. "And do you know what he found in his trap?" he asked. "*A mouse!*"

No one said a word. I wonder whether Henny Youngman got started this way.

"Are We Rich?"—June 3, 1971

The other day out of a clear blue sky Brucie asked, "Are we rich?"

I paused on my knees as I retrieved a dime from the sweeper bag, blew the dust off it and asked, "Not so you can notice. Why?"

"How can you tell?" he asked.

I straightened up and thought a bit. Being rich is a relative sort of thing. Here's how I can always tell.

"You're rich when you buy your gas at the same service station all the time so your glasses match.

"You're rich when you can have eight people to dinner and don't have to wash forks between the main course and dessert.

"You're rich when you buy clothes for your kids that are two sizes too big for the one you buy 'em for and four sizes too big for the one that comes after him.

"You're rich when you own a boat—without oars.

"You can tell people have money when they record a check and don't have to subtract it right away.

"People have money when they sit around and joke with the cashier while she's calling in their charge to see if it's still open.

"You're rich when you write notes to the teacher on paper without lines.

"You're rich when your television set has all the knobs on it.

"You're rich when you can throw away a pair of pantyhose just because it has a large hole in it.

"You know people are loaded when they don't have to save rubber bands from the celery and store them on a doorknob.

"You're rich when you can have a home wedding without HAVEN FUNERAL HOME stamped on the folding chairs.

"You're rich when the Scouts have a paper drive and you have a stack of *The New York Times* in your basement.

"You're rich when your dog is wet and smells good.

"You're rich when your own hair looks so great everyone thinks it's a wig."

Brucie sat quietly for a moment, then said, "I think my friend Ronny is rich."

"How can you tell?" I asked.

"His mom buys his birthday cake at a bakery, and it isn't even cracked on top."

"He's rich, all right," I sighed.

When God Created Mothers—May 12, 1974

When the good Lord was creating mothers, He was into His sixth day of overtime when the angel appeared and said, "You're doing a lot of fiddling around on this one."

The Lord said, "Have you read the specs on this order?

"She has to be completely washable, but not plastic;

"Have 180 movable parts . . . all replaceable;

"Run on black coffee and leftovers;

"Have a lap that disappears when she stands up;

"A kiss that can cure anything from a broken leg to a disappointed love affair;

"And six pairs of hands."

The angel shook her head slowly and said, "Six pairs of hands? No way."

"It's not the hands that are causing me problems," said the Lord. "It's the three pairs of eyes that mothers have to have."

"That's on the standard model?" asked the angel.

The Lord nodded. "One pair that sees through closed doors when she asks, 'What are you kids doing in there?' when she already knows. Another here in the back of her head that sees what she shouldn't but what she has to know, and of course the ones here in front that can look at a child when he goofs up and say, 'I understand and I love you,' without so much as uttering a word."

"Lord," said the angel, touching His sleeve gently, "come to bed. Tomorrow—"

"I can't," said the Lord. "I'm so close to creating something so close to myself. Already I have one who heals herself when she is sick . . . can feed a family of six on one pound of hamburger . . . and can get a nine-year-old to stand under a shower."

The angel circled the model of a mother very slowly and sighed. "It's too soft."

"But tough!" said the Lord excitedly. "You cannot imagine what this mother can do or endure."

"Can it think?"

"Not only think, but it can reason and compromise," said the Creator.

Finally the angel bent over and ran her finger across the cheek.

"There's a leak," she pronounced. "I told you that you were trying to put too much into this model."

"It's not a leak," said the Lord. "It's a tear."

"What's it for?"

"It's for joy, sadness, disappointment, pain, loneliness and pride."

"You are a genius," said the angel.

The Lord looked somber. "I didn't put it there."

Motherhood—Love and Laughter—September 1974

Every once in a while, my flip approach to motherhood arouses the wrath of a few readers.

"Why did you have children?" . . . "You're a terrible mother!" . . . "I feel sorry for your family!" filter across my desk.

When I was born, I was 40 years old with a cup of cold coffee in one hand, a sponge in the other and the original Excedrin headache. My parents exclaimed, "Good grief! We've given birth to a 130-pound parent!" Or so it seemed.

As I sat in the middle of three children one night, chipping the enamel off my teeth by biting a knot out of a shoestring that a child had been getting wet all day long, I began to think about motherhood.

There seemed to be several avenues open to me: (a) take myself seriously and end up drinking gin just after the school bus left; (b) take the children seriously and end up drinking gin before the school bus left; (c) admit to the fear and frustration and have a good time with it.

It hasn't been easy. Everyone loves a child. Face it. They're young, adorable and innocent. The world is on their side. My three-year-old once sunk her entire set of teeth into my shoulder, causing me to go to the doctor for possible stitches. He gave the child a tetanus shot and barked at me, "What did you do to provoke the child?"

In a public restaurant one night, I rapped one kid for loosening the tops on salt shakers, another for making rivers out of the gravy, and socked one in a chair for rearranging the furniture (with diners still in them), only to have a couple stop by the table and cluck, "Some people don't deserve children."

I defy any parent who has been on a trip with a child who kicked the seat for 50 miles, threw his shoes out the window, lost his pet snake in Cleveland during the five o'clock traffic and spilled his slush down your back to tell me she has never considered abandoning him at the next Shell station.

What mother has never fallen on her knees when she has gone

into her son's bedroom and prayed "Please, God. No more. You were only supposed to give me what I could handle."

And while we're being honest, what grandmother has never heard her small grandson beat on the piano with his fists for three hours and not looked apprehensively at the clock? (TV blames it on irregularity, but the truth is they're going bananas.)

To my critics, I can only assure you there is love in every line. And remind you that he who laughs . . . lasts!

How to Communicate with Toddlers—December 1974

A father in Champaign, Illinois, is inquiring how to communicate with toddlers.

You all know what toddlers are. They're the little people about two feet tall who walk under coffee tables and are the only ones in the house who can take the caps off the child-safe aspirin bottles.

Specifically, the letter writer was having difficulty advising his toddler in the following areas:

1. There are basic differences between food and clothing. You eat food and wear clothing. Food goes in; clothing goes on.
2. Do not bite anything that will bite back. This includes the dog, other babies, electrical cords and your father when he is watching professional football on television.
3. Washing your face after a meal is not considered cruel and unusual punishment. It won't do any good to report Mommy and Daddy to the police.
4. Your pacifier is not a permanent part of your face. Removing it is not considered major surgery and does not normally require an anesthetic.
5. Don't hide your tennis shoes in the oven when Mommy is making supper. It makes the roast taste funny.
6. Don't use the drapes in the living room to wipe your hands and face unless they are patterned.
7. Diaper rash does not have to be terminal.

I sympathize with the father from Illinois, but I don't know what to tell him. All my kids were born on a Monday, and you know how sloppy the production is on a day following the weekend.

I never met three children who could understand me less. When I laid out the pajamas, put the sides up on the crib and turned on the night-light, they came alive like the "big midnight show," standing on their heads, bringing out all the toys and playing patty-cake with the dog.

When I picked up the phone, like mechanical robots on schedule they gargled bleach, rolled potatoes across the floor, climbed on top of the TV set and took off all their clothes.

When I said "No," they giggled; "Not now," they bit me; "Come to Mama," they ran into the traffic; "Let me see what is in your hand," they ate it; "The strained lamb is good for you," they blew it back in my face.

Communicate with a toddler? I'd sooner take my chances with an untrained, excited puppy on a new white carpet.

The Twelve Days of School—September 1975

Please sing to the tune of "The Twelve Days of Christmas."

On the first day of school, my children said to me, "Aren't you glad that our education's free?"

On the second day of school, my children said to me, "I need five notebooks, six fountain pens and an unabridged dictionary."

On the third day of school, my children said to me, "We need Crayolas, your old Victrola, one pencil box and a buck for a lock and a key."

On the fourth day of school, my children said to me, "I need a gym suit, tennies and shower cap, a sewing kit, some pinking shears, and five yards of string, one tailor chalk, two thimbles, one bias tape and something called emery."

On the fifth day of school, my children said to me, "We need insurance, don't forget our lunches and a deposit for our lab breakage fee."

On the sixth day of school, my children said to me, "You forgot my workbook, name tags on my soccer socks and the loan of your car till after three."

On the seventh day of school, my children said to me, "I need a camera, hockey stick and pink tights, a tuba in key, one chess set, one nose plug, one leotard, for my extracurricular activities."

On the eighth day of school, my children said to me, "Do we have some old shoes, food we will never use, books we're not reading, money we aren't needing, for some hard-pressed, needy family?"

On the ninth day of school, my children said to me, "I had my picture took. It'll cost you ten to look, for twenty you can buy the book; no stamps, no checks, just money."

On the tenth day of school, my children said to me, "Wanta join the PTA, the Boosters and the Blue and Gray, the band is selling key rings, and you know how you're always losing keys."

On the eleventh day of school, my children said to me, "Where is my cigar box? Did you pay my milk bill? I need fifty cents. We're going to plant a tree."

On the twelfth day of school, my children said to me, "Why are you crying, you're finished buying, aren't you glad that our education's free?"

"Things My Mother Taught Me" Assignment
—September 28, 1975

One of my kids had an English assignment the other night to do a paper on "Things My Mother Taught Me."

I couldn't help but be flattered as he wrote feverishly in his notebook for the better part of 45 minutes. When he was finished, I asked, "Do you mind if I read it?"

He shrugged. "Okay, if you want to, but don't get it dirty."

THINGS MY MOTHER TAUGHT ME
Logic: "If you fall off that swing and break your neck, you are not going to the store with me."

Medicine: "If you don't stop crossing your eyes, they are going to freeze that way!" (There is no cure, no telethon and no relief for frozen eyes.)

Optimism: "You are going to enjoy yourself at that birthday party or I am going to break every bone in your body."

Philosophy: "You show me a boy with a pet snake and I'll show you a boy who wants his mother dead!"

ESP: "Put on the sweater! Don't you think I know when you are cold?"

Science: "You put your hand out the car window and it'll blow off." (Gravity: What goes out, must blow off.)

Insight: "Do you realize that fifty million children in Southeast Asia consider broccoli a treat . . . like ice cream?" (How do you get a broccoli deficiency?)

Finance: "I told you the tooth fairy is writing checks because computerized billing is easier for the IRS."

Challenge: "Where is your sister and don't talk with food in your mouth. Answer me!"

Ethics: "If you are too busy to take out the garbage, you are too busy to need an allowance."

Genealogy: "Shut that door. Or were you born in a barn?" (You're asking me?)

Suspense: "Can you guess what I found under your bed today?"

Humor: "When that lawn mower cuts off your toes, don't come running to me."

I took off my glasses and put down the paper. Son of a gun. I would have been willing to bet during all those years he hadn't heard a word I said.

A Baby's Bill of Rights—November 13, 1975

On the eve of the two hundredth anniversary of our country, it is only fitting that groups everywhere reaffirm their rights.

To date, we have had declarations of the status of women, senior citizens, children and even dieters. Today, I wish to speak on behalf of a group that cannot speak for itself but nonetheless occupies a very special place in our world.

A BABY'S BILL OF RIGHTS

Article the first: People who chew garlic shall not be allowed within three miles of a baby, under penalty of drowning by spitting.

Article the second: Excessive bail shall be set for turkeys who tickle a baby's feet until he faints or throw him up in the air after a full meal.

Article the third: Where a crime of the kidneys has been committed, the accused should enjoy the right to a speedy diaper change. Public announcements, details and guided tours of the aforementioned are not necessary.

Article the fourth: The decision to eat strained lamb or not to eat strained lamb should be with the feedee and not the feeder. Blowing the strained lamb into the feeder's face should be accepted as an option, not as a declaration of war.

Article the fifth: New and innovative ways should be sought to test whether or not food is too hot for a baby's taste. If God had meant for parents to test food with their tongues, He would have made tongues disposable.

Article the sixth: Babies should enjoy the freedom to vocalize, whether it be in church, a public meeting place, during a movie or after hours when the lights are out. They have not yet learned that joy and laughter have to last a lifetime and must be conserved.

Article the seventh: No person may be made to wear a sweater when the parent/grandparent is cold or run around under a cold garden hose when the aforementioned is hot.

Amendment one: No baby shall at any time be quartered in a house where there are no soft laps, no laughter or no love.

Happiness and Motherhood—April 24, 1980

Researchers are finally getting down to some real serious studies on the postnatal depression. Do you know what they've discovered?

You're not supposed to have a good time after the baby is born.

It's something a lot of us suspected, but were never really sure about.

My postnatal depression was longer than most. I went into it seven months before the baby came, and it lasted until the kid was 17. Then it began to taper off.

Had it not been for *As the World Turns* and pacifiers, I'd have slipped into humming and braiding my hair. Every day I'd put a pacifier into whatever part of his face was open, get a plate full of buttered noodles and sit in front of the TV set and watch someone who was worse off than I was.

Every time I went to the pediatrician, I'd try to search the faces of the other mothers for some sign of exhaustion.

I only saw one mother break, and that was when her son, a real hellion, had skated across the carpet shocking everyone with his static electricity, rearranged the furniture, licked the drinking fountain, taken a book away from another child and finally submerged his hand in the aquarium. She just sat there, numb, and finally said softly, "Think piranha."

Another rare moment of honesty that suggested motherhood was less than perfect came on Mother's Day in church when a new priest looked out and said to the mothers, "I know what you're thinking. You're tired. You feel pulled in nine different directions. You think no one understands you, and you're saying to yourself, "Mary and her one kid. Big deal!"

According to the new theory, ambivalent feelings are perfectly natural. It doesn't mean you love your child any less; it means you're realistic about the demands on your personal life.

A new mother in Colorado wrote recently about her two children, one two years old, the other three months. She put the toddler on a potty seat so she could bathe the baby. She lathered up the baby when the meter man appeared. The dog suddenly went into heat. The phone rang. The toddler jumped up and overturned the potty on the new shag rug. He then stuck his head in between the washer and the wall to see what the meter reader was doing and got stuck. The baby got cold and began screaming. Strange dogs began running through the house. She moved the washer and her son emerged bleeding. "What would you do?" she asked.

I'd do now what I should have done years ago . . . cry!

Disposable Diapers—February 8, 1990

The question being asked by baby boomers isn't, "Is there life after throwaway diapers are abolished?" but, "Is that life worth living?"

Disposable diapers were something my generation used to fantasize about. That and catheter implants. I used to stand at my picture window in the suburbs, watch a blizzard raging outside and pray, "Please, God, I don't care if the milk gets through or the mail or even the school bus . . . but please give wings to the diaper-service truck."

Maybe it's because we had gone through the dip-and-flush era on our hands and knees in front of the commode. It was not a pretty sight. If we drifted, the flush sucked the diaper and our arm right into the septic tank on the front lawn.

When diaper service came into being, we rejoiced. True, dropping a soiled diaper into the can the day before pickup meant risking the sight of a good eye, but it was better than what we had had.

When paper products became state-of-the-art here, disposable diapers were a natural. Today, mothers use 16 billion of them a year. That's 3.6 million tons a year going into sanitary landfills. Environmentalists say you have to start somewhere. Why not go back to cloth diapers that you dip and flush, wash, bleach, soften and use again?

Could we talk about this? As a mother, I'd rather do away with foam cups and have hot coffee poured into both of my hands and drink fast than do away with disposable diapers. Want to cut back on paper products? Abolish those little paper dresses that doctors use to make you forget why you came to their office in the first place. Just bring a bathrobe from home.

It's not as if we don't have other options. Think how much wastepaper we could save by doing away with the 18 or 19 subscription cards that drop out of a single magazine each month. Ask yourself, Do we need all that paper wadded up in the toes of new shoes? There is absolutely no reason in this world to keep turning out gift boxes year after year. My mother has enough of them stored to supply every major city in this country for the next 10 years.

You need priorities. What is more important, filling out eight pounds of insurance forms for a crack in your windshield or changing the diaper of a child who just ate mud? There have been few contributions to society in this century that have made such an impact on our population as the disposable diaper. I don't think people really care if their hamburger is housed in a white foam condo or if plastic rings are really necessary to bond their six-pack. But to do away with paper diapers would once again bring mothers to their knees . . . literally.

Let us hope manufacturers can come up with a diaper that is environmentally sound. To go back to cloth would send us back to the day when breathing and raising a baby at the same time were incompatible.

Spit—March 18, 1990

I received a birthday card from my daughter that said she loved me. When I opened it up, it continued: "But I never forgave you for cleaning my face with spit on your hanky."

We laughed. She, because she thought I was embarrassed. I, because I never used a hanky. I used my fingers.

In truth, I thought the sentiment was rather ironic, coming from a kid who drank from the water jug in the refrigerator and deposited enough crumbs in it to make it look like a Christmas paperweight.

She is not yet a parent, so how is she expected to know that mothers are endowed with a spit supply that develops during pregnancy, much like milk glands? After birth, there is an increased amount to fulfill the demands of child raising.

Mothers need all the spit they can get. At first it seems gross, but you soon adapt to it. How else do you remove a milk stain from a bib? Lipstick kisses from a cheek? Chocolate from lips? Bird doo and mud from shoes? Ice cream from noses? Spilled food from shirts?

Mothers need saliva to tame flyaway hair and cowlicks, remove mustard from car seats and get fingerprints off walls and doorknobs. They need it to condition swim goggles. (You don't think kids are going to use their own spit, do you?) With each child, I had a fear that my spit would dry up before I had her trained to soap and water.

Parents do a lot of gross things in the name of motherhood and fatherhood. It doesn't matter on what economic level you live, when a child hands you a shoe with a knot in the shoestring that he has wet on all day long, the first thing you do instinctively is put it in your mouth and try to loosen up the knot with your teeth. If we had an ounce of pride, we'd say, "You put that shoe in my face one more time and I'll cut its tongue out!"

And what is the first thing you do when a child wants to get rid of his gum? You stick out your hand and say, "Spit it out in here." You have absolutely nothing in mind as to what you're going to do with it. It just seems the thing to do.

There isn't a mother alive who has watched her child play in his food until it looks like road kill and, when he doesn't want it, hasn't eaten it herself rather than waste it.

We are born to sacrifice, but my daughter is too young and too inexperienced to know these things. I live for the day when she has spit on three children, a Naugahyde sofa, a steering wheel, a light switch and the handles of a shopping cart, and doesn't have enough saliva left to put on mascara.

Then she'll know.

All My Children

Children Cornering the Coin Market—January 5, 1965
(Erma's first syndicated column)

It's time we quit kidding ourselves. The only group that can alleviate the national coin shortage is children.

I don't know what the appeal will be to get them to lighten their loafers, empty their socks and unfatten their little ceramic pigs, but it had best be soon.

It has been an insidiously slow process, but our national economy now rests with a group of plotting little bandits who have amassed a fortune in coins for emptying garbage, cutting grass, minding babies, scraping plates, bringing in milk, clearing snow-laden driveways, redeeming baby teeth and racking up A's on their report cards.

A large boost to their independent solvency has been the Friday night allowance. How much can this amount to, you ask? I thought you'd never ask.

We doled out 15 cents a week until we received the "Chintzy Employer of the Month" award on our block. A grievance committee informed us our children could make more in a Chinese rice paddy. They pointed out that we subscribed to three newspapers, had two cars in the driveway and an outside TV antenna, yet underpaid our children. Before we started receiving CARE packages from some European family, we thought it best to grant an increase. The kids now rake in a quarter a week.

But the flow of currency does not stop there. Ages four to nine are retirement years for most youngsters. They live solely off their loose teeth. They spit these out like popcorn as the financial urgency hits them, and before you can whisper in the darkness, "Mother, have you got change for the tooth fairy for a half-dollar?" a little hand in the darkness reaches out, snatches the coin, whisks it under the pillow and snores a little to keep you from feeling like a complete fool.

The mound of coins continues to grow as the little Kool-Aid tycoons and garbage financiers continue to amaze and to amass. Any adult can only marvel at their grasp of finances.

"Mother, you are not cognizant of the fact you are four weeks in arrears in your allowance to me. Computed in simple compound interest over a four-week period, you have forced me to miss the current fiscal dividend from my bank, costing me an additional . . ."

(Oh shut up!) This yet, from a son who has not mastered his threes timetables.

For those parents foolish enough to float a loan from a child, a word of warning. They are less than discreet in their business dealings. In the middle of a dinner party, they are likely to emerge in their pajamas, complete with ledger, and query, "Daddy, when are you going to pay me the $40 you borrowed out of my bureau drawer to make the car payment last month?"

The coins continue to roll in from the most unexpected sources. One pitch that has been pretty successful has been the appearance of our youngest at bedtime. He appears pink and scrubbed in his "jammys" and clutches a little coffee can (keep it simple) and goes to guests and grandparents, chanting through adorable gums, "Christmath ith coming . . . the geese are getting fat . . . please put a penny in the old man's hat."

He then jingles his little can, and the guests laugh (but not much) and drop a coin in it. He started it last August, had a peak month in December and is still pulling it off.

I could go on forever on how children hoard coins. The problem is who is going to pry them away from them. This is how a child reasons. Paper money is nice. You can make planes out of it, paste it on walls and windows, color it or use it for bookmarks. But a drawer full of coins! Why, that's better than owning your own bottle of catsup!

My Son, the President—October 30, 1965

There's been a decline in the past decade of little boys who aspire to the presidency of the United States.

I can remember when every other male infant was hopefully named Franklin Delano Roosevelt Schmaltz or William Howard Taft Feeney and was primed from the cradle to occupy the White House when he grew up.

Not today. Boys don't want to write historic speeches on brown paper bags any more. They want to write secret code messages on their eyeballs and be 007 spies. They don't want to ride a charger at Appomattox and return General Lee's sword with honor. They want to dress up their GI Joe dolls.

They don't even want to be a general throwing a half dollar across the Potomac. They want to stand on the shore and convince him that his half dollar in their bank would earn him $4^1/_2$ percent dividend at interest compounded from day of deposit.

There's probably a couple of good reasons for the lagging interest of presidential aspirants. The presidency is no bargain. The campaign price tag is prohibitive . . . the personal price paid after election is exorbitant. But has that ever stopped an ambitious, pushy mother? Indeed not!

"You're going to be president of the United States," I said, collaring my son. "And already we're getting a late start. Bring me that old photograph album."

"Aw Mom," he growled. "I've got a game this afternoon."

"That's what Millard Fillmore said when his mother collared him. Now then, some of these pictures will have to go. You know how those national magazines are when a president is named. They dig up all the old photographs they can find. Burn this one of you on the rug in the nude. And this one. Your bloomers are hanging suspiciously heavy around your ankles. And get rid of those old report cards. No sense asking for trouble. Now, who's your idol?"

"Willie Mays."

"Oh, good grief. Let's pick Thomas Jefferson. He talked a lot and would be good for at least two terms of quotations. Now, about your handwriting . . ."

"It's not bad."

"That's your problem. You've got to learn to write illegibly or no one will read anything you write. Now, what about sports?"

"I like baseball."

"No, no, who ever heard of a president liking baseball? Besides, they'd never stand still for a baseball diamond on the White House lawn. You be thinking about a sport that you can do in the Rose Garden in front of a dozen reporters or so."

"Aw Mom, this is nutsy."

"Nutsy! Don't you want to sit at that big desk and know that the eyes of the world are upon you . . . that everything you do or say affects them in some way? And that your strength is their strength . . . your weakness, their weakness . . . your promises . . . their promises?" (He pulled himself erect and began to hum the "Battle Hymn of the Republic.") "And just think, boy, it all began here today in this room with Mama."

He looked at me impersonally, his head held high with pride. . . . "Mama who?"

"I Don't Want to Go to Grandma's"—May 1966

"I don't want to go to Grandma's."

The first time you hear your child say it, it's as shocking as dancing on a grave, spitting on the flag or knocking apple pie!

How dare she disfavor this woman who looked into her wrinkled, newborn face, as she lay toothless and bald, and said proudly, "She's beautiful!" How dare she discard this woman who let her bake cookies with her dirty hands, who let her pound on her piano with sticky fingers.

When did the magic go? She used to be in the car before her parents had their coats on. Grandma let her do grown-up things.

When did the magic go? Maybe it was the day she looked anxiously out at the "big table" in the dining room and Grandma saw the look and said, "Maybe you should start eating with the adults now." (Before that she had food fights in the kitchen with her cousins.) A door closed that day on childhood. Had she tried the door, she would have realized it swung only one way. She never could go back again. The trip through the door leading to the "big table" was awkward, not nearly the fun she thought it would be. There was cigar smoke that made her cough and talk about washing machines and politics. It was boring being in the crack between childhood and maturity.

From that day forward Grandma's house was never the same. The player piano sounded out of key and wasn't fun anymore. The front steps no longer were an adventure. Children's conversation was silly, and adult conversation was meaningless. There was nothing to do at Grandma's.

Why did the magic go?

It was time to move life along. There were experiences to gather, friends to cultivate, interests to be indulged and decisions to be made. There were things she had to do alone . . . away from the family. It was time to expand her world.

And Grandma's house? For several years, it diminished—along with Grandma. She took along books to cushion the boredom.

It wasn't until she had children of her own that she had time to reflect on the house and its occupants and what they had meant to her. And she hungered for it. The magic had returned.

"I don't want to go to Grandma's."

Let the door close softly, Grandma. They'll be back.

Going Deaf from Rock 'n' Roll—January 23, 1967

"Pardon me, madam," said the young man at the door. "I'm doing a survey among mothers to see whether or not they agree with an acoustical engineer from Arizona that rock 'n' roll may cause teenagers to go deaf."

"No, I don't need rolls or bread today. . . . If you've got any of those little buns with the jelly inside, though—"

"No, madam," he said, raising his voice, "you don't understand. I'm not a bakery man. I'd like to get your opinion on what hearing experts are saying about rock 'n' roll music and whether or not you think excessive—"

"Oh, Excedrin! You want me to do a commercial! My, yes, I have headaches all the time. It's this loud music. You see, we've got four radios in the house. Along about four o'clock it sounds like the U.N. General Assembly singing a serenade in four languages to Red China. So I simply crawl under the sink with a shaker full of Excedrin and—"

"Madam," he said, facing me squarely, "we're not doing a commercial. We're doing a survey. Do you have a teenager in your home?"

"You're going to have to keep your lips in full view of my eyes at all times," I explained. "And talk a little slower!"

"I'm sorry," he said. "Do you have a teenager in your home?"

"I think that's what it is," I said hesitantly.

"You're not sure?"

"Well, it's difficult to tell. The bangs are two inches above the hemline and there's a lump on the hip shaped like a small transistor, two button eyes and a long cord that connects the hip to the ear."

"That's a teenager," he added impersonally. "Now, have you noticed any impairment in her hearing since she started listening to rock 'n' roll music?"

"Nothing unusual." I pondered. "She still doesn't respond to simple commands like: Clean your room. Change your clothes. Get the door. On the other hand she picks up phrases like: Have you heard the joke about. . . . The bank balance is down to. . . . Let's feed the kids here and slip out to dinner . . . like she was standing in the middle of the Capitol rotunda in Washington."

"Then the increased decibels have made no change in your teenager?"

"Pardon me while I get the phone."

"I didn't hear anything ring," he said.

"It's always like that after I've listened to three hours of Maurice and His Electric Fuse Foxes. Just a ringing sound in my ears. Would you believe that once the guitar player got hiccups and it sold three million records? Are you saying something, young man? I told you you'd have to keep your lips in full view of my eyes at all times. *And speak a little slower!*"

Daughter Learning to Drive—July 18, 1969

I saw an old school chum of mine last fall and couldn't believe my eyes. She looked haggard and tired. There were lines around her eyes, and she seemed preoccupied and unsure of herself.

"What in the world is wrong with Evelyn?" I remember asking. "If it's something terminal, I want to know."

"It's not that simple," said my companion. "Her son is learning to drive."

My daughter has been driving for three days, five hours and 17 minutes. Compared to Evelyn, I look like Pat Paulsen with a migraine.

I find myself sitting around in the evening, and for no apparent reason I will lift up my right foot and jam it down on an imaginary brake pedal.

Sometimes I will lay down my fork and say mechanically, "I don't wish to excite you, but would you mind turning off your windshield wipers? They are tickling the neck of the pedestrian riding on your hood whom we picked up going down the opposite direction of a one-way street."

The nights are the worst. The other night I dreamt she got her license.

My husband cannot understand what all the shouting is about When he takes her out he carries on a conversation, listens to the radio and occasionally catnaps, but then he has the kind of courage it takes to get your teeth cleaned without taking an anesthetic.

Heaven knows I tried to make her feel comfortable and relaxed. The first day I took her out I said softly, "This, my child, is an automobile. It is a vehicle to be enjoyed. It will take you along many happy roads of pleasure. It will afford you many happy hours on the highways and open up new horizons of relaxation and leisure. It is mechanically engineered to take you where you want to go and return you on the best highways the country has ever known. Remember, seven out of ten people drive a car. Little old ladies do it. People who wear glasses do it. Even people who can't type do it. Relax, take your time and hang loose."

She turned the key in the ignition.

"Thirty million Americans die each year on the highway!" I shouted hysterically.

She put the car into gear.

"If I go through this windshield there won't be a Mother's Day that you won't feel terrible."

She eased the car onto the highway.

"Just because they haven't recalled this model doesn't mean we're home free. Speed kills. There's a drunken driver waiting for you over the next hill. Drive defensively. You go over twenty and I'm using my ejection seat button. The light is green. What color are you waiting for?"

There is talk of lowering the driving age. It might be a good idea. There was a time when I had more patience. But who ever heard of a five-year-old behind the wheel of a car?

Phone Messages—October 22, 1969

I caught the tail end of one of my husband's lectures to the children the other night on Who Took the Phone Message I Didn't Get?

I have heard it before. It is one of his better efforts, in which he explains what a pencil is, tells of the humiliation he suffers at the office, and ends up with excerpts from President Truman's famous Give 'Em Hell speech.

The children blink and point an accusing finger at each other and promise never to let it happen again. It will.

Frankly, I am in favor of raising the age of children answering the phone to 23 years old. I base this on several facts. First, I have been savagely beaten, kicked and maimed on the way to my own telephone. Second, spies detained in Cuba get more messages through the Red Cross than I get in my own house. Third, at the age of 23, it is likely the children are married and have a phone of their own.

Sometimes when I am feeling overly sadistic about it, I can imagine how history might have been altered had a youngster been on the line taking messages.

"Anyone call today?" asks General Eisenhower.

"Oh, yes," answers his son, "a girl with a deep voice called Winnie Burchill."

"That's Churchill. What did he say?"

"I don't remember."

"Think."

"It was something about an invasion. He'll be ready to go on either June second, eighth or ninth or December fifth or eleventh. One of those days. He said the weather was either going to be sunny or rainy. I don't remember. Hey, did you notice what the base movie was when you passed by?"

Or what if Neil Armstrong had called directly home and gotten one his youngsters on the line.

> Mrs. Armstrong: "Was that the phone ringing?"
>
> Child: "Yes, it was Daddy. He just called from the moon."
>
> Mrs. Armstrong: "Why didn't you call me?"
>
> Child: "You were hanging out the wash."
>
> Mrs. Armstrong: "Well, what did he say. Is he all right?"
>
> Child: "He said he wants you to tell the world he took a little step for mankind and a giant leap just for the fun of it. Something like that."
>
> Mrs. Armstrong: "What else did he say?"
>
> Child: "He didn't bring me anything so I hung up on him."

Who knows? Maybe Grant wanted to surrender to Lee and a teenage corporal wrote the message on a breath mint and ate it. Maybe General Custer was supposed to fight at Big Little Horn and someone goofed the message up to read Little Big Horn. Maybe Julius Caesar never got the phone message saying, "Jeane Dixon said forget the Senate today."

Oh, well, we'll never really know for sure, will we?

Working Mom's Telephone Crisis—May 28, 1971

In talking with a working mother the other day, she disclosed one of the little-discussed hazards of holding down a job with one hand and tending a family with the other. She called it the Telephone Crisis.

At least once a day a working mother will be summoned to the business phone to hear the voice of her child say, "Mom, can I make a raft and mess around on the Ohio River with Huckleberry Hickey?"

Striving to keep her carpetland composure, the mother, remembering she is a professional, will clutch her throat and shout, "You leave the house and I'll break your head!"

"If you want to find out how indispensable you really are," said one mother, "just get a job and wait for the phone to ring. My kids have had me called out of conferences involving thousands of dollars to electrify me with such breathless decisions as:

1. Can I split a Pepsi with Kathy?
2. Guess what the dog dug up?
3. Did you wash my white shorts for gym tomorrow?
4. I got an 83 on my health test.
5. Rick just got his driver's license. Can I go with him to town and see how he does in traffic?

The plight of the working mother and the Telephone Crisis reaches a feverish pitch in the summer months when the children are at home. There is perhaps nothing that strikes fear in a mother's heart as much as the following sequence:

"Hello, Mom. This is Debbie."

"Give me that phone! Mom, this is Wesley and make her stop slapping."

"You're gonna get it. I'm telling! Mom, tell him it's his turn to set the table."

"I thought you told her she couldn't have fifteen girls in here at once."

"I'm telling. Mom, did you know . . . quit it! You're hurting me."

"You're not even bleeding much. Mooooommmmm!"
Click.

Until the Telephone Crisis is resolved, it is safe to assume there will not be a woman in the White House. Can you imagine getting a busy signal on the Hot Line?

I've Always Loved You Best—July 20, 1971

It is normal for children to want assurance that they are loved. Having all the warmth of the Berlin Wall, I have always admired women who can reach out to pat their children and not have them flinch.

Feeling more comfortable on paper, I wrote this for each of my children.

To the firstborn . . . I've always loved you best because you were our first miracle. You were the genesis of a marriage, the fulfillment of young love, the promise of our infinity.

You sustained us through the hamburger years: the first apartment furnished in Early Poverty . . . our first mode of transportation (1955 feet) . . . the 7-inch TV set we paid on for 36 months.

You wore new, had unused grandparents and more clothes than a Barbie doll. You were the original model for unsure parents trying to work the bugs out. You got the strained lamb, open pins and three-hour naps.

You were the beginning.

To the middle child . . . I've always loved you best because you drew a dumb spot in the family and it made you stronger for it.

You cried less, had more patience, wore faded and never in your life did anything first, but it only made you more special. You are the one we relaxed with and realized a dog could kiss you and you wouldn't get sick. You could cross a street by yourself long before you were old enough to get married, and the world wouldn't come to an end if you went to bed with dirty feet.

You were the continuance.

To the baby . . . I've always loved you best because endings generally are sad and you are such a joy. You readily accepted the milk-stained bibs. The lower bunk. The cracked baseball bat. The baby book, barren but for a recipe for graham piecrust that someone jammed between the pages.

You are the one we held on to so tightly. For, you see, you are the link with the past that gives a reason to tomorrow. You darken our hair, quicken our steps, square our shoulders, restore our vision and give us humor that security and maturity can't give us.

When your hairline takes on the shape of Lake Erie and your children tower over you, you will still be "the baby."

You were the culmination.

Mike and the Grass—May 1973

When Mike was three, he wanted a sandbox, and his father said, "There goes the yard. We'll have kids over here day and night, and they'll throw sand into the flower beds, and cats will make a mess in it, and it'll kill the grass for sure."

And Mike's mother said, "It'll come back."

When Mike was five, he wanted a jungle-gym set with swings that would take his breath away and bars to take him to the summit, and his father said, "Good grief, I've seen those things in backyards, and do you know what they look like? Mud holes in a pasture. Kids digging their gym shoes in the ground. It'll kill the grass."

And Mike's mother said, "It'll come back."

Between breaths when Daddy was blowing up the plastic swimming pool, he warned, "You know what they're going to do to this place? They're going to condemn it and use it for a missile site. I hope you know what you're doing. They'll track water everywhere and have a million water fights, and you won't be able to take out the garbage without stepping in mud up to your neck. When we take this down, we'll have the only brown lawn on the block."

"It'll come back," Mike's mother said.

When Mike was 12, he volunteered his yard for a camp-out. As they hoisted the tents and drove in the spikes, his father stood at the window and observed: "Why don't I just put the grass seed out in cereal bowls for the birds and save myself trouble spreading it around? You know for a fact that those tents and all those big feet are going to trample down every single blade of grass, don't you? Don't bother to answer. I know what you're going to say. 'It'll come back.'"

The basketball hoop on the side of the garage attracted more crowds than the Olympics. And a small patch of lawn that started out with a barren spot the size of a garbage can lid soon grew to encompass the entire side yard.

Just when it looked as if the new seed might take root, the winter came and the sled runners beat it into ridges. Mike's father shook his head and said, "I never asked for much in this life—only a patch of grass."

And his wife smiled and said, "It'll come back."

The lawn this fall was beautiful. It was green and alive and rolled out like a sponge carpet along the drive where gym shoes had trod . . . along the garage where bicycles used to fall . . . and around the flower beds where little boys used to dig with iced-tea spoons.

But Mike's father never saw it. He anxiously looked beyond the yard and asked with a catch in his voice, "He *will* come back, won't he?"

Live-in Neighbor Child—September 30, 1973

There isn't a family in the world that at one time or another hasn't had a live-in neighbor child.

He's the kid who sleeps in the woodwork, materializes each morning at your breakfast table, spends the entire day with you, and the next thing you know you can't really remember where he lives or who he belongs to.

We were sitting around the breakfast table one morning when my husband asked, "How many children do we have?"

"Three," I replied.

"We have four at breakfast," he tallied. "Which one isn't ours?"

I was stumped. One had my eyes, another the same color of hair as my husband, but the other two we both could have phoned in.

"Okay," I announced, "will the real Bombecks please stand up?"

They exchanged glances dramatically. One slid back his chair like he was going to stand up but didn't. Slowly, the other three rose to their feet.

"If that doesn't tear it," I snarled, looking at Tim, who was still seated. "I not only thought he was mine, I just got him toilet trained."

I have often wondered about the mothers of these children who disappear for five or six years to play. Do they rent out their rooms or keep them available? Do they feel guilty when they list them as a deduction on their income tax?

I think it's flattering when a child joins your family, but there has to come a time when you send him home.

A neighbor child has been with you too long when you postpone your vacation because you can't get anyone to sit with him.

He's been with you too long when his teacher wants to have a parent conference with you.

He's been with you too long when you punish him by sending him to his house.

He's been with you too long when you call his mother and she says, "Huh?"

He's been with you too long when he appears with all of you on your Christmas card.

Tim has been with us too long. The other day a car driven by his father picked him up. Before I realized what I was doing, I was calling the police to report a missing child.

Kids: Life's Greatest Mysteries—July 29, 1975

My goodness, the children have only been out of school for six weeks. Time flies when you're under sedation, doesn't it?

As I was hiding from them in the backseat of the car just last week, it occurred to me that I don't know children at all. I'm raising three of them, and yet they remain one of life's greatest mysteries.

For example, I don't understand how come a child can climb up on the roof, scale the TV antenna and rescue the cat . . . yet cannot walk down the hallway without grabbing both walls with his grubby hands for balance.

Or how come a child can eat yellow snow, kiss the dog on the lips, chew gum that he has found in the ashtray, put his mouth over a muddy garden hose nozzle . . . and refuse to drink from a glass his brother has just used?

Why is it he can stand with one foot on first base while reaching out and plucking a baseball off the ground with the tips of his fingers . . . yet cannot pick up a piece of soap before it melts into the drain?

Explain to me how he can ride a bicycle, run, play ball, set up a camp, swing, fight a war, swim and race for eight hours . . . and has to be driven to the garbage can.

It puzzles me how a child can see a dairy bar three miles away but cannot see a 4-by-6 rug that has scrunched up under his feet and been dragged through two rooms.

Why is it a child can reject a hot dog with mustard served on a soft bun at home . . . yet eat six of them two hours later at 50 cents each?

How come I can trip over a kid's shoes under the kitchen sink, in the bathroom, on the front porch, under the coffee table, in the sandbox, in the car, in the clothes hamper and on the washer . . . but we can never find them when it is time to cut the grass?

Why is the sun hotter delivering papers than it is goofing around . . . when it is the same sun?

How come they can't remember what time they're supposed to be home, but they remember they did dishes a week ago Wednesday two nights in a row because we had spaghetti and a spoon got caught in the disposal and they traded off?

I'll never understand how a child can't even find his English book when it is under his right hand but can find his mother hiding out in the backseat of a car.

I Loved You Enough to . . . —January 6, 1976

"You don't love me!"

How many times have your kids laid that one on you? And how many times have you, as a parent, resisted the urge to tell them how much?

Someday, when my children are old enough to understand the logic that motivates a mother, I'll tell them:

I loved you enough to bug you about where you were going, with whom and what time you would get home.

I loved you enough to insist you buy a bike with your own money even though we could afford it.

I loved you enough to be silent and let you discover your friend was a creep.

I loved you enough to make you return a Milky Way with a bite out of it to the drugstore and confess, "I stole this."

I loved you enough to stand over you for two hours while you cleaned your bedroom, a job that would have taken me 15 minutes.

I loved you enough to say, "Yes, you can go to Disney World on Mother's Day."

I loved you enough to let you see anger, disappointment, disgust and tears in my eyes.

I loved you enough not to make excuses for your lack of respect or your bad manners.

I loved you enough to admit that I was wrong and ask for your forgiveness.

I loved you enough to ignore what every other mother did or said.

I loved you enough to let you stumble, fall, hurt and fail.

I loved you enough to let you assume the responsibility for your own actions at age 6, 10 or 16.

I loved you enough to figure you would lie about the party being chaperoned but forgave you for it—after discovering I was right.

I loved you enough to accept you for what you are, not what I wanted you to be.

But, most of all, I loved you enough to say no when you hated me for it. That was the hardest part of all.

Parents Get Apartment—June 6, 1976

We knew the kids would take it the wrong way, but we had to do it anyway.

"Children, your father and I want to get our own apartment."

One looked up from his homework and the other two even turned the volume down on the TV set. "What are you saying?"

"We are saying we'd like to move out and be on our own for a while."

"But why?" asked our daughter. "Aren't you happy here? You have your own room and the run of the house."

"I know, but a lot of parents our age are striking out on their own."

"It'll be expensive," said our son. "Have you thought about utilities and phone bills and newspapers and a hundred little things you take for granted around here?"

"We've thought it all through."

"Spit it out," said our daughter. "What's bothering you about living with us? Did we ask too much? What did we ask you to do? Only cook, make beds, do laundry, take care of the yard, keep the cars in running order and bring in the money. Was that so hard?"

"It's not that," I said gently. "It's just that we want to fix up our own apartment and come and go as we please."

"If it's your car you wanted, why didn't you say so? We could make arrangements."

"It's not just the car. We want to be able to play our phonograph when we want to and come in late without someone saying, 'Where have you been?' and invite people over without other people hanging around."

"What will you do for furniture?"

"We don't need all that much. We'll just take a few small appliances, some linens, our bedroom suite, the typewriter, the luggage, the card table and chairs, the old TV you never use, some pots and pans and a few tables and chairs."

"You'll call every day?"

We nodded.

"Mom, do me a favor. Don't wear those white socks when you meet your new neighbors. And Dad! Let your hair grow."

As we headed for the car I heard our son whisper sadly, "Our parents have grown up." His brother said, "They'll be back in a week!"

Children Are Like Kites—May 15, 1977

I was autographing books at one of those little rattan tables in the bookstore when I found myself looking into the saddest eyes I had ever seen.

"The doctor wanted me to buy something that would make me laugh," she said.

I hesitated about signing the book. It would have taken corrective surgery to make that woman laugh.

"Is it a big problem?" I asked. The whole line of people was eavesdropping.

"Yes. My daughter is getting married." The line cheered.

"Is she twelve or something?"

"She's twenty-four," said the woman, biting her lip. "And he's a wonderful man. It's just that she could have stayed home a few more years."

The woman behind her looked wistful. "We've moved three times, and our son keeps finding us. Some women have all the luck."

Isn't it curious how some mothers don't know when they've done a good job or when it's basically finished? They figure the longer the kids hang around, the better parents they are. I guess it all depends on how you regard children in the first place.

How do you regard yours? Are they like an appliance? The more you have, the more status you command? They're under warranty to perform at your whim for the first 18 years; then, when they start costing money, you get rid of them?

Are they like a used car? You maintain it for years, and when you're ready to sell it to someone else, you feel a great responsibility to keep it running or it reflects on you? (That's why some parents never let their children marry good friends.)

Are they like an endowment policy? You invest in them for 18 or 20 years, and then for the next 20 years they return dividends that support you in your declining years or they suffer from terminal guilt?

Are they like a finely gilded mirror that reflects the image of its owner in every way? On the day the owner looks in and sees a flaw, a crack, a distortion, one tiny idea or attitude that is different from his own, he casts it aside and declares himself a failure?

I see children as kites. You spend a lifetime trying to get them off the ground. You run with them until you're both breathless . . . they crash . . . you add a longer tail . . . they hit the rooftop . . . you pluck them out of the spout. You patch and comfort, adjust and teach. You watch them lifted by the wind and assure them that someday they'll fly.

Finally they are airborne, but they need more string so you keep letting it out. With each twist of the ball of twine there is a sadness that goes with the joy, because the kite becomes more distant, and somehow you know it won't be long before that beautiful creature will snap the lifeline that bound you together and soar as it was meant to soar—free and alone.

Only then do you know that you did your job.

Summertime Blues—August 3, 1978

"Summertime, and the livin' is easy. . . ."

There are 35 unwashed glasses on the countertop by the sink. I don't own 35 glasses.

The front door has not been shut all the way since June 10.

The water jug in the refrigerator has a piece of lettuce floating in it.

The washer has a better pulse than I do.

There are six cars in the driveway. None of them are ours. One of them runs.

The phone rings constantly. It was for me once. A kid wanted to be picked up at the ballpark.

I put baking soda in the refrigerator. Someone poured milk on it and ate it.

I tried to take a shower by myself. A note slid under the door. It read, *Can I split a Pepsi?*

There is a bucket, a volleyball and a stack of poker chips in the middle of the living room. It's a new game.

My husband says the house is always hot. Today, I discovered the furnace is on.

A man selling real estate in Mexico knocked on our door and asked for Mr. Bruce Bombeck. Brucie is seven years old.

The kids used limes to liven up their Coke. Limes are $1.49 a pound.

They're going to put a streetlight at the end of our driveway.

I found a suitcase full of dirty sweaters under a bed.

Someone ran through our house with black heel marks that are now permanently transferred to our yellow tile.

My daughter said my sewing machine needle misses the hole and breaks off on the bobbin plate.

Someone has been in the hall bathroom with the door locked for 15 days.

The dog looks fat.

I found an application for college in the stove drawer.

Gym shoes that make you jump higher and make more basketball points just went up two bucks.

"So hush, little baby, don't you cry. . . ."

Local or Toll Call Girlfriend?—February 1, 1979

A lot of mothers I know are downright meddling when it comes to their children's selection of a boyfriend or a girlfriend.

They want to know how old, how tall, what their father does, where they live, the scope of their education, what their plans are for the future, and how they feel about children.

I don't care about any of those things. All I want to know is, "Is he or she a local call or a toll?" I don't remember names or faces of old flames. All I remember is their area code. One of my sons once dated an area code 513 for six months. It was marriage by Ma Bell. I figured we were spending $35 a month to share such insights as:

"What are you doing?"

"Nothing, what are you doing?"

"I don't want to interrupt you if you're doing something."

"I told you I wasn't doing anything."

"You sure?"

"I'm sure."

"So, what's new?"

Another one of my kids showed an interest in a lovely girl who lived just a few miles from us. It was great. I didn't have to worry about a deep involvement because they were never off the phone.

He set his alarm to call her in the morning. At night I used to go in and remove the phone from his ear as he slept. It was like hanging up an umbilical cord. As soon as they left each other at school in the afternoon they would shout, "I'll call you when I get home!" I offered to feed him intravenously.

The suggestion by my husband to put a timer by the phone with sand running through was ridiculous. However, I did slip a calendar under his door and circle the month.

Panic didn't set in until one day when I was standing near and saw him dial "1." "Who are you calling?" I asked.

"You know," he said, "the same person I've been talking with for the last month."

"But I thought she was a local call."

"Don't worry," he said, "it only costs about eight cents a minute.

Besides, this isn't just some silly kid infatuation. This is a person I genuinely care for and want to spend the rest of my life with. She's important to me. She's special and there isn't anything I wouldn't do for her."

"I'm glad to hear you say that," I said, "because according to the phone bill you owe us $36.86 in long-distance charges."

I learned something that day. When toll charges enter the room, love goes right out the window.

Marching to a Different Drummer—November 3, 1979

In 1955, I gave birth to a child who "marched to a different drummer."

I predicted then if he didn't shape up, he'd goose-step his way right into the unemployment line or the boys' industrial school.

As a child he wandered away from home to see parades . . . got his arm caught in a construction pipe . . . and figured out if he coughed on his brother's cupcake he got an extra dessert.

He sold our canceled checks door to door, registered us for a free ham (and a visit from an encyclopedia salesman), made the first overseas phone call by direct dialing from a private home without directory assistance and made history by catching a broken leg at camp.

In 1966, I wrote that parents are awed by genius, adjust to the average child and are compassionate toward the slow learner. But the child who stands apart and is none of these things only puzzles, confuses and tries their patience.

They fear for the future of this rare, unpredictable child, who is not only out of step with the world but, if there's a puddle or a pile in front of him . . . will step in it.

What has happened to this child-turned-man whose destiny filled me with apprehension?

He lost his billfold in the Grand Canyon, but the trip back to look for it was "worth it." He forgot birthdays, but when he remembered, the gifts were warm and personal and melted your heart. He set a record for having a tape deck installed and stolen within three hours but held no malice. He left his space maintainer in a sandwich he was reheating in the microwave oven but paid for a new one with money from his paper route. He borrowed the car and, when the radiator boiled over, poured Orange Crush in it, but he was contrite.

His mail consists of brochures from causes and needs all over the world. His desk is scattered with unpaid traffic tickets and his billfold holds three duplicate driver's licenses. He runs his car on empty, writes 35 checks a week and has never bought a bottle of shampoo.

I have never heard him say, "I'm too busy to talk to you." Never heard him complain, "The world is rotten." Never known him to be intolerant.

He dreams impractical dreams. He tries the patience of Job.

But with his childlike trust and his zest for living, who am I to say that the drummer he marches to will not take him to the stars?

Parenthood Is Worth the Risks—September 2, 1980

There's at least one in every crowd, the woman who does not want to bring a child into "this lousy, mixed-up world."

I met one the other night who said children were just ego trips for parents who like to see their own image staring back at them over the breakfast table. She added, "I can't come up with one reason for having them."

What a pity. According to my children, there were a lot of reasons I had them.

I needed a personal slave: someone to answer the phone, get my sweater, find my glasses, get my keys out of the door, unload the groceries, go to the store, let the dog out and move the hose.

I needed someone around the house to eat the leftovers the dog wouldn't touch.

I needed someone to shove out of the car to throw his body over the last picnic table while we found a place to park.

I needed a live-in who would assist in raising a younger brother and sister by taking them to the bathroom every five minutes and sitting with them for free on New Year's Eve.

I needed an excuse for my saddlebag hips and flabby upper arms.

I needed material for the Christmas newsletter and a three-times-a-week column.

I needed someone to mail letters for me when it rained.

I needed someone to practice medicine on. ("Turn down that record or you'll go deaf!")

I needed someone to spy on and make me feel important.

That's their story. Mine is even more biased.

I brought children into this lousy, mixed-up world because when you love someone and they love you back, the world doesn't look that lousy or seem that mixed up.

I gave them life because they have the same right I was given to make up their own minds as to what makes a good or a bad world.

More than an image over the breakfast table, they are special to this universe now and will be long after I am gone.

Some people must take the risk of being a parent. If we don't, who will be left to listen to the young people who lament, "I don't want to bring children into this lousy, mixed-up world"?

Favorite Child—May 10, 1981

Every mother has a favorite child.

She cannot help it. She is only human.

I have mine.

That child for whom I feel a special closeness. The one I reach out to in a rare moment, to share a love that no one else could possibly understand.

My favorite child is the one who was too sick to eat the ice cream at his birthday party, had measles at Christmas and wore leg braces to bed because he toed in.

She was the fever in the middle of the night, the asthma attack, the child in my arms at the emergency ward.

My favorite child spent Christmas alone away from the family, was stranded after the game with a gas tank on E, lost the money for his class ring.

My favorite child is the one who screwed up the piano recital, misspelled *committee* in a spelling bee, ran the wrong way with the football and had his bike stolen because he was careless.

My favorite child is the one who fell asleep over an assignment on China that the teacher never bothered to grade, flunked her driver's test five times and told us she could hardly wait to get out of the house.

My favorite child is the one I punished for lying, grounded for insensitivity to other people's feelings and informed he was a royal pain to the entire family.

My favorite child slammed doors in frustration, cried when she didn't think I saw her, withdrew and said she could not talk to me.

My favorite child always needed a haircut, had hair that wouldn't curl, had no date for Saturday night and a car that cost $600 to fix.

My favorite child said dumb things for which there were no excuses. He was selfish, immature, bad-tempered and self-centered. He was vulnerable, lonely, unsure of what he was doing in this world . . . and quite wonderful.

The one I've loved the most is the one whom I have watched struggle and—because the struggle was his—done nothing.

All mothers have their favorite child. It is always the same one, the one who needs you at the moment for whatever reason—to cling to, to shout at, to hurt, to hug, to flatter, to reverse charges to, to unload on, to use—but mostly, to be there.

The First Day of School—September 3, 1981

This column could be entitled: Confessions of a child entering school for the first time who according to adults has "nothing to worry about."

My name is Donald and I don't know anything.

I have new underwear, a new sweater, a loose tooth and I didn't sleep last night. I am worried.

What if the school bus jerks after I get on and I lose my balance and my pants rip and everyone laughs?

What if I have to go to the bathroom before we get to school?

What if a bell rings and everyone goes in a door and a man yells, "Where do you belong?" and I don't know?

What if my shoestring comes untied and someone says, "Your shoestring is untied. We'll all watch while you tie it"?

What if the trays in the cafeteria are too high for me to reach?

What if the thermos lid on my soup is on too tight and, when I try to open it, it breaks?

What if my loose tooth wants to come out when we're supposed to have our heads down and be quiet?

What if teacher tells the class to go to the bathroom and I can't go?

What if I get hot and want to take my sweater off and someone steals it?

What if I splash water on my name tag and my name disappears and no one will know who I am?

What if they send us out to play and all the swings are taken? What do I do?

What if the wind blows all the important papers out of my hands that I'm supposed to take home?

What if they mispronounce my last name and everyone laughs?

What if my teacher doesn't make her D's like Mom taught me?

What if I spend the whole day without a friend?

What if the teacher gives a seat to everyone and I'm left over?

What if the windows in the bus steam up and I won't be able to tell when I get to my stop?

I'm just a little kid, but maybe I'm smarter than I think I am. At least I know better than to tell a five-year-old with a loose tooth who has never been out of the yard by himself before that he has "nothing to worry about."

Third Child—November 5, 1981

Someone, who has wisely remained anonymous, once said that children are like waffles. The first one should be used to season the grill and then tossed out.

Studies made on first children say they're not all that bad. They are usually shy, serious and sensitive, are academically superior and are more likely to be an Einstein.

Second children, on the other hand, are relaxed, independent, cheerful, lean toward creativity and are more likely to be a Picasso.

No one has had the courage to find—let alone study—child No. 3 and the ones who follow, whom I call et ceteras.

Is there life after the first two children? What are the et ceteras like?

I have discovered the third child has a few attributes of his own. He has itchy feet and joins other families for three or four months, often without being noticed. He is not intimidated by anyone, has a great sense of humor and is apt to be a game show host.

Part of their uniqueness is that third children have no history. There are no footprints of them in the baby book, no record of their baptism, no snapshots of their birthdays and no report cards to show they ever were.

Their childhood diseases are uneventful, their first words fall on deaf ears, and toilet training is a lonely affair with no one to applaud their efforts.

The third child learns early that he is odd man out and has broken the family symmetry.

Kitchen chairs come four to a set, breakfast rolls four to a package and milk four cups to a quart. Rides at Disneyland accommodate two to a seat, the family car carries four comfortably, and beds come in twos, not threes.

The third child is the one who gets called the other two's names before the mother finally remembers his. He goes through a lifetime of comparisons: "You're not going to be as tall as your brother . . . as smart as your sister . . . as athletic as your father."

I personally feel there's a lot to be said for the et cetera children, who get a fast family shuffle and who thrive on neglect and somehow appear one day all grown up.

They not only know who they are and what they are, but they've dealt very early with the two things that most children fear the most: competition and loneliness.

Mother–Son Dialogue—January 13, 1987

Parents are always complaining that their kids never talk to them. I have *never* had a problem communicating. I can question them openly about anything and they will respond.

Take the other night. One of them came in late and I padded out into the hallway, where mother and son had a real dialogue at 2 A.M.

"Is that you?"

A: "Who did you think it was?"

"What time is it?"

A: "What time do you think it is?"

"We had your favorite dinner tonight: pork chops and apple-sauce. Did you eat?"

A: "Don't I always?"

"What do people do at 2 A.M.?"

A: "Have you forgotten?"

"Yes. Did you see Greg tonight?"

A: "Did he call?"

"Did I say he did?"

A: "Did he or didn't he?"

"No, but Lisa did."

A: "What did she want?"

"She didn't say. Did you get gas for the car?"

A: "Didn't I say I would?"

At this point he went into the bathroom and I had to continue the conversation through the crack in the door.

"Are there an5y towels in there?"

A: "Aren't there always?"

"When will you stop taking things for granted?"

A: "Do I do that?"

"Did I tell you to be home at six Friday? It's Grandma's birthday."

A: "Don't you remember?"

"Is the water hot?"

A: "Why wouldn't it be?"

"Do you want me to call you late in the morning?"

A: "How late is late?"

"Nine-ish?"

A: "Are you serious?"

"I'm going to bed. It's wonderful that we can talk together like this. A lot of kids, when they reach your age, become un-communicative, and you don't know what they're doing or what they're thinking. Am I lucky or what? Don't answer that."

Different Mother for Each Child—June 26, 1990

Often when I'm interviewed, I'm asked what kind of a mother I am. That's like asking me to make up my own test and grade it. Who knows? I showed up for it. I worked a lot of overtime. Had a lot of help from Drs. Spock, Denton and Ruth. Not one of my kids is working on a *Mommie* book. Only one has an agent. I suspect that if you talked with each of the three, you would get a different answer because I was three different people. No one got the same mother.

Child No. 1 got the Antiseptic Queen, a thin, nervous woman endowed with patience and dedicated to staying at home boiling things all day long, as if she were living through a typhoid epidemic. She boiled pacifiers, toys and diapers, recorded the baby's BMs and took pictures every four days for the baby album. She hand-smocked little dresses, served homemade baby food in a warmer dish with little ducks floating around the rim and actually needlepointed a 4-by-6 rug of a sailboat for the nursery.

Child No. 2 got Super Sufferer, who had stretch marks on her face from overeating and dragged around in her husband's shirts. She couldn't get a meal together until seven and fell asleep during a root canal. With regularity, she flunked the wife/mother quizzes in magazines. She told her children the tooth fairy resorted to checks because the IRS needed proof of the deductions. Apathy reigned. The baby food included a hot dog on a paper plate. The musical potty seat played "The Impossible Dream," and she once rescued the pacifier from the coffee grounds and rinsed it with the garden hose before sticking it into the baby's mouth.

Child No. 3 got Mother Mellow, who didn't much care what he did just so long as he had clean hands and his own door key. Birth and graduation pictures were on the same film. The sailboat rug faded when it was washed and was now used for a dog bed. She was a woman with no nervous system even when the baby bit into a tube of paint tint and urinated blue for a week. This mother actually revealed a sense of humor and admitted to mistakes from time to time. She ironed on demand and just the parts that showed. The only items in the baby book were a footprint and congratulations from the insurance agent.

Small wonder kiss-and-tell books are written by the firstborn.

Housewife's Lament

Soap Operas—June 1, 1965

I don't know what my husband thinks I'm made of!

After spending a day ironing in front of my television, I am so emotionally involved in the tormented lives of my soap opera heroines, you'd think he would sense that I can't take on his problems, too.

Just last week he came barging in and said, "Hello."

"What do you mean by that!" I said, flipping open the tablecloth.

"Just hello," he said.

"No one says 'hello.' You sound funny. If you're going to share some big, fat trauma with me, forget it! I've just lived through three miscarriages, two trial separations, a nasty, interfering grandmother, a broken-down actress who's a lush visiting her daughter in prison, a cheating wife, a custody suit, and a neurological workup. Besides, I blew three quiz games, and underbid on a weekend for two in a poverty pocket. I'm exhausted."

He shook his head. "It's ridiculous how you involve yourself in these make-believe stories. Got any coffee on?"

"I knew it. You want to talk. Some days I feel like Ma Perkins, who just pours coffee while the entire world comes through her kitchen and puts problems at her feet. Get your own sugar. What's the problem?"

"No problem."

"There has to be. No one drinks coffee in the afternoon without a problem. I know. Joanne went through this on *Love's Eternal Guiding Flame Is Flickering but Still Searches for General Hospital's World of Tomorrow*, and her husband got sacked. You didn't get sacked, did you?"

"Isn't there anything else on daytime television but stories and games?"

"Sure, there are Pinky Lee reruns. And Boston Blackie repeats. But it's not fun when you know the dialogue."

"Don't these stories ever have any happiness in them?" he persisted.

"Yes. When Lisa lost her baby, her mother was happy."

"That's weird."

"Not so weird. Lisa wasn't married. It solves the problems for all of them. Of course, big-mouth Bruce had to complicate things for them. He's the orderly in the hospital. In a pig's eye! I wouldn't let him tidy up my curler tray. Anyway, he blew it all over town. More coffee?"

"These soap opera heroes—don't they ever work?"

"Work! Could you put in a day's work if your mother-in-law accused you of doing her daughter in and was trying to take the children away from you? That's the trouble with men. They've got no feelings for other people."

"I do have a little problem. Could we eat later, so I can get a haircut before dinner?"

"I knew it. Tell you what, I don't want to miss my night soap operas, so I'll fix you a tray. I wouldn't ask you to eat alone, but when you're an illegitimate child, whose convict father is fresh out of his oxygen tent after being shot by the town's only insurance salesman, you need friends."

Lost Identity—September 18, 1965

I never know what to say to women who ask my opinion on how they can find their "lost identity."

I'm a poor one to ask. Not only has my identity been lost for years, but so has my front door key. (And if you think I get my jollies taking out the bathroom screen and shinnying down the shower head to get into my house each evening, you're crazy.)

When I was first married, I fancied I identified with Debbie Reynolds and Dr. Schweitzer. Several years and three children later, I reshuffled standards and now identify with Jane Withers, taking the stains out of her sink, and Pa Kettle.

I'd be a fool to pretend I hadn't noticed the real me lost in a cloud of impersonal pronouns throughout the years. For example, at the office, it's "Oh, you're Bill's wife." On the playground, it's "So you're Andy's mother." At the neighborhood coffee klatch, it's "I'd know you anywhere. You're the Wednesday Volkswagen in the car pool." Even at the bank, it's "Well, if you're 002-968-994-05, why didn't you say so?" You know how it goes.

Actually, what I represent to other people isn't half as important as what I represent to myself. One day, as I stood studying my reflection in a skillet lid, I plopped it down, went back to the bedroom, put my hair up in curlers and changed my dress. I put a dab of perfume behind each ear and returned to the kitchen. When asked where I was going, I snapped, "I'm going out to the garbage can all by myself!" No one understood. But I felt better.

Identity is more than a tag or a label. It's a feeling that takes a little time out of each day to develop—time that a housewife doesn't usually have.

The slick magazines are forever trying to build the feminine image by pointing out that the modern-day mother is a taskmaster of a hundred skills—"She must be chauffeur, dietitian, doctor"—and a list of 20 specialized fields, ad nauseam. Rubbish! I could be replaced at the car wheel by a chimpanzee (who could probably even be taught to park!). My meals are a living monument to the frozen foods industry. As for my medical background, if I can't cure it with a Band-Aid or a kiss, I use my tongue paddle to dial a doctor.

I contend it's the absence of time to herself that breaks a homemaker's back. Some days it's like living in the eye of a hurricane. It's refereeing a family of differences. It's puppeteering a houseful of personalities. It's making more decisions in a single hour than an umpire makes in nine innings. It's the constancy of a job that runs from one night into the next day and into that night and into the next morning.

Have you ever slipped out to the car and slumped down, only to have six beady eyes discover you and squeal, "We found her"? Have you ever locked yourself in the bathroom and watched entranced while a note slid under the door that read, *Are the Popsicles frozen yet?* Have you ever been in a group and been too embarrassed to confess that the last book you read was *Guadalcanal Diary?* Have you ever gone to dinner with a group of friends and been horrified to discover you mechanically buttered everyone's bread and cut up their meat into bite sizes?

This is what a woman is talking about when she says she's lost her identity. Only I like to think it isn't lost at all—just buried temporarily under a stack of ironing, a book that needs covering or a basket of mending.

When the Memory Starts to Go—June 9, 1967

As a youth, the thought crossed my mind several times. How would I know when I began to deteriorate?

Would I quit running after buses? Would I wear a stocking cap to ward off a chill when I emptied the garbage? Would I forget to moisten my lips when I smiled? Or would it be a little thing—like having my legs go asleep and require medical attention every time I fell out of a foreign car?

Surprisingly, it is none of these things. Deterioration begins with the memory.

It's true. Since reaching 40, I can't seem to remember a thing, including the fact that I reached the age of 40.

If I were cute about it, like Scarlett O'Hara stomping her foot on the veranda and pouting, "I swear, Ashley Wilkes, I can't remember promising you to promenade!" I wouldn't mind.

But it's not like that.

There's my husband penciling buttons on his T-shirt because I forgot to pick up his dress shirts at the laundry.

There's my child in a cafeteria with a dampened blouse for lunch because I gave him the wrong bag.

And in some little lunchroom, somewhere in the city, my very best friend, what's-her-name, is throwing down breadsticks waiting for me to join her for lunch, unaware that I wrapped my gum in her memo and discarded the same.

There are other evidences of forgetfulness.

Friends have noted a fantastic increase in the number of miles I walked to school as a child, the number of bridesmaids at my wedding, my take-home pay on my first job and the number of hours I labored with my first child. (My husband says, given a few more years, I will enrich the story to the point where I excused myself from a campfire and delivered the baby myself in a barren field using only a few leeches, fig leaves and strips of buffalo hide.)

Lord knows I've tried to be a list maker. It is all very executivish. There is a pad of paper at my bedside. At the top is printed the day of the week, followed by the day's schedule: Get up. Put the dog out. Get the kids up. Bring the dog in. Get the husband up. Put the kids out. Bring the milk in. Put the husband out.

Before the schedule, I was getting the milk and the dog confused. It certainly made an interesting cereal bowl.

Those who have preceded me down forgotten-memory lane are hard-put to explain why you forget simple daily routine things, yet remember explicitly things that aren't worth a hill of beans.

For example, I can still remember the New York phone number of the "Major Bowes Amateur Hour" (Murray Hill 8-7933). I can't remember who carries our automobile insurance.

I know the verses and chorus of the "Beer Barrel Polka." I can never remember my brother-in-law's birthday.

Do you know before I went to the hospital I bought birth announcements and put them away so I'd have them and have been looking for them ever since?

Oh, well, the kid's eight years old now, so what does it matter?

Subversive Window Washer—September 29, 1967

A wonderful thing happened in our neighborhood last week. Wanda the window washer moved.

Wanda wasn't a bad sort. It's just when you get a woman of her kind who washes windows every 10 days the neighborhood gets a bad name.

I remember the day she moved in. We were all poking our heads through the cracks on our doors (our windows distort bodies), when right off we saw her unpack this big stepladder.

"Don't panic!" I told the group. "It's probably a garage prop. Undoubtedly got it for a wedding present and doesn't know what it's for."

Within minutes, she was shinnying up the rungs with a bucket in her hand and polishing the panes until we were nearly struck blind by the glare.

After that performance, homemade FOR SALE signs sprang up like crabgrass. We tried to reason with some of the homeowners, but they stood firm.

"We're selling before property values decrease," they insisted. "Sure, now it's only a window washer, but tomorrow it'll be a grass trimmer, a porch scrubber, a garbage can cleaner or even some nut who waxes the driveway."

Those of us who stood firm got it from all directions, especially our husbands.

"Hey," said my husband one evening, "is that woman across the street washing her windows again?"

"What windows?" I said, trying to divert his attention.

"You told me our windows weren't washable, that you had to send them out to be cleaned."

"Our windows aren't that dirty or I'd wash them."

"Aren't that dirty?" he shouted. "We're the only house in the block growing mushrooms for houseplants!"

"Can't you see what Wanda the window washer really is?" I asked. "She's a subversive. She was sent to this good upper-middle-class neighborhood of slobs to cause unrest, discontent and hostility. In time, she'll cause us to fight with our husbands, argue with our neighbors. The next thing you know, we'll divide politically and the country will be taken over by Communists."

The new neighbor moved in yesterday.

"How do you feel about washing windows?" we asked cautiously.

"The same way I feel about biting fingernails," she said. "It's a filthy habit. Besides, it's un-American."

Now, there's the kind of woman you'd like your son to marry.

Sewing-Basket Blues—November 21, 1969

You show me a woman who likes to mend and I'll show you a real weirdo. I know. I met a woman once who liked to mend and she was weird.

She ran around with a threaded needle stuck in her collar and a pair of scissors hanging on a piece of bias tape around her neck. She'd sneak up behind you and clip off ravelings from your seams and whip a threaded eye for your hook sooner than you could say, "Keep your cold clammy hands to yourself."

There is an old saying around our house: "When you say good-bye to a button, you say hello to drafts." As soon as a Bombeck child reaches the age of reason I sit down and explain to him how it is at our house.

"Some mommies have sewing baskets. Sewing baskets are round little boxes, sometimes square, that hold a needle and thread, a tape measure, chalk, scissors, bobbins and button box. This is Mommy's sewing basket. It is an old shoe box that I keep in the stove drawer. You'll notice it is different. It holds a box of paper clips, a roll of masking tape, a package of home permanent papers, a razor blade, a burnt-out bug bulb, a bookmarker with a prayer to St. Anthony and an iced tea spoon. Put your hand down; I answer questions at the end. Now, you must hang on to your buttons or you will have (a) a cold winter, (b) a hot summer, (c) an embarrassment for all seasons.

"If your sleeve rips, wear a sweater. If your hem falls out, turn your waistband up. If your pants rip, crouch. Anything you can't clip, paste, pin or tape, start praying you'll outgrow it. That's all. And good luck!"

I don't know why I have such an attitude toward mending except I regard it with the same excitement as hosing out the garbage can. It's menial, tedious, unimaginative and beneath me. There are parts of housekeeping that are quite creative. Mending is not one of them.

My husband finds my theory impossible to live with.

"The button fell off my coat."

"You know the rules of the house."

"I know the rules. I can't clip it, paste it, pin it or tape it, and I've grown as big as I'm going to get."

"Where's the button? Thank goodness there's a hole in it."

"What are you doing?"

"Looking for the weather report for tomorrow. Maybe you won't even need the coat."

"Give me a simple reason why you cannot sew on a simple button."

"I can't find my glasses. The House Needle is missing. If I did it for you, I'd have to do it for everybody. The thread doesn't match. I hurt myself when I sew. Take your pick."

"Forget it," he snarled.

"Have you thought of a belt?" I said brightly.

"Many times," he sighed.

Ironing—June 10, 1971

An ad in a Midwest newspaper read WANTED: Woman to do ironing for housewife 10 years behind in everything. Must have strong courage and sense of humor.

Now there's a woman I could live next door to in perfect harmony. I iron by appointment only. I learned long ago that if I ironed and hung three dresses in my daughter's closet, she would change three times during dinner.

The other day my son wanted me to iron his jeans for a class play. "Which leg faces the audience?" I asked with my iron poised in midair.

"Boy," he said, "you're sure not like Mrs. Breck."

I hadn't thought about Mrs. Breck in years. She was an antiseptic old broad who used to live two houses down from me. She had an annoying habit of putting her ironing board up on Tuesdays and putting it away again at the end of the day. (What can you expect from a woman who ironed belt buckles?)

One afternoon I dropped in on her as she was pressing the tongues in her son's tennis shoes.

"You know what you are, Mrs. Breck?" I said. "A drudge."

"Oh, I enjoy ironing," she said.

"You keep talking like that, and someone is going to put you in a home."

"What's so bad about ironing?" She grinned.

"No one does it," I snapped. "Did you ever see the women on soap operas iron? They're just normal American housewives. But do you ever see them in front of an ironing board? No! They're out having abortions, committing murder, blackmailing their boss, undergoing surgery, having fun! If you weren't chained to this ironing board you too could be out doing all sorts of exciting things."

"Like what?" She chuckled, pressing the wrinkles out of a pair of sweat socks and folding them neatly.

"You could give Tupperware parties, learn to scuba dive, learn hotel management while sitting under a hair dryer, have an affair with the Avon lady's unemployed brother-in-law, sing along with Jack LaLanne, collect antique barbed wire, take a course in Hebrew flower arranging, start chain letters. . . . I don't know, woman, use your imagination!"

I read the newspaper ad again. It intrigued me, so I dialed the number and waited.

"Hello, Mrs. Breck speaking."

Son of a gun. It sure makes you feel good when you had a part in someone's success, doesn't it?

The Mother Who Drives—June 11, 1972

When I am reincarnated, I want to come back in this world as a mother who doesn't drive.

I have noted with some bitterness that mothers who do not drive have time to paint sunsets, knit coats, bake bread and write symphonies.

Not only that, they are fully dressed by nine in the morning, have a deep bronze tan by May 20 and somehow seem taller.

Fifteen years of car pools does something to a woman. It makes her a little strange. For example, I cannot sit in a chair and delicately cross my legs at the ankles like other women. Instinctively, my right foot extends in an accelerator position and remains there until I stand up.

Also, I mumble a lot. That comes from spending years on the telephone trying to figure out that if Mary Jane's husband goes to the doctor's office on Wednesday, she will have to bundle the baby up and take him to work and trade with Martha, who is having a cyst removed. On the other hand, if Peter was really exposed to measles that means he will have them by Wednesday and Ada, who has already exchanged with Charlotte because Charlotte has trouble starting (the car, not Charlotte), would have to trade with Muriel because she has the convertible with the top that is stuck and it is her hair appointment day (she also cannot drive on rainy days).

Probably the most disconcerting hazard of being a "listed parent" in a car pool is that intellectually I have become stagnant. My vocabulary at the moment is down to four basic sentences. "Fill it up with regular," "Lock the door," "Keep your feet on the floor" and "Didn't you go before you left home?"

The other night at a party I was standing alone, holding my handbag in front of me like a steering wheel, when a handsome man approached me and said, "You look like you could use a drink. What'll it be?"

I handed him my Shell card and said, "Fill it up with regular." He laughed and steered me toward the kitchen where the bar was set up.

"Lock the door," I said mechanically. "And keep your feet on the floor."

He looked around nervously. "Listen," he said, "I just remembered I have some unfinished business to attend to. Would you excuse me, please?"

"Didn't you go before you left home?" I snapped.

If Ralph Nader doesn't recall me soon, it may be too late.

Making Paycheck Stretch—October 1972

I read some pretty incredible things in the newspaper, but the story I can't get over is the one about the woman from Michigan who grocery shops for staples once a year.

She makes up a grocery list 13 pages long, fills up 14 shopping carts, transfers it to 56 paper bags, coughs up $571.88 to pay for it, loads it in two cars and shouts gaily over her shoulder, "See you next year!"

I once bought eight boxes of cake mix on sale, four for a dollar, and by the end of the week we had a cake every day and two on Sunday. I can't save a thing around the house. When my husband taught school we used to get paid the fifteenth of every month. On the sixteenth, we ate like a Weight Watcher who has just fallen into a vat of baked potatoes and sour cream. For 15 days, we had three meats at every meal, five vegetables and a choice of four desserts.

The first of the month, we began to panic. By the time the last week rolled around, I was dyeing the rice brown trying to palm it off as ground beef and sucking on dental floss.

One night (the thirteenth of some month), my husband picked at a mound of cocktail onions and Spam and said, "If you can't manage the food any better than this throughout the month, why don't you plan your menus ahead and I'll hide the stuff so you won't use it all up the first couple of weeks."

As I contemplated our dessert for the evening (Kool-Aid over crushed ice), I had to agree it might work.

The first night he came through the door, I grabbed him by the shirt and said, "Where are they?"

"Where are what?" he asked.

"The bananas. I've been looking all day for the bananas."

"They're scheduled for salad tomorrow night."

"I don't want to wait until tomorrow night," I said testily. *"I'd kill for bananas, and you know it!"*

Our domestic bliss didn't end with bananas. I tore the attic up one day looking for the canned Boston brown bread to go with the cream cheese. And to ration a woman's coffee is dehumanizing.

I got to thinking about that doggone woman in Michigan. Could a person really stock up once a year or did she get home, unload her 56 shopping bags and tell her youngest, "There's nothing for lunch. Pedal down and get some lunchmeat and potato chips."

Anyway, I decided to try it. I went to the supermarket, made a grocery list 18 pages long, filled up 20 shopping carts, transferred 58 paper bags, coughed up $602.19 to pay for it, and then loaded it into two cars and shouted over my shoulder, "See you next year!"

As I drove by I heard a smart-mouthed carry-out boy say, "You said that last week, lady."

A Housewife's Prayer—October 1974

Prayer of a housewife who gets out once a year and tonight is the night.

Please, Lord, don't let the spots on Laurie's chest mean what I think they mean, and if they do mean what we both know they mean, grant that our sitter has had chicken pox.

Give me the humor to smile when I turn on the bathwater and realize that someone has left the knob on SHOWER and it drenches an $8 hairdo.

Grant me the serenity to put on my fake eyelashes without gluing my left eyelid permanently to my cheekbone.

Do not let me despair when my husband arrives home thirty minutes late, with a three-day beard that can't wait, a front seat full of dirty Little League bases that smell like a stable, then tells me he has to stop at a discount house to cash a check.

Smile upon me this one night so that I may not have to endure a klutz on one side who hums the overture and Typhoid Annie who is sitting behind me and is coughing down my back.

In your infinite wisdom, help us to ignore our name as it is being paged in the restaurant, as we all well know it is the sitter saying that Michael demands an entire bottle of Pepsi and she will not be responsible for his plumbing if he has a whole one instead of half.

Walk with us as we get the table by the kitchen door and I get the bent fork and my husband's soup is cold.

And when it rains (as we know it will) lead us into the nearest gas station so that we may buy the refills for our windshield wipers that my husband has been putting off for three years . . . saying the world is due for a drought.

Comfort us as we go fifteen miles out of our way for a gas station that is open all night and the sitter is angry because we are late and it is a school night and we have to write her a check for the tip and she's never had chicken pox . . . before tonight.

If I ask too much, Lord, give me the strength to say, "Who needs a night out? I'd rather stay at home."

Mom Last to Get Cold—October 16, 1975

There is one negative aspect of being a housewife that no one has ever touched upon: We get all the diseases last.

Not only that, we have to take what everyone in the family brings us. It's like being social director in a house of pestilence.

A couple of weeks ago, my husband dragged home in the middle of the day and said, "I don't want to panic you, but I may be going to the big car pool in the sky."

"What's the matter?"

"My head aches. My body is burning up. I am nauseated. My chest is tight and I can't make a fist. Call a specialist and bring me *TV Guide*."

After calling his office and his sister, setting up the card table for his reading material, canceling his dental appointment and lugging trays to his bed, I heard another call for help.

It was my son who complained. "I'm hot, feel like throwing up and am wobbly. Can I have ice cream for dessert?"

I put him to bed, called the pediatrician, took his mitt over to the alternate first baseman, went to school for his homework assignment, bought a coloring book, played 30 games of Old Maid and picked up a prescription at the drugstore.

By the next morning, his brother complained his nose was stuffed up, his head hurt and could I get the electric football game out of the attic.

The traffic at the front door was like a freeway. My husband received a planter from the secretary pool, Miss Wartz brought over 30 get-well wishes from the class, and Grandma dropped by with a light pudding and molding clay.

The morning they all went back to their respective jobs, I awoke feeling lousy. "I don't want to panic you," I said to my husband, "but if I were on *Marcus Welby, M.D.*, I could only be a one-part episode."

"Nonsense," he said. "You've just got what the rest of us had, and we lived."

It wasn't fair. Everyone else had a cold that was the "real thing." My cold had no status, no respect—and could well have been stamped MADE IN JAPAN.

My good friend called me up and said, "Didn't I tell you? Someday they will make one tombstone for housewives everywhere with a standard inscription. It will read, *I told you I was sick.*"

"I Was 37 Years Old at the Time"—August 7, 1976

For years, you've watched everyone else do it.

The children who sat on the curb eating their lunches while waiting for their bus.

The husband you put through school who drank coffee standing up and slept with his hand on the alarm.

And you envied them and said, "Maybe next year I'll go back to school." And the years went by and this morning you looked into the mirror and said, "You blew it. You're too old to pick it up and start a new career."

This column is for you.

Margaret Mitchell won the Pulitzer Prize for Fiction for *Gone With the Wind* in 1937. She was 37 years old at the time.

Margaret Chase Smith was elected to the Senate for the first time in 1948 at the age of 49.

Ruth Gordon picked up her first Oscar in 1968 for *Rosemary's Baby*. She was 72 years old.

Billie Jean King took the battle of women's worth to a tennis court in Houston's Astrodome to outplay Bobby Riggs. She was 31 years of age.

Grandma Moses began a painting career at the age of 76.

Anne Morrow Lindbergh followed in the shadow of her husband until she began to question the meaning of existence for individual women. She published her thoughts in *Gift from the Sea* in 1955, at 49.

Shirley Temple Black was Ambassador to Ghana at the age of 47.

Golda Meir in 1969 was elected prime minister of Israel. She had just turned 71.

This summer Barbara Jordan was given official duties as a speaker at the Democratic National Convention. She is 40 years old.

You can tell yourself these people started out as exceptional. You can tell yourself they had influence before they started. You can tell yourself the conditions under which they achieved were different from yours.

Or you can be like a woman I knew who sat at her kitchen window year after year and watched everyone else do it and then said to herself, "It's my turn."

I was 37 years old at the time.

Dumpy Paper Dress—March 31, 1977

Do you know what depression is?

It's sitting in your doctor's examination room.

In a paper dress.

On a cold table.

And it's the high spot of your week.

Your eyes rove around the room and come to rest on the doctor's diploma. The year he graduated. I've got shoes older than that.

Darn. Forgot to grease my cracked heels. I wonder if anyone else goes in without hose in the wintertime. You have to make a choice in this world. Wear white socks and alienate your children or go sockless and live with cracked heels.

This dress is not to be believed. I look like a Christmas package that arrived in February. I wonder who their fashion coordinator is, Mr. Hefty? All I need is a twist tie around my neck and someone would put me at the curb.

The nurse is coming.

"Are you decent?"

"No."

"I mean are you in your gown?"

"That's not the same thing."

"Care for a magazine while you're waiting? Here's *Esquire.* There's a great article in it on Mary Tyler Moore."

"I can't handle Mary Tyler Moore today. I'm depressed, and that could put me over the brink."

"Would you rather read *The Cysts Digest?*"

"I'll take Mary."

"It says Robert Redford saw her walking along the beach and wanted to introduce himself, but he was awed by her and respected her privacy."

"I have that problem," I said. "Thirty million men out there respect my privacy. And the more they respect it, the more I seem to have. Give me *The Cysts Digest.*"

"Now, what seems to be your problem?" she asked, clicking her ballpoint pen and leaning over my card.

"I'm depressed. I'm not happy with my life. All my appliances are going. My goldfish died. I need a root canal. I'm talking back to bumper stickers. My hair is greasy. My menus are boring. I fell apart last week when I opened the refrigerator and discovered the date on my yeast had expired. I pray every day for patience . . . but I can't wait around for the answer."

The doctor came in. "What seems to be the trouble?"

"I'm depressed," I said simply.

"You should be," he said. "That's a rotten-looking dress."

See what I mean?

Handbags—October 25, 1977

The first and only time I was on a ski slope, I had the attention of every person within a two-mile radius.

It could have been my color-coordinated pants and jacket.

It could have been my oversized goggles.

It could have been my knitted cap with the signature of a leading skier on it.

My husband seemed to think it was because I was the only woman on skis carrying a handbag.

I can't help it. Do men actually believe women enjoy lugging around a handbag everywhere they go? By the time everyone in the family unloads their stuff on me, I feel like an anvil salesman.

I don't know when it all started, but somewhere in history someone decided women were the keepers of the nose tissue, fingernail clippers, breath spray, Band-Aids, change for rest rooms, pins, hair spray, sticks for chapped lips, road maps, combs and scratch pads. I never see a film clip of Queen Elizabeth with that large handbag slung over her arm that I don't half expect to see Prince Philip lean forward and say, "Got any gum, Ducky?"

History used to be kinder to women. Did you see Joan of Arc carrying a Gucci to war? Did Pocahontas lug around a pouch to match her moccasins? And I don't know where Lady Godiva carried her credit cards, but it wasn't in a handbag. I would have noticed.

Believe me, there is nothing that detracts from a woman's aura of mystery and intrigue like wearing a black suede over-the-shoulder bag with a pale blue bathing suit.

I think it's time we women stopped carrying supplies for the entire family. If children don't have room to carry their own toys, if men don't have pockets in their pants, tougho.

Things are clearly out of control. I didn't mind rummaging through my bag for the ring at the wedding ceremony. I didn't raise my voice when I went to surgery with a tote bag over my chest. But the other day, I realized things had gone too far. My husband said, "These LifeSavers are stuck together. Where did you have them?"

"When I went to the sauna—"

"You didn't!"

Bizarre Accidents—November 29, 1981

I read the other day where a woman was grocery shopping and, in trying to reach the last package of frozen broccoli, lost her balance and fell head first into the freezer.

A man walking by grabbed her by the ankles, dragged her out and drove her to the hospital, where she was treated and released.

I have to believe that falling in the freezer was the easy part. The real trauma came when she had to deal with the people who fill out insurance forms. I can see it now:

"Was this an accident?"

"Yes."

"Was there any other way to get the broccoli out of the case?"

"Probably."

"Have you gotten broccoli out of the case like this before?"

"Many times."

Mothers know exactly what I am talking about. Most of the accidents that happen with children border on the bizarre. They never do anything in a conventional way. I always had the kid with the penny shoved up his nose, the arm wedged in a sweeper bag, a lip caught in a mousetrap. Things that everyone told me 30 years from now I'd laugh at—and I'm still waiting.

I was only five years into child raising when I stopped asking, "How in the world could something like this happen?" After a while, I fully accepted strange happenings and prepared myself to defend them while riding to the emergency room.

"How did your son split his head open?"

"He did a swan dive into two feet of water."

"You can't do that."

"Right."

I used to watch nurses at the desk who would try to jam "got pant leg caught in mixer" onto insurance forms or "cut tongue while hiding Fort Apache soldier set from cereal box in his mouth to annoy brother" and wonder what some of the other insurance claims read like.

I'd surely love to have seen their faces when a woman reported recently her buttocks were lodged in an emergency exit when she was in the rest room of a bus and the bus swerved, forcing her into the window.

Can't you hear them asking at the hospital, "Was this your assigned seat?"

Turning into Mother—June 1, 1989

I rummaged through a stack of old gift boxes in my closet before I found what I was looking for. It was a knotted, crumpled ribbon. Feverishly, I salvaged what I could and steamed out the wrinkles with an iron. My shoulders slumped as I realized that I had just come full circle. I had turned into my mother!

How could I have allowed this to happen? I love my mother dearly, but all the little things that have driven me nuts throughout the years have now found a home in my body.

I carry my lipstick in one of those little holders with a mirror. There is a piece of bright-colored yarn around the handle of my suitcase so I can spot it easily. I keep a litter bag in my car. Can you believe any of this?

Every time I change the color of my shoes, I change handbags to match. I never used to do that. And the other day I found myself throwing a measuring cup in the dishwasher when I had measured only water in it.

Maybe I have misjudged my mother. Is it possible there was a time in her life when she never considered rinsing out bread wrappers and hanging them out to dry with little clamp clothespins? Was it Grandma who passed on to her the habits of never calling anyone after 10 o'clock at night and never washing her hair just before she went to bed?

The first trait I picked up was a shock. When I pulled out of our driveway one day, I immediately got into the left lane on our boulevard.

"Why are you doing that?" asked my daughter.

"I have to make a left turn," I said.

"Mom! You don't make a left turn for another thirty blocks."

"I want to be there just in case no one will let me in."

"You sound just like Grandma," she said. "She's always doing that."

The comparison bothered me. I have always considered myself to be a free spirit, a monument to rebellion. I worked at it while I was growing up. If my mother said someone was a creep, I saw him as a role model. If she said a philosophy course wouldn't pay the rent, I minored in it. If her prime concern was getting all the tomatoes canned before they went bad, mine was saving the world. Other than the fact that she gave me life, shared the same home and loved me, we had little in common.

I was riding with my daughter the other day when she entered the expressway and immediately got into the left lane. "I know," she said, "the exit ramp is a few miles down, but sometimes no one will let you in."

I smiled. It's only a matter of time before she'll be saving boxes and ironing old ribbons.

Love and Marriage

Get Well for Mom—April 3, 1966

Notes pinned to the pillow of a mother who has flu by a well-meaning husband who has inherited the house and kids.

Monday A.M.

Dearest:
Sleep late. Everything under control. Lunches packed. Kids off to school. Menu for dinner planned. Your lunch is on a tray in refrigerator: fruit cup, finger sandwiches. Thermos of hot tea by bedside. See you around six.

Tuesday A.M.

Honey:
Sorry about the egg rack in the refrigerator. Hope you got back to sleep. Did the kids tell you about the Coke I put in the Thermoses? The school might call you on this. Dinner may be a little late. I'm doing your door-to-door canvass for liver research. Your lunch is in refrigerator. Hope you like leftover chili.

Wednesday A.M.

Dear Doris:
Why in the name of all that is sane would you put soap chips in the flour canister! If you have time, could you please come up with a likely spot for Chris's missing shoes? We've checked the clothes hamper, garage, backseat of the car and wood box. Did you know the school has a ruling on bedroom slip-

pers? There's some cold pizza for you in a napkin in the oven drawer. Late tonight. Driving eight Girl Scouts to tour meat-packing house.

Thursday A.M.

Doris:

Don't panic over water in hallway. It crested last night at 9 P.M. Will finish laundry tonight. Please pencil in answers to following:

1. How do you turn on the garbage disposal?
2. How do you turn off the milkman?
3. Why would that rotten kid leave his shoes in his boots?
4. How do you remove a Confederate flag inked on the palm of a small boy's hand?
5. What do you do with leftovers when they begin to snap at you when you open the door?

I don't know what you're having for lunch! Surprise me!

Friday A.M.

Hey:

Don't drink from pitcher by the sink. Am trying to restore pink dress shirt to original white. Take heart. Tonight, the ironing will be folded, house cleaned and dinner on time. I called your mother.

Cleaning Out the Attic—December 28, 1966

Actually, we didn't have to clean the attic last Thursday.

The builder checked the sled runner coming through the ceiling in the boys' room, the sag over the kitchen and the cracks in the hallway and said engineering-wise it would be another full two weeks before the entire structure gave way.

We picked Thursday because we were still in a festive mood. This is important. On previous occasions when we were not in a festive mood, we had to summon a marriage counselor to hang a picture together. (The time we hung wallpaper in the dining room as a team we were written up in the *Ladies' Home Journal* feature, "Can This Marriage Be Saved?")

"Let me start off by saying," said my husband, "that you can't be illogical or sentimental about this stuff."

"Well, that's pretty pompous, coming from a man who still has his Jack Armstrong signet ring, a book of shoe stamps from World War II, and his first bow-wow!"

"Those are collector's items," he explained. "That's different. I'm talking about junk. Right now, we are going to establish a rule of thumb for saving things."

We sat down on a carton marked RAIN-SOAKED HALLOWEEN MASKS. "Now," he continued, "if we can't wear it, frame it, sell it or hang it on the Christmas tree, out it goes! Understand?"

At the end of two hours we hauled four pitiful items to the curb: a broken Hula Hoop, an airline calendar showing Wiley Post spinning a propeller, an empty varnish can and one tire chain.

"This is ridiculous," he growled, crawling back into the attic. "Let's take this stuff one by one. What's this?"

"That's our summer cabin inventory."

"What summer cabin?"

"The one we're going to buy someday. So far we have a studio couch, a lamp with a bowling pin base, six Shirley Temple cereal bowls, two venetian blinds and a chair with a rope seat."

"And this?" he sighed.

"That's my motherhood insurance. They're all my old maternity clothes, bottle sterilizer, potty chair, layettes, baby bed and car seat. You lay a hand on this stuff, and we'll both live to regret it!"

"And all this trash?"

"That belongs to you. Consecutive license plates from 1937, old fertilizer bags, a rusted hand sickle, a picture of the Cincinnati Reds autographed by Bucky Walters, the medical dictionary wrapped in plain brown wrapper, cartons of English quizzes from the class of 1953, 18 empty antifreeze cans, a box marked OLD FURNACE FILTERS and a bait box that's trying to tell us something. Do you want me to start tossing?"

"Tossing! Don't talk nonsense! Go out to the curb and get back that tire chain. I just found its mate under this insulation! You never know. Edsels may come back!"

Interpreting the Checkbook—April 24, 1967

It was right after I mailed our house payment check to our own address . . . no, I'll take that back; it was right after I let my husband's insurance policy lapse that he said quietly, "Maybe paying the bills is getting to be a little too much for you. Why don't you let me take over writing the checks?"

I can remember licking his hand and promising him I would never rest until they memorialized him on a five-cent postage stamp. "I'll show you how the checkbook works," I said excitedly.

"I *know* how the checkbook works," he answered patiently.

It was a full two days before he cornered me and said, "What does NS beside a check stand for?"

"It stands for No Stamp," I answered. "That means I wrote the check and put it in an envelope and put it on the bookcase, but I didn't have a stamp to mail it, so I bent an arrow down to the deposit line and added the check to the balance."

"Maybe you'd better explain how the checkbook works," he said wearily.

"Well, when the arrow goes *up*, that's something different. That's when I start writing checks earlier in the week than when I actually have money in the bank. Then, when I deposit your check, I make an arrow *up* to that point so I will have a balance to subtract from. You got it with the arrows now?"

"I think so," he said.

"Good. When there's an SG, that means Somebody Goofed on the balance. I don't sweat it anymore. Remember I used to bite my cuticles until they bled? Well, I draw a big, black, wavy line. That means we begin with brand-new figures—the bank's. Now, JM means Just Mailed, so you naturally subtract the entry. It's not too tricky to understand, once you get the symbols down."

"On this check to a sorority, you've got TB beside the entry."

"Yes. That stands for Tough Beans. It's an expression I picked up from the kids. You see, when a check is older than six months, the bank has to check with you personally to see whether or not you want it to go through. When I see that check has never been canceled or returned, I simply put TB beside it and spend the money all over again."

"I see what you mean," he said slowly. "One more question; I almost hate to ask, but what's APR?"

"Good grief," I said, aghast, "that's a simple abbreviation for April. I thought everyone knew that. If you think you can't handle the checkbook you'd better say so. You can't fool around with money, you know."

Men Have a Six-Word Limit—July 23, 1969

I have publicly stated that men speak approximately six words a day in their own homes. A few readers have challenged me and want to know what the six words are.

I should have qualified my statement. The six words are not necessarily spoken in sequence, nor are they necessarily spoken to wives.

A friend of mine, for example, has a husband who saves his six words until the Carson show has signed off and she is fast asleep. Then he snaps on all the lights in the bedroom, punches his pillow, shakes her out of a sound slumber and says, "Did you turn off the hose?" (6)

Some men will blow their quota at one time.

They'll garage the car, make tracks to the kitchen, take the lid off the fry pan and announce loudly, "I had it for lunch." (5) Then, realizing he has used only five words, he will add, "Yuck!"

Others will spend a half dozen words in obscenities directed toward Bobby's bicycle in the driveway.

My week gets off to a slow start but builds to a feverish climax.

Monday: Me: "Say something."
              Him: "What ya want me to say?" (6)
Tuesday: Me: "What kind of day did you have?"
              Him: "Don't aggravate me. You wouldn't believe." (6)
Wednesday: Me: "Try me."
              Him: "Where's the rest of the paper?" (6)

Thursday: Me: "We had a crisis here today."
          Him: "The dog isn't lost, is he?" (6)
Friday: Me: "Guess what? Know who called today? And is coming to dinner? And is bringing her new husband with her? And can't wait to talk your arm off? Are you ready?"
          Him: "No. No. No. No. No. No." (6)
Saturday: Me: "I'll be out for a while. I've got some errands to do at the shopping center."
          Him: "Admit it. My chattering gets on your nerves." (8)
Sunday: Me: "Do you know you spoke eight words to me yesterday? I wouldn't be surprised if you were starting a new trend."
          Him: "Don't count on it." (4)

Part of man's silence is woman's doing. We created the strong, silent, masculine image. The silence represented deep thought, a repression of emotions. A quiet man was an island of mystery, a challenge to probe and discover as years went on. I always thought a quiet man was subtle and romantic.

But that was before I started arguing with the tropical fish over which channel we were going to watch.

Car Hits a Tree—January 24, 1971

The other night a tree I had never seen before swerved in front of me at the end of our driveway and clipped my right fender.

"That is the most ridiculous story I have ever heard," said my husband.

I knew he would say that. He said that when one of the kids pushed a button on the automatic umbrella in the backseat, poked me in the ear and caused me to run through a barrier in the parking garage.

He said that the time a crazy, wild, out-of-control grocery cart attacked the car and caused me to sideswipe a row of balled evergreens along the curb.

He's one of those "logical drivers" who doesn't believe garbage cans are out to get you (even the sober ones).

"For your information," I said, "I am not the only driver who has had weird experiences behind the wheel of a car. I was reading a story the other day about some of the reasons motorists gave their insurance companies for having an accident. One man said, 'I'm a preacher so I couldn't have been "at fault." Another one said, 'I was driving down the road when I received a message from the Lord. Being a religious man, I bowed my head; that's when I hit the car in front of me.'"

"Oh, good grief," said my husband, shaking his head.

"It's possible," I said. "One poor victim reported, 'I was fascinated by seeing this here wheel roll down the road. After the accident, I found it was off my car. I never seen a wheel go so—'"

"That doesn't make any sense at all," he insisted.

"Sometimes it really isn't our fault," I said. "Take pollution. It caused at least one accident. The man said he was speeding up to pass the awful odor. Sometimes there's nothing else you can do. Like the poor guy who said, 'I started up and the car ahead didn't, so I drove into him.' I ask you, what would you have done?"

"Let's get back to your instant landscaping story."

"You mean you do not believe a tree would appear out of nowhere and clip my fender?"

"That's right."

"Would you believe the dog wouldn't stop breathing until he steamed up my windows so bad I couldn't see the tree growing?"

He shook his head.

"Okay," I said, "and this is your last chance. The devil made me do it."

Daytime Husband, Nocturnal Wife—March 22, 1971

Someone asked my husband at a party the other night to what he attributed his long marriage and he said, "It's the happy mating of a man and a hamster. I work all day while she sleeps, and I sleep at night while she runs around her exercise wheel."

I thought that was a pretty rotten thing to say, considering the fact that I must assume all the worry and the anxiety of raising a family and running a home when there aren't enough daylight hours.

Once I am in bed I must worry if the front door is locked; if the coffeepot is unplugged, the guard rails up on the bunk beds, the car lights out, the bread out of the freezer to defrost for breakfast, the check is in the milkbox for the milkman, and if the toilet will stop running. Frankly, I don't know how men can be so insensitive to what is going on.

Last week I shook my husband and whispered, "What's that?"

"What's what?"

"That barking."

"It's just a wild guess, but it could be the dog."

"I know it is the dog, but what is he barking at?"

"Maybe the furnace blower went on again."

"You don't care about anything, do you?"

"Like what?"

"Like in all the years we've been married, never once have you gone around to the children's beds and checked to see if they were breathing all right."

"Oh, good grief. Why do you insist on lying there all night with your eyes open?"

"Because that is when I do my best thinking. Last night I think I figured out where Howard Hughes is. Tonight I am trying to figure out how to stay on the Stillman diet without a nose plug. Tomorrow, who knows? I may find a cure for ground hamburger."

"Where are you going?"

"To see why the dog is barking."

At dawn I crawled into bed. My husband stirred. "What was the dog barking about?"

"Someone had put gym shoes on the register to dry. I knew he was barking at something."

"You've been down there all that time blowing on a pair of gym shoes?" he asked.

"No, I decided to do the ironing. Did you really mean that crack about our marriage?"

"No." He yawned. "You've given me fourteen wonderful years."

"We've been married twenty-one years," I corrected.

"So," he sighed. "Fourteen out of twenty-one isn't bad."

Keeping Track of Valuable Papers—June 1972

We had an insurance claim to make the other day, and my husband asked, "Where is the policy?"

"It's obviously in my folder marked IMPORTANT PAPERS."

"Which is—?"

"Which is lost," I said. "I haven't seen it since we moved."

"You mean it has been lost since last June?"

"No, it's been lost since we moved from the flat to the farm in 1968."

"That's incredible," he said. "That means we can't put our finger on our insurance policies, our deeds, our car registrations, our will—or our marriage license, for that matter."

"I'll look for it this afternoon," I said.

By that evening, I was all smiles. "I have some good news and some bad news," I said.

"Let's have the good news first," he said.

"Well, I found our car registrations being used as bookmarks in *The Man in the Gray Flannel Suit,* our life insurance policies turned up in your shirt drawer, and the deed to the house was in the attic in a box marked MATERNITY CLOTHES. The will turned up in the suit jacket you wore the day we made it. And I found our folder marked IMPORTANT PAPERS in the sewing machine drawer."

"Now we're getting somewhere," he said, excitedly opening the box. He picked up a decayed blossom and said, "What is this?"

"It's a dried gardenia you got me for the military ball. And here are 400 Top Value stamps, a batch of spelling papers from the seventh grade you once taught, a dental appointment card for our son from 1962, your dog tags from the army, a Korean flag, a renewal card from *Reader's Digest,* someone's baby tooth and an expired library card."

"These are important papers?" he asked, his eyes widening.

"I'm not finished. There are three tokens for Fantasy City, a typing certificate for 40 words a minute in my name, the dog's inoculation record, the laundry instructions for something Celanese, two tags that read, DO NOT REMOVE THESE TAGS, and, voilà! our house insurance policy. Aren't you pleased?"

He sat silently for a moment, looking at the contents of the IM-PORTANT PAPERS file. "What's the bad news?" he asked tiredly.

"I found our marriage license," I said quietly.

Husband Born Late—October 8, 1972

There are no records to prove it, but I have every reason to believe my husband was an 11-month baby. And he's been running two months late ever since.

Through marriage (and bad association), I have become a member of that great body of tardy Americans who grope their way down theater aisles in the dark, arrive at parties in time to drink their cocktails with dessert and celebrate Christmas on December 26.

Frankly, I don't know how a nice punctual girl like me got stuck with a man who doesn't need a watch . . . but a calendar and a keeper.

Would it shock you to know I have never seen a bride walk down the aisle? I have never seen a choir or a graduate in a processional. I have never seen the victim of a mystery *before* he was murdered. I have never seen a parking lot jammed with people. I have never seen the first race of a daily double or a football team in clean uniforms.

The other night I had it out with my husband. "Look, I am in the prime time of my life and I have never heard the first thirty seconds of the Minute Waltz. Doesn't that tell you something?"

"What are you trying to say?" he asked.

"I am saying that once before I die I would like to see a church with empty seats."

"We've been through all this before." He sighed. "Sitting around before an event begins is a complete waste of time when you could be spending it sleeping . . . reading . . . working. . . ."

"Don't forget driving around the block looking for a parking place. I don't understand you at all," I continued. "Don't you get curious as to what they put into first acts? Aren't you just a bit envious of people who don't have to jump onto moving trains? Aren't you tired of sitting down to a 44-minute egg for breakfast each morning?"

"I set my alarm clock every night. What do you want from me?"

"I have seen you set your alarm clock. When you want to get up at six-thirty you set it for five-thirty. Then you smack it and say, 'Don't tell me what to do, buddy.' Then you reset it for six. At six when it goes off you hit it again and shout, 'Ha,-ha. I was only kidding. I got another half hour.' You reset it for six-thirty, at which time you throw your body on it and say, 'I don't need you. I don't need anybody.' Then you go back to sleep."

"I just happen to believe there is no virtue in being early. What time is it?"

"It's eight o'clock. You're supposed to be at work at eight."

"Yes. Lucky I've got twenty minutes to spare."

I have a feeling I will go through life and never again hear "The Star-Spangled Banner."

Husband Dreads Hammering Nails in the Wall
—November 23, 1972

You know what the real basic difference is between a man and a woman?

A woman can walk through the Louvre in Paris and see 5,000 paintings on the wall. A man can walk through the Louvre in Paris and see 5,000 nails in the wall.

I don't know what there is about a nail in the wall that makes strong, virile men cry.

The first time I was aware of this phenomenon was a week after my husband and I were married. I passed him in the kitchen one day while carrying a small nail and a small hammer.

"Where are you going with that hammer and nail?" he asked, beginning to pale.

"I am going to hang up a towel rack," I said.

He could not have looked more shocked if I had said I was going to drive a wooden peg in the heart of a vampire.

"Do you have to drive that spike in the wall to do it?"

"No," I said, resting on the sink. "I could prop the towel rack up in a corner on the floor. I could hang it around my waist from a rope, or I could do away with it altogether and keep a furry dog around the sink to dry my hands on."

"What is there about women that they cannot stand to see a smooth bare wall?" he grumbled.

"And what is there about men that they cannot stand to have the necessities of life hung from a wall?"

"What necessities?" he asked. "Certainly you don't need that mirror in the hallway."

"You said that about the light switches."

His eyes narrowed, and I had the feeling he was going to zap me with his big point. "Do you realize," he asked slowly, "that there is not one single wall in this house where we can show a home movie?"

"Radio City Music Hall only has one!" I retorted.

And so the nail vs. the bare wall has gone on for years at our house. He wouldn't hang a calendar over my desk because in 12 months the nail would become obsolete. He wouldn't hang the children's baby pictures because in two years they'd grow teeth and no one would recognize them. He wouldn't let me put a hook in the bathroom so I wouldn't have to hold my robe while I showered. He wouldn't let me hang a kitchen clock anywhere but on a wall stud, which happened to be located just behind the refrigerator.

I have waited 23 years for my revenge. Yesterday, he reported he ran over a nail with his car.

There's an object lesson here, but I won't insult your intelligence by pointing it out.

My Husband the Prince of Darkness—February 20, 1973

The poet who said "It is better to light a candle than to curse the darkness" did not know my husband.

He has dedicated his entire life to flipping off light switches, giving rise to his theory that "It is better to break your leg in the darkness than to curse the light bills."

By his description, our house is lit up like a pleasure boat cruising up the Potomac. He lies. Had we lived in England during the blitz, ours would have been the only house that never needed blackout curtains.

It is like living with a hamster with long arms. For example, I will turn on the bathroom light switch, and 15 seconds later the light will flick off. From the darkness, a voice will proclaim, "Unless you've rearranged the furniture in there, you know your way around, don't you?"

His tour through the house every evening has become rather predictable. "Who's in the kitchen?" *(Click.)* "Who's in the hall closet?" *(Click.)* "Who's in the bedroom?" *(Click.)* Then we are in for his dramatic tally. "I have just turned off thirteen lights."

The most frustrating patch of darkness is the garage. He pulled the car in the other evening and doused the lights. I fumbled with the car door while he fumbled for the house key. Finally, he shouted, "Are you all right?"

"Don't talk to me," I said. "I'm counting my steps like the blind boy in *Butterflies Are Free*." Inside the house he inched his way through the darkness.

"It's twenty-two steps to the family-room light switch," I said.

"I don't want the family-room light switch," he said. "I want to turn on the stove light. It's a smaller bulb."

"How about a sparkler?" I asked.

"I've had enough of your smart remarks about my war against waste," he said. "Today I bought a lamp that illuminates the entire room. No more stumbling around. No more squinting. You and your lack of regard for money will love it!"

I followed him into the bedroom, where he proceeded to turn on the light above our bed.

Recoiling from the glare into the corner, I had the strangest sensation either Moses was going to write something on a mountain or a new supermarket was being opened.

As he lay in bed reading, and as the lids of my eyes were being broiled to medium well, I could only wonder if Thomas Edison could be named as co-defendant in a divorce suit.

Husband Has Clothes for All Occasions—May 8, 1979

Whenever a group of women get together, they always discuss at what age a husband is capable of dressing himself.

I stopped dressing my husband two years ago when it became

clear he had a wino dress wish. He simply did not care that a striped tie and a plaid shirt were incompatible, or that trousers worn to the ankle were to be slipped on only on the way to the rowboat in the event of a flood.

We had words over it, and I said, "From here on in, you are on your own." This year, I am going one step further by severing the marital discord entirely and letting him do his own packing for vacation. It's risky, but he has to assume the responsibility sometime.

Last year, just before vacation, I checked over his suitcase and he had proved once again his readiness for any occasion.

He had clothes in which to accept the Nobel Peace Prize.

He had clothes to parachute behind enemy lines dressed as a mercenary.

He had clothes to commandeer a torpedo boat through a squall.

He had clothes to barter for mules and guides in a Colombian jungle and clothes to celebrate Halloween behind the Iron Curtain.

He had clothes for snorkeling, discoing, safaris, high teas and low ceilings, clothes for lounging and clothes to leave behind as tips.

He also packed eight pairs of shoes, a tripod and coats for all seasons. There wasn't a porter in the world who could have put an inch of space between that suitcase and the floor. I was not about to travel with the luggage of an anvil salesman.

Naturally, I brought some reason to the contents, taking care to stuff the shoes neatly with underwear, put the necessary items into plastic bags and layer the suitcase with cardboard to guard against wrinkles. It would be his last brush with systematic packing.

Yesterday he told me his packing was complete. I opened the closet door. There was nothing left in it except a red vest and bow tie left over from high school.

"In case you decide to wait tables, you may have nothing to wear," I said dryly.

He grabbed it off the hanger and stuffed it into his flight bag.

Jim Is Retired—May 19, 1985

See Jim. Jim used to run and jump and chase accounts. Jim is going to stay home now. He has a new watch. He will tell you what time it is even when you don't ask.

It is time to get up.

It is time to remove the oil stain from the driveway before it spreads to the rest of the house.

It is time to alphabetize your spices.

It is time to eat. (Lunch/dinner/breakfast/break/snack/party.)

It is time to use the packet of yeast before it expires at noon tomorrow.

Sometimes Jim will act like a houseguest.

"Where do you hide the iced-tea glasses?"

"The hall bath needs toilet tissue."

"There is someone at the door selling something."

"I'd put the dishes away, but I don't know where they belong."

Sometimes Jim will act as if he has hired you for the summer.

"Who was that on the phone, and what did they want?"

"Where are you going, and what time are you coming back?"

"I don't think the grass can wait another day."

Retired men like Jim bring efficiency to the home.

"It is cheaper to make your own tea bags than to buy ready-made."

"Don't heat up the oven for one baked potato. Do a dozen and freeze them."

See Jim drive a nail by the door to hold your car keys.

See Jim drive a nail by the phone to hold a pencil.

See Jim drive a nail in the desk to hold your unpaid bills.

See Jim drive you crazy.

You are surprised. You did not know you married a man who knew so much about dishwashers, wax buildup, hand washables, stain removers and children.

Jim is surprised. He does not know how you have managed to stumble through 40 years of running a house without him.

Everyone is surprised he is busier than ever.

You're not.

My Social Life—November 3, 1985

There is no delicate way to say it. My social life is somewhere to the right of a sedated parakeet.

It happens. The Zelda and F. Scott Fitzgeralds of their time who vowed 36 years ago to let the good times roll have turned into Ma and Pa Kettle.

During the last 20 years, it has been an uphill fight to get my husband out of his running shoes and into hard soles. This madcap who used to bounce around a dance floor like a Ping-Pong ball and have confetti in his bathrobe pocket is now reduced to a TV remote switch and deep breathing by 9 P.M.

Most of the time, women are the social animals who plan dinners and movie dates, buy season tickets to concerts, organize bowling and tennis games and keep them on the move. Then one day the nonsocial "ani-males" become militant. They rebel.

"Are we going out again? I feel like I'm on a treadmill. How do you expect me to work every day and keep up this pace all night? Don't you ever get the desire to just stay at home and relax? I suppose next month you'll want to go out again!"

For me, it gets tougher and tougher to sell my husband on a social outing. He's at that time of his life where his heart will take no surprises. If it's a movie, he wants to know if he's going to like it. If it's a party, he wants to know when we're coming home. If it's a game, he wants to know if the score is going to be close. If it's a lecture, he wants to know if it's worth staying awake for. If I mislead him, I am held personally responsible and points are mentally racked up against me.

They say you can always tell how exciting your life is by the hour you get into your nightclothes. Sometimes we have to change our pajamas because we dribbled our dinner onto them. I cannot tell you the times we have said to startled guests who just dropped in unexpectedly that we both have the flu.

The other night as I sat needlepointing in my nest of pillows and his recliner body was draped over the recliner chair, the phone rang. He jumped back to reality and said, "Who could be calling at this hour?"

"I don't know," I said.

He hesitated before he picked it up. "They don't call to tell you you've won the lottery at eight-thirty at night. It must be bad news!"

There are some people who tell me I should be flattered that my husband wants to stay at home. These are the same unstable people who believe age has nothing whatsoever to do with the way you feel.

I always knew a man's home was his castle. I just never thought he'd pull up the drawbridge at 5:30 in the evening.

Clippers—April 26, 1987

I was leafing through a magazine in my gynecologist's office the other day when I encountered a page with three holes in it left by a "clipper."

Slamming it shut, I looked around in horror. I didn't know why or when, but my husband was there or had been there as surely as if he had left his business card.

He belongs to a sick little group of people who feel compelled to rip out any story or cartoon that catches their fancy. It's not enough to read it and enjoy it. They have to own it.

By the time I sit down to read our paper, it has more holes in it than a screen door on a rental cabin. Thanks to his handy razor blade, he has deftly committed surgery on two thirds of the contents. Small wonder that people accuse me of having a current-affairs lobotomy. All I can discuss intelligently is the masthead on the editorial page and the advertising rates in the want ads. Everything else has been removed.

Last week, he ripped out the weather map and was folding it carefully to store in his pocket. "What are you going to do with that?" I asked.

"I'm sending it to the Cochrans in Ohio," he said, "so they can see how cold they were."

"Why would you want to do that? They live there. They already know how cold it was."

"Yes, but they didn't know that it made our newspaper."

I knew better than to look for logic. I didn't find it when he sent the day's horoscope to his sister in Florida, telling her she'd hear from a stranger that day. By the time she received it, her son had probably called anyway.

In my mind, I have constructed a profile of these clippers. They are people who preface every sentence with, "I don't suppose you read that amusing story the other day about . . ." and then proceed to open their billfolds and read the entire story out loud to you. Their letters always have a cartoon falling out of them attacking the weakest part of your personality. They paste apropos stories on your bathroom mirror (FIVE MILLION WOMEN WANT YOUR HUSBAND). They never leave home without a Swiss Army knife in case they find a paper in the airport that someone has left.

I met a man the other day who fit the profile, and as I was about to walk away he told me how he clipped my columns and covered the refrigerator with them.

On second thought, a man has to have some vices.

Car Heater—December 11, 1988

My husband and I go through this every winter. We climb into the car, and before we back out of the garage I say, "Turn on the heater. I'm freezing."

He recites, "I cannot turn on the heater yet. The car isn't warmed up."

"What's to warm up?" I shout. "If we have a heater, why don't we just turn it on?"

With this, he flips open the glove compartment and hands me a diagram of the engine of a car, which he made 30 years ago. "Find the radiator," he commands. "Now look for the engine block."

Then he proceeds to tell me how wind goes through the radiator, which is full of fluids. The wind cools the fluids, and with the help of a pump, also cools the engine. I know there is no stopping him once he gets started on this discourse.

He explains how the heater has a thermostat in front of the water pump. It traps the water in the engine until it reaches a certain temperature. Then it is released and the car can heat up.

As I fold the diagram and put it back, I ask, "So why do they have a whole panel of buttons regulating heat, and when you push them cold air pours out?"

As we drive in silence, I finally approach the subject again. "Do you suppose it will heat up before we get to where we are going?"

"The car has no way of knowing how far we are going," he says patiently.

"Joyce has a car that can heat up her coffee and has a digital clock that tells her what time she will get someplace if she maintains a certain speed. There's even a little voice that tells her when her door is open, her brake is on and she is driving too fast. And you are telling me that this car has no idea when it is going to release a little heat?"

"Her car probably doesn't heat up any faster than ours does."

"You don't know that," I snap. "You're just being stubborn. Just because you have a heavy coat and a jacket under it, you're not even cold. Women don't wear as many clothes as men. No wonder we're sick all the time. We're sitting around waiting for the heat to kick in."

We ride in silence a while longer. Finally, I say, "I hate to say this, but I think you don't turn on the heat because it uses more gas and you're cheap. It's just like the thermostat at home. It's easier to curse the cold. I've never told you this before, but I'm afraid to fall asleep at night. I'm afraid I'll never wake up."

He leans over and pushes the heater button and hot air pours out. "We had heat all the time, didn't we?" I say.

"We did not have heat all the time. We've been arguing for ten minutes."

He's been saying that for 30 years.

Husband Reads at Night—March 14, 1989

We've talked before about my husband, the Prince of Darkness. I've told you how he has dedicated his life to turning off lights. How he turns off the porch light before our guests have reached their cars in the driveway. And how he figured the Donald Duck night-light cost 8 cents a year and pulled the plug on it.

Well, I want to correct an erroneous impression I may have left with you. There is one moment when the cost of a light is no object. It can never burn too long or too brightly. In fact, it is the only 200-watter in the entire house. I'm talking about the light by the bed he shines in my eyes when I am trying to sleep and he wants to "read a little to get sleepy."

A lighthouse should have such a light. Night baseball games and operating rooms should benefit from such radiance.

The other night I asked, "How long are you going to read?"

He said, "Whenever I get sleepy. Why?"

"Because I want to know how much Number Thirty sunscreen to use on my eyelids."

"It's not that bright," he said.

"It's like looking at Queen Elizabeth in a snowstorm. It is the whitest white I have ever seen."

"Do you want me to ruin my eyes?" he asked.

"If that's what it takes," I said.

I personally do not know why it takes so much light to peruse a dull book he has been reading for three years.

Lately, a new wrinkle has evolved in his discovery of light. He has started to bring to our bed boxes of snacks and a television tuner. Even if I were not blinded by the light, the sound of him grinding up a hard pretzel in his teeth would jolt anyone out of a coma. (Did you know it takes 133 chews to masticate a small Triscuit?)

The volume on the television set is low enough to know Carson is saying something, but you don't know what. It is loud enough to hear the laughs.

I once sat up in the middle of this orgy and said angrily, "I cannot believe you are the same man who, when the power goes out, tells me God is punishing me for leaving the garage light on all night. The man who turns off the Christmas tree lights when we leave the room to answer the door."

He stopped chewing and said, "Why don't you just sit up and join me? It would be more cost-efficient if you did."

I almost punched his light out.

Husband Preempts His Christmas Gifts—December 10, 1992

I know the symptoms well. My husband looks up from the paper and says, "Good grief, it's the middle of December already. I've got to start shopping."

With that pronouncement, he pushes himself away from the table and goes on his annual buying spree—for himself.

He discards from his drawer all the boxer shorts where the elastic has died in the waistband and buys new ones. He renews his *TV Guide* subscription and buys a new warm-up suit on sale and a book he wants to read. He tracks down his favorite ski pajamas and buys three pairs. He carts in new sweaters and replaces his old billfold that is falling apart.

He shops for a coffeecup holder for his car, new luggage tags and a pen to replace the one he lost.

Boxes and tissue fill his room as he pulls out shirts that were too cheap to pass up and a pair of glasses he's always wanted that you wear to tie flies.

If I were Santa Claus, I'd smack him right across the mouth.

Men at best are impossible to buy for.

The styles of their clothes rarely change. Their hobbies are limited. They don't succumb to cosmetic promises to take years off their lives, nor do they do busywork like needlepointing or knitting. Their jewelry is limited.

What they don't have they don't need, and what they don't need they don't want.

We have the same argument every year. "I suppose you bought yourself a flu shot."

"Actually, I did. Why?" he says.

"I was going to surprise you with it," I said.

"You know me; I don't need anything."

"You need someone to put you under sedation until Christmas," I snapped. "How would you like it if two weeks before Christmas I went out and bought everything I wanted and left you with nothing to buy? You'd be devastated."

"Try me," he said.

I thought my father was hard to buy for. He didn't like to read and he had only one hobby: golf. We golfed him to death.

When he could no longer play the game, we were stuck with his other passion: peanut brittle. One year, he got five cans of peanut brittle, including one made with jalapeño peppers.

I told my husband, "Do you realize I am the only shopper in town who returns gifts before Christmas?"

He said, "I'll do it for you. I have to go out again this afternoon. I have my eye on a tie for my brown suit."

Home Sweet Home

Household Hints—September 11, 1965

"Hey, if you write a column for the newspaper," said the voice on the telephone, "how come you don't tell women how to get stains out of their stainless steel sinks?"

I mumbled something about being blackballed by the PTA hospitality committee for my blunders in the kitchen and said good-bye. But not before she had stirred up a hornet's nest of memories.

Some 15 years ago, I actually did a household hints column for the local newspaper. To this day, homemakers in the area are still trying to salvage bits and pieces of the damages I caused. Queries on "How do I clean my bathroom?" would get an answer like "Burn incense daily. At the end of five years . . . move."

What really amazed me was how seriously women took their housekeeping chores. To some, it was a way of life. Their plaintive pleas rolled in daily. "How do I clean my alabaster?" ("Madam, I didn't know birds got dirty.") "How can I prevent scrub water from running down my arm to my elbows?" ("Hang by your feet when you wash the walls?") "Is there a formula for removing chocolate from over-stuffed furniture?" ("No, but there's one for beating the stuffing out of the little boy who ate chocolate on the overstuffed furniture.")

After several irate calls from women who had tried my little balls of paraffin in their rinse water to make their chintz look chintzier (one woman said if her curtains had wicks they'd burn right through Advent), I promised my editor I would try these things at home first. My home began to take on all the excitement of a missile at countdown.

From these experiments came some pretty profound results.

To make a towel for the children's bath, simply take two towels and monogram each with an *F.* One *F* will represent face . . . the other, feet. Then simply toss both towels into a corner on the floor. This sounds primitive, but after three days they won't even want to know which *F* they're using, and at least the towels will always be where they belong . . . on the floor.

For mildew or musty odor on the shower curtains, simply take a sharp pair of scissors and whack it off. Actually, the more mildew, the more interesting the shower curtains become.

To clean piano keys, try having your children wear chamois gloves moistened with clear water. I daresay their practice sessions won't sound any different, and you'll have a clean keyboard.

To remove gum stains, pick off as much gum as possible, then soften it by applying egg white. An egg white is better to live with than chewing gum.

A sterilizer that has boiled dry will make an interesting conversation piece. Small rolls of dust under the bed will entertain small children for hours. (Likewise in-laws, malicious neighbors and the board of health.)

I thought I had touched all bases on how to live with housework until I received a note from a woman who had solved her ironing problem in a unique way. She wrote, "Two to four times a year, before holidays, I pack the unironed clothes in a bag or box and label them EASTER GRASS, OLD CHRISTMAS TRIMMINGS, FOURTH OF JULY FLAGS (RAIN-SOAKED) or HALLOWEEN PICTURES. By the time they're discovered, the children are married or living away from home."

Now, there's a woman who makes sense.

The Home Handyman—January 18, 1966

I am one of those devoted wives who is trying to up the retirement age for men to 95.

The motives are purely selfish. I don't think I could stand Mr. Fixit around the house for longer periods than my present four hours a day, Saturdays, Sundays and holidays.

The mail I'm receiving bears me out. On one card was a plaintive *Help!* In another letter was penciled, *I'm being held prisoner by an idiot with a set of wrenches in a house that has been without running water for 23 days.*

The home handyman usually fits into one of two categories. First, there's the home improvements dropout. He's the one who is fired with enthusiasm over a project at the outset. Within minutes of a request, he has laid wall-to-wall ladders over the living room, has a myriad of paint cans open and ready for spilling and the good draperies spread about the floor to pick up paint spatters. Then he smiles, climbs into his coat and says, "I just remembered, I'm off to study the tootse fly in South America. Don't touch anything until I get back!"

Some dropouts are not so inventive. They simply pull the stove out from the wall, take the oven door off, remove the back panel, spread shelves around the kitchen, then announce, "I don't have tools like the rest of the fellas. I do the best I can with a Boy Scout hatchet and crude tools I've been able to fashion out of boulders and buffalo hide. But when you don't have the right tool for the job . . ." (Along with the cold dinner, there isn't a dry eye in the house.)

Other dropouts are easily identifiable. They're the ones with the screens in during the winter and the storm windows in during the summer months. They spread grass seed in the snow and put up TV antennas in an electrical storm.

The second species is the perennial putterer. He never sleeps. And he never puts off till tomorrow what he can bungle tonight. Simple appeals, like "But it's the dinner hour," "But the company's *here,*" and "Please, I'm in the middle of a shower," all fall on deaf ears. He comes on like a herd of turtles at a cocktail party.

One of these perennial putterers was a man from the Midwest who was asked to reach behind the washer and put a simple plug into a simple outlet. He hoisted himself to the top of the washer, where his foot promptly broke the washer cycle dial. He lowered himself behind the appliance, inserted the plug halfway and blew out all the power on the kitchen circuit.

Shocked (but literally), he backed into the dryer vent, disconnecting it. Simultaneously, he dropped his flashlight in an opening between the walls. For an encore, he rapped his head on the utility shelf and opened a hissing valve on the hot water heater with his belt buckle.

I hear stories like that, and I wonder if the age of 95 is too conservative to shoot for.

The American Clothesline—April 20, 1967

Never do I feel the sun on my face and the wind gently billowing my skirt that I do not hold my right hand over my heart and mourn the passing of the housewife's answer to Radio Free Europe: the American clothesline.

Like the American buffalo, Irish tenors and the nickel cup of coffee, the clothesline is virtually becoming extinct. And with it goes the greatest communications medium the world has ever known.

When I was a kid, the neighbors stretched a clothesline the day they moved in. And we watched and learned. "How many of them are there? Boys or girls? Ages? Do they have nice underwear?" (Mama always said you could judge a woman by the underwear she hung and her character by the way she acted when her clothesline broke.)

By the time I had a home of my own, I could read Monday's wash like a gypsy reads tea leaves.

New diapers: "She brought the baby home."

Navy bell-bottoms: "His leave came through."

Extra sheets: "The in-laws from Kansas City."

Sleeping bags: "She finally found a camp to take those boys."

Blankets: "Stay away. They've got the virus again."

Training pants: "Well, it's about time."

Curtains and slipcovers: "She starts earlier every year."

Wading boots and fishing nets: "I'd leave the bum!"

Bathroom wall-to-wall carpet: "Status seekers!"

The clothesline was more than a flapping news bulletin. It was a little game housewives played. The women used to run a footrace to see who could get their wash out on the line first. If the sun ever rose on an empty clothesline, I think it had something to do with the success or the failure of your marriage. At least, it seemed that way.

It was also a test of skill and endurance to see how swiftly you could transfer a pair of steaming long johns to the clothesline in sub-zero temperatures without having them freeze in the basket in a cross-legged position.

As for me, it was group therapy . . . a lull in the busy day . . . a wave and a hello . . . a breath of fresh air . . . a glance upward at the sky . . . the smell of rain . . . the chill winds of winter to come . . . the fluffed-up chenille and the sweet-scented sheets that would never see an iron.

Why, if I had a clothesline today, I wouldn't be going crazy over the suitcases airing on my neighbor's patio. I'd have known before they did whether they were going or coming.

Getting Locked Out—July 8, 1968

Ever since my mother's house was robbed of a Swiss watch, a bottle of Scotch and a box of Girl Scout cookies, I have been suspicious of every strange man in the neighborhood who has booze breath, crumbs in his beard and the right time.

If anyone ever broke into our house, they'd leave a donation, but still my husband insisted I start locking the doors every time I left it.

This is a kick in the head for me, as I have a thing about keys. They're like umbrellas. I only want to be bothered with them when I need them.

I am inclined to mail them with my letters, use them as bookmarks, toss them into ashtrays and, often as not, leave them hanging in the lock on the outside of the door.

Since last February, I have broken into my own home 38 times. There are several approaches to the problem of being locked out.

First, there's Plan A, or the Crowd Teaser, as it is often called. Haul a ladder from the garage, have the kids steady it at the bottom while you climb to a small opening in the attic no bigger then the lid of a kidney bean can, and proceed to shinny through.

The dogs are the first to notice the commotion and will stage a bark-in. Their noise will in turn attract the mailman, neighbors, salesmen and meter readers from a 12-mile radius.

Eventually, a social worker will ascend the ladder slowly and try to talk you down by telling you that you are loved and needed, your acne will clear up, and you have no right to throw away your own life.

Plan B is a bit more subtle . . . but not much. You find a window with only enough space for a draft to go through and try to squeeze Sparrow Legs (he's the only kid in the family who fits in a supermarket cart, remember?) and drop him into the house, head first.

This is risky, as once little Sparrow Legs is in the house, he runs off to his bedroom to play with his trucks and cars and forgets all about the key and the rest of his family hovering together on the front porch.

Plan C was a favorite of ours. To avoid embarrassment and public ridicule, we'd go into the garage, shut the door and read aloud from the fertilizer bags until Daddy came home with his key.

I hesitate to mention Plan D, which is a little theatrical. We would go to the back of the house and make a human pyramid like the Wallenda family, while the smallest would gain entrance to the attic through a louvered opening. Invariably, however, my husband would notice the hole in the ceiling where a foot went through, and we had some explaining to do.

Breaking and entering is hard work. That's why I say to anyone who craves a Swiss watch, a bottle of Scotch or a box of Girl Scout cookies, it's almost easier to go straight.

No Pencil in the House—February 17, 1969

We have 26 appliances in our home, two cars in the driveway, a few savings bonds put away, and I am a "standing" at the beauty shop.

We do not own a pencil.

On the surface we would appear to be a family of some comfort. If Onassis knocked on the door and wanted to buy our house for a highway phone booth, I would have to sign the agreement with (a) an eyebrow pencil, (b) yellow crayon, (c) cotton swab saturated in shoe polish, (d) an eyedropper filled with cake coloring, or (e) a sharp fingernail dipped in my own blood.

Pencils are weird little devils. I discovered this quite by accident. One day I took a spanking-new pencil, sharpened it and put it by the telephone. Three days later the same pencil showed up in the vegetable crisper of the refrigerator.

I put it back by the phone. It popped up in the medicine chest.

I put it on a string and attached it to the telephone. It broke its lead. I sharpened it. It broke the string.

It was clear that lousy pencil was not an ordinary inanimate object. It possessed the human qualities of free will and intellect.

As I studied this strange creature, other things became apparent. It enjoyed no sex life whatsoever. Other household items, like coat hangers, straight pins and paper clips, propagated themselves.

Not pencils. They never begot anything but frustration. They came into this world alone, and they dropped behind the stove and out of your life.

They also had an affinity for never being where they were needed.

The other morning I had to write an admittance note for my daughter. "Get Mama's all-occasion cards," I yelled. (We haven't had stationery for six years.)

She gave me the box.

"Okay, what'll it be? Happy Birthday to a Nephew Who Has Been Like a Mother to Me, Sorry You're Sick or Thinking of You in Your Hour of Sorrow?"

"The birthday, I guess."

"OK, now get me a pencil."

"Where?"

"Try the desk, the sewing basket, the stove drawer, Daddy's workbench in the garage and my black purse."

"Not there."

"Very well, try the glove compartment of the car, the clothes hamper, the toy box, the pocket of my blue housecoat, the sink drain, the mailbox, the guitar case and the base of the big oak tree." (Shouting hysterically) "All right, you little devils! Come out, wherever you are! You've had your fun. I'll show you. You'll go to bed without your din-din!"

And some people worry about the Russians.

The Husband Who Prunes—September 15, 1969

There is something about a pair of pruning shears that turns a mild, conservative husband into a raving madman. If you watch closely you can almost see the physical features change. His ears become pointed, his teeth extend over his lower lip, and his muscles fairly ripple with the excitement of leveling all those wonderful trees and bushes even with the group.

There is a rumor that seven states are considering overpruning as a cause for divorce, second only to incompatibility and adultery. I hope our state is one of them.

No judge would dare deny me freedom after he heard the story of my privet hedge.

The first year I planted the hedge my husband knocked them down with a hose spray. The second year he inadvertently ran them down with his power mower. By the third year they had barely strength enough to grow leaves when he said, "They look a little raggy. Maybe I should prune them."

"You won't prune them as severely as you did our maple tree, will you?"

"What maple tree?"

"That's what I mean."

"Women do not understand the principle of development," he explained. "If you want the hedge to become bushy, you must prune it to promote growth and fullness."

Whack!

"Murderer."

"Look," he said. "Didn't I prune your roses back last year and didn't they do better this summer?"

"Better than what? I had to repot them and give them penicillin shots."

Whack!

"Now you've done it," I said. "That side is lower than the other."

"So, what's the problem? I'll just even it up a little."

"The last thing you evened up were those evergreens on either side of the garage."

"What evergreens?"

Whack!

"Did anyone ever tell you you're vicious? I mean, there has to be a sadistic streak in a man who destroys beautiful things."

"For heaven's sake, will you keep your voice down? They'll grow back."

"Hush. Look around you. This yard looks like a testing ground for nuclear weapons: a few battered twigs, a few twisted roots, a mound of dirt here and there."

Whack, whack, whack!

I rest my case.

Garage Sales—June 6, 1971

What is faster than a speeding bullet? More powerful than a locomotive? Able to leap tall buildings in a single jump?

Women at garage sales, that's who.

I had to see Garage Power firsthand to believe it. Before moving out of state, I found myself with a few excess trinkets. (Who am I kidding? The attic was so full of junk the county couldn't get the door open to condemn it.)

My girlfriend Esther said, "You are a natural for a garage sale."

"Why do you say that?" I asked.

"Because you are cheap."

I sniffed. "I don't think you understand that spreading one's personal wares out in a garage for public exhibition is not only crass, it smacks of being tacky."

"I made thirty-two bucks off of my junk," she said.

"Why didn't you say so?" I asked excitedly. "Get the card table and let's get started."

The garage sale began at 9 A.M. By 7:30 A.M. I had 15 cars parked on the driveway, 18 on the lawn, two in a ditch and a Volkswagen trying to parallel park between two andirons in my living room.

They grabbed and bought anything that wasn't pumping water, cemented in the ground, growing from seed or spitting sparks at them when touched.

They bought cocktail toothpicks that were billed as "like new," radios guaranteed not to play ever, plastic flowers that had died, toothless rakes, buckets with leaks, books of German military commands, and a ukulele that only knew one song, "The World Is Waiting for the Sunrise."

At one point I tried to shove through the crowd with a package in my hand. A woman grabbed it from me and said, "I'll give you thirty-five cents."

"No, really," I stammered. "This isn't—"

"Forty cents," she said, grabbing it, "and that is my last offer."

It is the first time anyone ever paid me 40 cents for my garbage.

By 4 P.M. I watched tiredly as a woman tried to coax my husband into her trunk.

"Esther," I said, "this is the most incredible sight I have ever seen."

"What's in that package under your arm?" she said.

"It's nothing." I hesitated.

"It's mildewed laundry!" she shouted. "How much did you pay for it?"

"Thirty-five cents, but some of it still fits."

Relaxing with "Country Gardens"—October 26, 1975

I wish all of you had known me when I was tense.

Those were the good times. There was color in my cheeks, my hands were steady, and people said my laughter was like the sound of Tiffany when you thumped it with your finger.

But that was before I started to crewel Country Gardens.

Everyone I knew was into some kind of stitchery, and one day as my friend Terri sat needlepointing a calendar, I said, "How do you have the patience?"

"Patience?" She laughed. "This is the most relaxing thing I do all day. You're tense. You should get yourself something to unwind."

That's when I bought Country Gardens, a stamped piece of linen in a kit with 28 colors of yarn and instructions for 18 stitches.

Ever since, Country Gardens has never left my side. It is like an appendage growing out of my fingers. I started it one morning when the kids left for school. At three when they wandered home, I was still at it and I continued on through the night.

Unwinding was a full-time job. The children bugged me constantly, demanding food, answers to questions and first aid when they bled. The other morning as I stitched feverishly, one of them came up to my elbow and said, "Mom." I jumped a foot off the chair.

"Can't you see I'm relaxing?" I said. "I don't suppose you've ever heard of appointments. If you want me to make time for you I can, but don't just drop in. Besides, why aren't you at school?"

"It's Saturday," he said simply.

My husband says I am possessed. The other morning about 2 A.M., he leaned over and said, "You have relaxed enough," and flipped off the light. I don't know what kind of animal would turn off your light in the middle of a French knot. I cried myself to sleep.

Yesterday, Terri dropped in (without an appointment) and suggested I relax more. "You are pale, your eyes are red from strain, and frankly I get more fun out of burping my Tupperware than talking to you anymore."

I figure if I can work straight through without interruption, Country Gardens should be finished and framed by the first week of November. Then I may take a few days off and be tense.

After all, all play and no work can kill you.

Working Wife/Maid Communication—September 28, 1982

Some of the best fiction being written today is never serialized in the slick magazines and never makes it to *The New York Times* list.

They're messages between the working wife/bachelor and the woman who comes in to clean the house/apartment. Sometimes, they never even see each other. They communicate only by notes left on the refrigerator door.

The following is a series of written communiqués between Wilma and her employer, Mrs. Rutledge.

"Mrs. Rutledge, There is a cat mess at the end of the sofa. Wilma."

"Wilma, I know. Mrs. Rutledge."

"Mrs. Rutledge, What do you want me to do with it? Wilma."

"Wilma, You are limited on options. You can surround it with sand and use it as a putting green, gift-wrap it and amaze your friends, or clean it up. I prefer the last. Mrs. Rutledge."

"Mrs. Rutledge, I was going to clean up the you-know-what, but the sweeper smells funny and sounds strange and won't pick up anything. Can you fix it? Wilma."

"Wilma, The cat is missing. I suggest you check the sweeper bag. Mrs. Rutledge."

"Mrs. Rutledge, The cat was not in the bag. Maybe the cat mess is not a mess at all. It looks just like something in a green bowl in the refrigerator. Is it what I think it is? Wilma."

"Wilma, What do you think it is? Mrs. Rutledge."

"Mrs. Rutledge, I knew once, but I forgot. The sweeper works just fine. What did you do to it? Wilma."

"Wilma, I emptied the bag. Mrs. Rutledge."

"Mrs. Rutledge, You know that little problem I told you about two weeks ago about the cat? I think I solved the problem. I moved the sofa over it and you can hardly notice it now. Wilma."

"Wilma, You're fired! Mrs. Rutledge."

"Mrs. Rutledge, There is another cat mess I didn't tell you about. It's hard to find. I'm the only one who knows where it is. Goodbye. Wilma."

VCR—January 24, 1985

For weeks, we looked at the videocassette recorder in our living room without speaking.

Mentally, I had begun to think of other uses for it. Maybe we could put legs on it and use it for an end table or release the ejection slot and put a plant in it.

From time to time, my husband would leaf through the manual with an intensity usually reserved for a nervous flier reading about the evacuation procedures on an aircraft.

It wasn't until last Friday night that he cleared his throat and said, "Since we are going out to dinner, why don't we tape *Dallas* so we can watch it later?"

I put my hand over his. "I want you to know that whatever happens I think you're the bravest man I have ever met."

As we stood in front of the machine, my husband observed, "This is ridiculous. We look like all we need are padded coveralls and a bucket of water. Good Lord, we aren't dismantling a bomb. It's only a harmless VCR. Read! I'll punch buttons."

"You want me to read to you the page on how to use the manual?"

"Skip that and get on with how to set it when we're not here."

"You have to swing down the cover of the programming button compartment at the right of the clock and set speed switch to LP, SP or SLP before you insert the cassette."

"The clock is blinking."

"Then you screwed up. You have to go back and reprogram that particular memory position."

"How do I do that?"

"Press the DAILY button. *Not* the 2W, you ninny, or you're back to square one!"

"I think I've got A.M.," he said.

"Well, you want P.M. You should be able to select one of the eight programs by pressing the button with the number and the minutes and the hours. Do you see the days of the week flashing?"

"Everything is flashing."

"Don't forget to press the record stop time. Are the letters CH flashing? If so, you're ready for the channel selector switch. Hey, I think you've done it. I see J.R. and Miss Ellie."

"What you see," said my husband, "is the actual program on the regular channel. We might just as well sit down and watch it. I don't know the time, but we've obviously missed dinner."

"What Time Is It?"—November 2, 1986

We have three clocks in our house, and each of us has a wristwatch. If you want to know what time it is, you'd find out faster by driving over to the bank or calling Time of Day.

The clock on the VCR blinks on and off at 12 A.M. That is because the power went off in the house in the spring, and when the continuity is broken, that's how the clock lets you know that the continuity is broken.

We had every intention of resetting it until we saw the directions. I was to hold down the clock button while my husband performed steps 2 through 5, but he screwed up by pressing the hour-minute button before he pressed the day button, and after a while we figured we were too old to start again at Step 1, so we let it blink.

The clock in the bedroom is hooked up to all kinds of things, including a radio and a speakerphone. It blinks too because its continuity was broken, so we never know what time it is. We are only sure that every morning at six, a disc jockey awakens us with a promise to maintain our pool with premium service. We don't have a pool. We also don't have to get up at six, but we can't figure out how to make him go away.

The clock on the oven hasn't had the right time since we have owned the stove. That is because without my glasses I cannot see what I am twirling and mistake it for the timer. Thus if it is 4 o'clock and I put a roast in the oven, I inadvertently reset the clock to 4:45. I have been known to lose as much as $2\frac{1}{2}$ hours on a busy day in the kitchen.

I have a wristwatch that gives you the time in Hamburg, West Germany. That is where the watch was made and set. The directions that came with it are very complete and written in German.

I live for the day when I'll be walking along the street and someone will say, "Pardon me, but do you have the time in Hamburg? I want to call my wife before three."

Possibly the only source of time in the house is my husband's watch. It's a runner's watch, which means it looks like a time machine that is ready to blast off. He can give you the time if you have the time to wait for it. He must depress a small knob with a sharpened pencil and subtract four or five hours from the time he bought it depending on the season and whether we are on daylight saving time. It sounds like a lot of fiddling, but to reset it he would have to climb in the car and make sure the owner of the shop where he bought it is in.

A couple came over the other night and innocently inquired, "What time is it?"

My husband said, "I don't have my calculator with me. You tell them."

I blinked my eyes 15 or 20 times.
They left hurriedly. It wasn't that late.

Boston Fern—November 13, 1986

I bought a Boston fern last week, and as I placed it on the countertop a hush came over the entire family.

They were all remembering the one I brought home in 1981. Finally, my mother whispered to my husband, "I tried to talk her out of it, but you can't tell her anything." He said, "I hope you're not going to get emotionally involved with this one." One of my children shivered and said, "Is Mama going to be sick again?"

I assured him that this Boston fern was different in many ways. The one I bought in 1981 cost $45, an excessive amount for a plant that cost more than my first set of flatware. I was an emotional pygmy then and never considered it would die in three days. Relationships with the flora and the fauna were important to me five years ago, and I felt personally responsible for their demise. I've watched PBS, and I'm wiser now.

I know now that you can't take a Boston fern seriously. It'll tear your heart out. You have to know that from the moment you take it out of the nursery, it turns hostile. It doesn't want your water. It doesn't want your sun. It doesn't want your fertilizer or your Willie Nelson records. It just wants to die.

So why do people buy Boston ferns in the first place? Because they need to feel challenged. You reach a stage in your life where you know you're not going to be Miss America; you're not going to win the Pillsbury Bake-Off. Winning the lottery is a long shot, and you've been passed over too often to have a late-night talk show of your own. So you see how long you can sustain a Boston fern.

The fern was in the house three hours when it went limp. We all gathered around and offered advice. "It's too near the stove." "It's getting a draft from the air vent." "It's offended by the music on *Prairie Home Companion*." "You overwatered it." "You should have misted it." "It needs fertilizer." "It's Reagan's foreign policy." "You should have gotten a heat lamp." "The dust is killing it."

Within two days, the fern was in the final stages of deterioration.

I bit my lip and said, "These things happen." Then I threw myself on the plant and gave it leaf-to-mouth resuscitation. The family restrained me. "How much did you pay for it?" asked my husband. When will any of them ever understand that it isn't the money?

A few days ago, I was going by one of those silk plant stores. I couldn't resist going in and checking out the fake Boston ferns. There were only two. Both of them had leaves missing, and the edges were turning brown.

I felt better.

Repairmanese—March 3, 1988

We had a malfunction recently in our alarm and they sent a man to check it out.

When I asked him what the problem was, he said, "One of the little wires is sick."

Call it a gut feeling, but I felt he was talking down to me, so I said, "Could you put it a little more technically than that?"

He said, "We were getting a silent signal when your toggle switch was inadvertently moved to the program position, so I reset it and checked to see whether there were any problem zones from the protective circuit due to winds the other night."

I said, "Does that mean the boo-boo is gone and the sick wire will smile now?"

He nodded.

For years, I've been trying to speak Repairmanese, but the natives all sound like they have mouths full of Novocain. Besides, the language has 56 known dialects: electrical, plumbing, refrigeration, termite control, roofing and siding, painting, washer repair—you haven't lived until you've tried to speak washer repair.

All I wanted to know were a few well-placed phrases to repeat to my husband in order to justify a bill for $67.33. That's all I needed to know. By the time the washer repairman got finished with a 10-minute explanation, the only words I recognized were "pump" and "boxer shorts."

And by the time I translated it to my husband, he said, "I don't understand why the pump was wearing my underwear."

When we were building the house, it was like visiting the Tower of Babel. Everyone was speaking his own language at the same time. I remember saying something to the electricians about splicing a lot of wires together so two switches could have their hearts beat as one; they laughed for a week.

I haven't felt so intimidated since we were all watching Louis Rukeyser one night, and he told a stock market joke and everyone in the room laughed, including me. But I didn't have the slightest idea why. And I thought Carl Sagan was funny.

As the alarm system repairman prepared to leave, I said, "I understand why you weren't too technical. My job is the same way. I'm a writer, and if I told you my creative level was stagnating and that cadences and insights were eluding me, you wouldn't know what I was talking about either."

He said, "It means you don't have an idea for a column."

The man is obviously bilingual.

Eyeglasses in Every Room—June 27, 1989

It has taken me a lot of years and progressive astigmatism, but I have finally amassed enough eyeglasses to have a pair in every room of the house. I can't see out of half of them, but it doesn't matter. I don't need them anyway.

Every time I got an eye examination and was advised that I needed stronger glasses, I'd never throw the old ones out. I'd put them in one of the rooms. Moving from room to room playing "musical eyeballs" is a romp through my life.

The pair I keep in the bedroom were my very first glasses. I got them in high school and look like Sally Jessy Raphael with a migraine in them. The glass is almost clear, and the only reason I wore them is that I thought they made me look smarter. They're painted with red nail polish. Someone sat on them, and they're held together with a bunion bandage. The only thing I use them for is to help me set the thermostat each evening before I go to bed.

I bought the vintage pair in the living room soon after I was married. There was this silly mix-up where I cooked my turkey by its price with all the innards in the cavity. Nineteen hours is too long to cook a turkey. I got a pair of reading glasses.

The bathroom glasses are considerably stronger. They were prescribed when I confessed to going into a restaurant and pretending to drop the menu on the floor. I read it quickly before I leaned over to pick it up. A lot of people do that.

The granny glasses were a long time coming. I didn't succumb to them perched on the end of my nose until one day, at one of the kids' parent conferences at school, I realized I said, "Excuse me, you were first" to a coat rack. I got half glasses just so people would think I looked like an interested parent. They're jammed in a phone book in the hallway.

As we hit the kitchen, the glasses are a little more current. There's a flashy pair with fins going up the sides like an old Buick. I was talked into them by my husband, who got sick and tired of sitting at the table and telling me, "Your peas are at eleven o'clock, your steak at three o'clock, and the steak sauce at five-thirty." They're a bit stronger, but I can do without them any time I want.

My present glasses are also expendable. Really. I just use them to match up my shoes, put on lipstick, recognize my mother before she speaks, and tell time. But I got extra pairs for my handbags, the glove compartment of the car and my coat pockets just to keep everyone happy.

My family is always ragging me to get contact lenses. Hey, I'd be the first to get them if I felt they were crucial—but I don't need them!

Weekends—March 15, 1990

At about seven o'clock every Friday night my world as I know it falls apart.

My perfectly healthy teeth start to hurt because they know my dentist's office closes at six. They will not stop thumping until early Monday morning, at which time they will become perfectly healthy again.

The TV cable will go out. Count on it. Repeated phone calls will put me in touch with a recording giving me weekday office hours. By Monday it won't matter. I won't have time to watch it anyway.

Someone in the house will come down with a mysterious malady that I have come to call Friday Night Fever. It's not high enough for the emergency room, but not normal enough to ignore. It's only enough to make you crazy that if you don't act, you may need an attorney.

With all the weekend services available to people, it's incredible how some things sense when you can be brought to your knees.

If I run out of blank checks, it will be on the weekend. If our dog gets lost, it is always between Friday night and Sunday, when "Help" falls on deaf ears. Keys break off in doors only on weekends. And I have never had a prescription that needed a doctor's OK expire on any other day except Saturday or Sunday.

At first glance, you might think cars are just inanimate hunks of metal that are incapable of thinking. Get real. Most of them figure you're going to run their wheels off on the weekend, so they just refuse to go. If it is winter, the electric windows will go down and freeze there. They know you have to go the distance to find a mechanic on duty on the weekend.

Probably the worst part about weekends is the house. It dies. Toilets overflow, washers freeze, dishwashers overheat, dryers don't and water heaters won't, the septic tank smells, the sliding glass door won't lock, water pressure is reduced to a trickle and something crawls into the woodwork and expires.

I try to rejoice with the TGIF crowd who cross off Monday through Thursday on their calendars as if they are serving time, but the truth is I live in dread of those two days when all the things I depend on are no longer there for me.

The ones who gather in a bar named for their favorite day of the week anticipate a glorious two days away from their desks. I have to be realistic and realize that synagogues are open on Saturdays and churches on Sundays. Given my weekends, there's a reason for this.

Changing of the Closets—May 1, 1990

It's an ancient ritual that makes the Changing of the Guard at Buckingham Palace look like an impulse.

Every spring and fall, millions of women march into their bedrooms, fling wide their closet doors and stage the seasonal Changing of the Closets.

Generally, the shuffling of clothes from winter to summer and summer to winter is a feminine trait.

Most men can live with short-sleeved shirts jammed next to their wool sweaters, but women cannot.

With each item of clothing that is taken off the rod, questions are asked and decisions are made:

1. Can these pants be buttoned when they are around my waist? No. Are they attractive on me? No. Do they have a designer label in them? Yes. The aye has it. I save the pants.
2. Does this hat go with anything? No. Would anyone else wear it? No. Did it cost 40 bucks? Yes. The hat stays.
3. Did I wear this coat one day last year? No. Will I wear it next year? No. Is it still in style? Yes. I store the coat.

There are rules to abide by. Clothes have a statute of limitations. If I do not wear an item in five years, I must (a) have it altered, (b) go on a diet and meet it halfway, or (c) put it in the holding drawer for three years.

At the end of three years, these clothes are reviewed again and a decision is made to (a) reinstate them to active status by inserting elastic waistbands, (b) infiltrate them into the closet to make it look like I have more clothes than I do, or (c) rip off the buttons and use the clothes for dust cloths.

Like a drone, I make the trip back and forth from my closet to the one in the guest room. Every time I drop off a load of dark wools and leathers, I return with an armload of cottons and gauzes. The transition takes days—sometimes weeks. My husband understands none of it.

"If you are going to transfer all the clothes in the bedroom closet to the guest closet and put the ones in the guest closet in your bedroom closet, why don't you just use the guest closet every other season?"

How can you reason with a man for whom pomp and tradition have no meaning?

Swinging Was Respectable on Front Porch
—September 22, 1994

In a world where people fear who is hanging out in the shadows of automatic-teller machines to withdraw from you what you have just withdrawn and put signs in their car windows, "Don't bother to break glass. Everything has been stolen," I was cheered to read that the front porch is coming back.

After World War II, all activities moved to the back of the house. Owners put in barbecue grills, patios and pools; and then they built a fence around it so no one would see what a good time they were having.

For those of a generation who can't imagine the function of the front porch, allow me to fill you in. It was a place that had a swing that squeaked. There was a roof over it so that when it rained you could swing back and forth and listen to the sound of it falling and smell the fresh earth. Kids left their bicycles and wagons on it so people wouldn't trip over them on the sidewalk in the darkness.

After dinner, parents had their coffee on the porch to watch the parade of people taking walks. Sometimes they stopped to get caught up on the news of the neighborhood.

For daters, the front porch was the place where you kissed, shook hands and promised to call. (I swear to you that's the truth.)

We lived in a different world back then. We could never have imagined a time when you pulled the blinds and hid behind them at dusk. We could never have imagined forgoing all that drama going on outside with kids and neighbors to sit in a dark room and watch *Kukla, Fran and Ollie* on a 10-inch screen.

The porch was another room. I can remember my mother on a stepladder washing it down with a sponge every spring. There were flower boxes and a table to hold the lemonade. There was a welcome mat.

The four of us—my mom, dad, sister and I—talked about everything. We talked about Dad's job, our school, Mom's day, when we were going to get a dog. We watched stars. Sometimes we argued.

A newsboy ran through the neighborhood one night shouting "Extra!" Wiley Post and Will Rogers had been killed in a plane crash.

More than any other topic of conversation these days is the state of the world and its people. What's happened to us? Our cars have alarms and clubs on the steering wheel. Our doors have deadbolts and are lighted up like nuclear sites. We're afraid of other adults and their children. We all want our old world back, but we don't know how to get there.

Maybe, just maybe, it's a path that leads to a front porch. It was more than just a place; it was an arena for learning how to act and how to trust and how we belonged to a group of people more important to us than ourselves.

Martha Stewart—September 27, 1995

My mom was visiting recently, and we sat stunned as we watched TV's Martha Stewart getting ready for Christmas. In 20 minutes she made an elaborate gingerbread house that looked better than the one I am living in. She followed this with baking 300 cookies the size of whoopee cushions, which she decorated and hung from the Christmas tree.

Two grown women watching a homemaking god prepare for a holiday that is three months away is what is so incredible about the Martha Stewart phenomenon.

I find myself unable to turn off her program.

What does this mean? Are there other women out there who are returning to putting creativity back into their homemaking, to join those who never left?

That's what those of us who had Martha Stewarts for neighbors tried to get away from. You all remember her. She was the woman who hand-painted her garbage cans with sunflowers while we didn't attempt anything that didn't have connect-the-dots. She maintained an organic garden, knew how to change fuses and made elaborate Halloween costumes for her children while the rest of us cut holes in garbage bags and shoved the kids out the door.

She entertained with theme parties (Low-Fat Fertility Foods Nite). She baked every day and ate nothing.

It's been 20 years since I've thought about a windowsill garden, but the other night as I watched Martha stake her tomatoes with rings cut from her pantyhose, I said, "I can do that."

I have started going to flea markets looking for mismatched bargain dishes to bring interest to my table. I think I bought back most of the dishes I got rid of in 1958, but I'm not sure.

My husband can't figure out what has happened to me. The other night I watched Martha plan a lobster bake by the seashore. He watched with me as she poured half a cup of gin into the boiling water before she dropped in the lobsters.

"Why doesn't she just drink the gin and forget dinner?" he asked.
"Shhh."

Martha said, "The gin relaxes the lobster. If you were going to be dropped into boiling water and steamed, wouldn't you want a drink first?"

When she was ready to take it all to the seashore, she had little brushes handmade from rosemary and dill, butter with chili and limes in it, and fresh corn.

My husband said dryly, "But will it play in a carport?"

Martha is not married.

Dear Old Dad

When God Created Fathers—June 17, 1973

When the good Lord was creating fathers, He started with a tall frame.

A female angel nearby said, "What kind of father is that? If you're going to make children so close to the ground, why have you put fathers up so high? He won't be able to shoot marbles without kneeling, tuck a child in bed without bending or even kiss a child without a lot of stooping."

... And God smiled and said, "Yes, but if I make him child-size, who would children have to look up to?"

And when God made a father's hands, they were large and sinewy.

The angel shook her head sadly and said, "Do you know what you're doing? Large hands are clumsy. They can't manage diaper pins, small buttons, rubber bands on ponytails or even remove splinters caused by baseball bats."

And God smiled and said, "I know, but they're large enough to hold everything a small boy empties from his pockets at the end of a day, yet small enough to cup a child's face."

And then God molded long, slim legs and broad shoulders.

The angel nearly had a heart attack. "Boy, this is the end of the week, all right," she clucked. "Do you realize you just made a father without a lap? How is he going to pull a child close to him without the kid falling between his legs?"

And God smiled and said, "A mother needs a lap. A father needs strong shoulders to pull a sled, balance a boy on a bicycle or hold a sleepy head on the way home from the circus."

God was in the middle of creating two of the largest feet anyone had ever seen when the angel could contain herself no longer. "That's not fair. Do you honestly think those large boats are going to dig out of bed early in the morning when the baby cries? Or walk through a small birthday party without crushing at least three of the guests?"

And God smiled and said, "They'll work. You'll see. They'll support a small child who wants to ride a horse to Banbury Cross or scare off mice at the summer cabin or display shoes that will be a challenge to fill."

God worked throughout the night, giving the father few words but a firm, authoritative voice and eyes that saw everything but remained calm and tolerant.

Finally, almost as an afterthought, He added tears. Then He turned to the angel and said, "Now, are you satisfied that he can love as much as a mother?"

The angel shutteth up.

Consolidating Cereal, Ice Cream, Cookies, etc.
—December 8, 1974

I poured myself a bowl of cereal this morning, and out dropped the weirdest array of raisins, flakes, oats, puffs and squares I have ever seen.

"Whatya call this?" I asked one of the kids.

"Frosted, fortified, cracked Cranbran flakes."

I dropped my spoon and slumped. "Don't tell me. Your father is on his annual crusade to consolidate all the empty boxes cluttering up the cupboards into one box!"

"Right," said my son. "If you think the cereal tastes rotten, you should dip into the ice cream. He found six cartons, each with a different flavor, with a spoonful left in each box, and put them into one bucket. It looks like someone spit up at Howard Johnson."

"Please," I cautioned. "No more."

"Not only that, he mixed all the cookies left lying around into one bag, and every time you reach in it's like trick or treat. You don't know if you're getting one baked this year or not."

"I'll speak to him," I said. I found their father in the bathroom trying to siphon a cap of toothpaste into another tube. "I want to talk with you," I said.

"If it's about the jellies being mixed together into one jar, I think you'll find the flavor rather interesting."

"It's not just the jellies," I said. "You're becoming paranoid about empty boxes."

"What's wrong with that?" he asked.

"You're making skeptics out of the children. They don't believe in anything anymore. They grabbed a box marked pretzels off the shelf the other night and sank their teeth into banana-flavored corn chips."

"The banana corn chips weren't moving in their box," he said.

"That's not the point. You do it with everything. Mother asked for an aspirin. I gave her one of the pills that you mixed together into one bottle. I didn't know if it would cure her headache, sweeten her breath, dry up her cold, put her to sleep, make her regular again or control birth. I can't go on living with a man who grafts soaps together in the soap dish and puts cake coloring in old shampoo and pours it into herbal shampoo bottles."

"Go on out and have your cereal," he said softly. "You'll feel better after breakfast."

I checked the dog's food supply. The box was full. I felt better already.

Stepfather—January 6, 1980

In addition to imitation mayonnaise, fake fur, sugar substitutes and plastic that wears like iron, the nuclear family has added another synthetic to its life: step-people.

There are stepmothers, stepfathers, stepsons and stepdaughters. The reception they get is varied.

Some are looked upon as relief pitchers who are brought in late but are optimistic enough to try to win the game.

Some are regarded as double agents, who in the end will pay for their crimes.

There are few generalizations you can make about step-people, except they're all locked into an awkward family unit none of them are too crazy about.

I know. I've been there. Perhaps you've heard of me. I became a hyphenated child a few years after my "real" father died. I was the only stepchild in North America to have a stepfather who had the gall to make me go to bed when I was sleepy, do homework before I went to school, and who yelled at me for wearing bedroom slippers in the snow.

My real father wouldn't have said that.

My stepfather punished me for sassing my mother, wouldn't allow me to waste food and wouldn't let me spend money I didn't have.

My real father wouldn't have done that.

My stepfather remained silent when I slammed doors in his face, patient when I insisted my mother take "my side" and emotionless when I informed him he had no rights.

My real father wouldn't have taken that.

My stepfather paid for my needs and my whims, was there through all my pain of growing up . . . and checked himself out of the VA hospital to give me away at my wedding.

My real father . . . was there all the time, and I didn't know it.

What is a "real" mother, father, son or daughter? "Real" translates to something authentic, genuine, permanent. Something that exists.

It has nothing to do with labor pains, history, memories or beginnings. All love begins with one day and builds.

"Step" in the dictionary translates to "a short distance." It's shorter than you think.

Daddy Doll Under the Bed—June 21, 1981

When I was a little kid, a father was like the light in the refrigerator. Every house had one, but no one really knew what either of them did once the door was shut.

My dad left the house every morning and always seemed glad to see everyone at night.

He opened the jar of pickles when no one else could.

He was the only one in the house who wasn't afraid to go in the basement by himself.

He cut himself shaving, but no one kissed it or got excited about it. It was understood whenever it rained, he got the car and brought it around to the door. When anyone was sick, he went out to get the prescription filled.

He kept busy enough. He set mousetraps. He cut back the roses so the thorns wouldn't clip you when you came to the front door. He oiled my skates, and they went faster. When I got my bike, he ran alongside me for at least a thousand miles until I got the hang of it.

He signed all my report cards. He put me to bed early. He took a lot of pictures but was never in them. He tightened up Mother's sagging clothesline every week or so.

I was afraid of everyone else's father, but not my own. Once I made him tea. It was only sugar water, but he sat on a small chair and said it was delicious. He looked very uncomfortable.

Once I went fishing with him in a rowboat. I threw huge rocks in the water, and he threatened to throw me overboard. I wasn't sure he wouldn't, so I looked him in the eye. I finally decided he was bluffing and threw in one more. He was a bad poker player.

Whenever I played house, the mother doll had a lot to do. I never knew what to do with the daddy doll, so I had him say "I'm going off to work now" and threw him under the bed.

When I was nine years old, my father didn't get up one morning and go to work. He went to the hospital and died the next day.

There were a lot of people in the house who brought all kinds of good food and cakes. We never had so much company before.

I went to my room and felt under the bed for the father doll. When I found him, I dusted him off and put him on my bed.

He never did anything. I didn't know his leaving would hurt so much.

I still don't know why.

Speak "Thermostat"—December 19, 1982

My husband has been trying to teach our children to speak "Thermostat" for years.

They say the younger you start to teach them a foreign language, the faster they learn. This has not been the case. "Flush" did not come easy for them. Neither did "Lights."

"Thermostat" is one of the last of the foreign languages to be taught to children. It comes just after "Hang Up That Phone" and "Shut the Door." (Note to parents: Please do not proceed to "Thermostat" until they are speaking "Shut the Door" fluently.)

There are several methods of teaching "Thermostat." Some parents use the Berlitz concept. They put recordings beneath the pillows of children that instruct, "A thermostat controls the furnace. When the door is open, the bad cold air wants to come in and the furnace tries very hard to heat the outdoors. God never meant for a furnace to heat America or He would never have invented snow."

One of the first phrases a child learns about "Thermostat" is "My room is cold." "My room is cold" voluntarily triggers his motor activity. He will proceed to the thermostat and with nimble precision move the thermostat dial to 82 degrees (by sheer coincidence, the boiling point of his father).

This is followed by "My room is hot." However, a strange phenomenon occurs. Instead of turning the thermostat back, your child will open a window. He needs work in the language.

Our children were slow. We spent a year and a half on "How do you spell relief? S-W-E-A-T-E-R!" We spent another two years on "Daddy is not a rich man, and we can no longer afford three children."

It wasn't until last week when we took them on a field trip to the meter that they seemed to comprehend what we were talking about. We showed them how the little dials twirled around on the meter and how we were charged for each little twirl. They watched our lips closely as we formed the word *Bankruptcy*.

One of them said, "Wait a minute. Are you telling us that the colder it gets outside, the harder the furnace has to work to keep it warm inside?"

We nodded happily.

"And every time it clicks on it costs money?"

We jumped up and down excitedly.

"Why didn't you say so?"

My husband smiled. "Do you think we can progress to 'Thank You'?"

"I hate to push 'em before they're ready," I said.

New Generation of Fathers—June 21, 1987

In the minds of women, fatherhood used to be considered a part-time job. It was something men did at the end of the day between parking the car for the night and going to bed.

As a matter of fact, it has just been within the past 10 years or so that it has been included in men's résumés. It is now something that commands more respect.

Children used to go through life waiting for that dreaded threat to materialize: "Just wait till your father gets home."

When he got there, he was always a bit of an enigma. What did you know about the man . . . really? He paid all the light bills. You knew that because he told you so. His talents were specialized. They included putting film in the camera, picking up prescriptions from the drugstore, bringing the car around to the door when it was pouring rain, putting Christmas tree lights on the top branches. And he was the only one in the house who could use a curse word and not get his mouth washed out with soap.

When there was a knock on the door late at night, everyone looked to him to answer it. If he had a problem, children never knew about it. If he cried, they never saw it. If he screwed up, they never heard about it. Sometimes it seemed he wasn't so much your father as he was your mother's husband.

He never got the egg with the broken yolk. He got the newspaper before anyone tore it apart. When he was taking a nap, everyone went around in stocking feet. On vacations, the car never stopped until he was hungry or had to go to the bathroom.

He was the supreme court of family discipline. His word was final. There were no appeals. This included everything from going away to school to getting the car on Saturday night to washing your hair after midnight in the winter.

And yet . . . he had a special place in the family. There were some things you could discuss only with him because he had the advantage of distance. With less exposure to you, he saw you differently from the way your mother saw you. You could tell him secrets and he would keep them . . . tell him your dreams and he wouldn't look at you and tell you you had to clean your room first. Because he didn't talk a lot, when he did you listened. When he wasn't at home, there was no family until he got there.

A new generation of fathers is emerging who want to do more than replace fuses and sign checks for the orthodontist. They don't want to be spectators or reigning monarchs over a family. They want to be equal partners in it. They've even stepped up their hours.

This is healthy. They may lose some of the mystique, but they'll be more than paid for the extra hours.

Food for Thought

The Instead-of Cookbook—November 4, 1965

Why doesn't someone write a cookbook for the suburban woman with one car that is used by her husband? Some real clever woman could call it *Cookbook for the Suburban Woman With One Car That Is Used by Her Husband* and to the first 500 subscribers give away stomach pumps as bonuses.

You've got to understand how it is in the suburbs. You can stand in the middle of your living room and sneeze, and promptly 200 families will yell out their patio doors, "Gesundheit!" But when you need something at the store, you have to drag yourself out to a car and drive two miles or so as the crow flies. (Unfortunately, she's new in the neighborhood and a trifle unfriendly.)

If you don't abuse your standing with the neighbors, they are sometimes good for short-term loans of staples. However, I am in hock to my neighbor on the left for a cup of rice, a snow shovel, a hamburger patty, a fuse and a sheet of juvenile birthday wrapping paper, and to the neighbor on the right for a can of tomato paste, a thermometer (oral), a quart of skim milk and a bobbin of green thread. I may be a sleazy, undependable, no-good deadbeat of a neighbor, but I've got my pride.

If I were writing a cookbook, I would naturally include my Fake-It Casserole. You substitute a cup of noodles for a cup of asparagus. Then for the sour cream, you either add a tablespoon of vinegar to the milk you have on hand to curdle it or forget about it entirely and add a can of cream of mushroom soup.

If you don't have cream of mushroom soup, put in a cup of grated cheese. However, if you have the mushroom soup, add bread crumbs and some minced onion. If you have the cheese but not the soup, sprinkle a little Parmesan on top and slip it into the oven.

Bake it at 350 degrees for 20 minutes if you've the noodles and the sour cream, or at 325 degrees for 30 minutes if you've the asparagus and the grated cheese. If this recipe makes you tense, then for goodness' sake forget it and have pork chops and applesauce.

If it is true that necessity is the mother of invention, it is for certain that irrationality is the grandmother of desperation. (Don't read that again. It makes even less sense the second time around.) One afternoon last week after a dismal attempt at a banana nut loaf (using no bananas and no nuts), I decided to whip up chocolate chip cookies. The chocolate chip bits were only a two-mile bicycle ride away. I huffed and pedaled until my varicose veins begged for mercy. It took me two hours and ten minutes, round trip.

Back in the kitchen, I was ready to create when I discovered I was out of flour and brown sugar. I'll share with you my recipe for Miracle Worker Chip Cookies. Substitute a cup of oatmeal for the flour and add a teaspoonful of vanilla. If you don't have the vanilla, use lemon extract with a dash. . . .

Weight Watchers Dilemma—April 27, 1972

I have dieted continuously for the last two decades and lost a total of 758 pounds. By all calculations, I should be hanging from a charm bracelet.

I have done a lot of kidding around with Weight Watchers, but it is the only organization in which I ever lost a great deal of weight. But I fought them.

Every Tuesday morning, a group of us had to weigh in before the lecture. Our ritual was enough to boggle the imagination. We got together a checklist of precautions before we actually stepped on the scale.

Bathroom? Check. Water pill? Check. Have you removed underwear, wedding rings, nail polish? Check. Set aside shoes, corn pads and earrings? Check. Are you wearing a summer dress beneath your winter coat? Check.

The first week, I stepped on the scale and my instructor said, "You have gained." (Next week, I cut my hair.)

The next week, she said, "You have lost eight ounces, but that is not enough." (I had the fillings in my teeth removed.)

The third week, I had dropped a pound, but my instructor was still not pleased. (I had my tonsils taken out.)

Finally, she really chewed me out. She accused me of not sticking to the diet and not taking it seriously. That hurt.

"I didn't want to tell you," I said, "but I think I am pregnant."

"How far?" she said coldly, clicking her ballpoint pen to make a notation on my card.

"Possibly three days," I said.

She glowered. "Any other excuses?"

"Would you believe I have a cold and my head is swollen?"

"No."

"How about I was celebrating the Buzzards' Return to Hinkley, Ohio, and had butter on my popcorn?"

She tapped her pen impatiently on the card and stared at me silently.

"Lint in the navel?" I offered feebly.

"How about first one at the trough?" she asked dryly.

I learned quickly never to argue with a woman who had the scales on her side.

I saw my old instructor the other day. She eyed me carefully and said, "When are you returning to class?"

"As soon as I have my appendix removed," I said, returning her gaze.

I'm not sure, but I think I heard her moan.

Burning Calories—August 18, 1974

My doctor flipped the weight of the scale over another notch, looked at me with annoyance and said, "Man does not live by bread alone."

"You think I don't know that?" I said. "Any fool knows you have to make it into a sandwich, top it with homemade preserves or cover it with cheese sauce and make a casserole out of it."

"You are overweight again," he said.

"Like how much?"

"Like if you were scheduled to fight Muhammad Ali this fall, you would have to drop fifteen pounds to make the heavyweight division. How much exercise do you get?"

"I leaned over a week ago Thursday for what I thought was a gingersnap cookie in the carpet, but it turned out to be a cork coaster and I haven't taken a chance since."

"Do you go to the refrigerator a lot?"

"Yes, and sometimes I even run."

"I have here a list of activities that tell you how many calories you can burn up per hour. I want you to go over the list and try to do at least one or two activities a day."

The list was depressing. An hour of housework burnt up 80 to 180 calories, ironing 50 to 60 and writing 10 to 20. I would have to arm-wrestle King Kong to make a difference.

Then a brilliant idea hit me. If I could do some vigorous exercises, I could eat all the fat food I wanted and burn it off before it took root.

That night I had a piece of apple pie. Then I grabbed one of the kid's bicycles and pedaled for two hours. It was work, but it was worth it. I had paid for my folly.

The next night I had 40 potato chips. To make up for it, I did a little ironing that I had put back. (Actually I only ironed for eight hours and put the rest of it back again.)

The next afternoon I outdid myself. I found an Easter egg I had hidden from the kids in the freezer totaling 583 calories. I had to paint the house to work it off. The same night I had lobster in butter, which totaled 2,390 calories. Checking my list I discovered I would have to row across Lake Erie and back to balance the calories.

Then, a terrible pattern began to form. I was borrowing on my energy and putting IOUs in the refrigerator. I owed two hours of carpentry for a bowl of cereal in cream, three miles of jogging for a French doughnut, and eight days of shoveling snow for a piece of birthday cake.

As I sit here writing this column, I am in hock through 1975. As I told my doctor, the only way I can possibly catch up is to be an oarsman on a slave ship. He is making the necessary arrangements.

Dinner Is Ready—May 24, 1977

In the mid-twenties, physiologist Ivan P. Pavlov made a rather interesting discovery. Every time he brought food to a dog, he would ring a bell and the dog's mouth began to water. Later, just by ringing the bell, he could bring about a reflex action of saliva.

In the late forties, Erma Bombeck, a simple housewife in Ohio, made another interesting scientific discovery. By announcing to her family, "Dinner is ready," it was noted that the entire family swung into action like a precision drill team. For no apparent reason, her husband would exit to clean out the medicine chest, one child would pick up the telephone and begin dialing, another would go to the bathroom and lock the door, and once one of them took a bus to Detroit.

After a while, she wouldn't even have to say anything. When she appeared at the door, they all just took off and scattered.

Just when it seemed her frustration had reached a breaking point, she observed yet another phenomenon. Hours later as the family sat around the table and raised their forks for the first bite, the phone would ring. It became as predictable as rain the day you washed the car, and it was driving her crazy.

She tried everything. She scheduled meals at odd hours. She tip-toed to the table. She once went to the living room where they were all seated around the TV set and instead of announcing dinner said, "I'm not here to announce what you think I am." But the group could not be fooled.

Every night they sat down to warm lettuce and cold French fries, while members of the family filed in and out like they were visiting a 7-Eleven market. And every night as they prepared to eat the first bite, the phone rang.

Her husband said she was imagining things, until one weekend Erma was flat on the sofa with a virus and he was in charge of dinner. Flushed with heat from the stove, and from the pressure, he ran into the living room and announced, "Dinner is ready."

One son stood up and went to the mailbox, another went to the car to look for his tennis racket, the dog went to the door and scratched to get out, and Erma started to exit.

"Where are *you* going?" he asked hysterically.

"I'm going to be sick."

"Couldn't you wait until after dinner?" he asked miserably. "I've worked like a dog to get the fish sticks, the chili and the potato chips to come out even."

Twenty minutes later as we all gathered around the table, we waited to hear the inevitable ring of the phone. There was silence for five minutes . . . then 10 . . . then 20 minutes.

A smile crept across my husband's face. "I guess your theory has just sprung a leak," he said. "We're eating and the phone is not ringing."

I didn't have the heart to tell him he was only half right.

Dieting Is a Losing Battle—March 21, 1978

It's no use for me to diet. I know that now.

All those years when my knees rubbing together whispered "no, no" but there was a "yes, yes" in my mouth, I fought the battle.

All those years when I lost 10 pounds every Monday (five in my neck and five in my bust), I hung in there.

All those years when I embraced cottage cheese as a formal religion, I gave it my all.

But after yesterday, I have to admit, I'm beaten. I'm fighting the battle alone.

It started in the morning when I faced the refrigerator with my hand over my heart and once again pledged allegiance to hunger. I poured myself half a glass of tomato juice mixed with half a glass of buttermilk and tossed it down. I felt virtuous.

At lunch, I threw down a cup of bouillon and pretended celery was wicked.

I had dinner ready to serve by 3:30 in the afternoon. It was well-balanced and would be totally satisfying: broiled fish, an oil-free salad, asparagus and an apple.

At 4 P.M. I looked at the dinner again. It looked pale, so I surrounded it with a fruit salad with coconut in it.

At 4:30, with nothing to do, I rolled out a pan of biscuits to pop into the oven.

By 5, the asparagus looked naked without a sauce, so I opted for hollandaise.

By 5:30, I was furious. How dare my husband be late and force me to obesity? I added whipped potatoes to the meal.

By 5:45, as I stood watching the driveway, I got a horrifying feeling. How could you possibly serve dry whipped potatoes? I added a pan of gravy.

By 6, the fish looked terminal. I decided to get my husband's mind off the small main course by giving him a robust appetizer. I rolled out those little butter, cheese and flour things stuffed with olives and popped them in the oven.

By 6:15, I sliced the apples and covered them with a pie.

At 6:30, my husband walked into the kitchen. "I'm home!" he shouted brightly.

"You animal! You don't care about other people at all. How they look. How they feel about themselves. If I go to my grave with pantyhose around my hips, let it be on your conscience!"

He pretended he didn't know what I was talking about.

Seven Days to Make Garbage—May 3, 1981

It's a myth in this country that anyone can make garbage. I'm not talking about the frozen/quick-serve/packaged/just-add-water/three-minutes-in-the-microwave garbage. I'm talking about the made-from-scratch-leftover garbage for which American women are famous.

Garbage, if it's made right, takes a full week. Most men don't understand the process. They think you can take a leftover straight from the table, scrape it right from the plate and dump it into the can. That is not the way American garbage is made.

Let us walk through a week in the life of two tablespoons of leftover peas and a coaster-size piece of leftover pot roast:

Day 1: The leftovers go from the table to the refrigerator in an elaborate ritual of joy. In her eagerness to display her frugality, the woman transfers the peas and beef to a smaller dish with the haunting chant, "Don't touch this. I'm saving it for vegetable soup." Everyone believes her . . . or pretends to.

Day 2: The leftovers enjoy a place of prominence in the refrigerator and are seen every time the door opens. A few times the container is reexamined, but from a distance comes the familiar chant, "Don't touch it. I'm saving it for vegetable soup."

Day 3: The leftovers are moved to a less prominent shelf and occasionally patted and reassured they will be the makings of vegetable soup.

Day 4: A traumatic time in the life of future garbage. It either is tossed prematurely or shoved to the rear of the refrigerator on a shelf next to a bowl containing three tablespoons of peach juice and a pit.

Day 5: Traditionally on the fifth day, a leftover is opened, exposed to air and passed around to see if anyone can identify it. If it is recognizable, it is shoved in a dark corner and allowed to ripen for another day.

Day 6: This is the crucial day in which the peas and beef curdle, turn green, harden and grow fuzz.

Day 7: Excited cries resound through the kitchen as the children dance around the refrigerator chanting, "Is it garbage yet?" Mother removes the leftovers, folds back the foil and pronounces the peas and beef dead.

In no other country do women prepare their garbage for burial the way they do here. First, they wrap it in newspaper, next put it in a brown paper bag, then a plastic one, and finally put it to rest in the garbage can in the garage. It's a time-honored tradition of American women, who for years have vowed, "I will bury no garbage before its time."

Thawing Hamburger—March 9, 1982

There is one thing I have never taught my body how to do, and that is to figure out at 6 A.M. what it wants to eat at 6 P.M.

I suppose there are some people who roll out of bed and can hardly wait for the day to go by to get at those cabbage rolls, but I'm not one of them.

I am always surprised when it is time to eat and there is nothing on my plate.

When my children were younger, I figured out there were two kinds of mothers: those who dragged out of a warm bed and put nutritious chili in a wide-mouth thermos, and those who stuck a stick of gum and a holy picture in a sack with instructions to "Trade up!"

When 43 percent of the women in this country went out into the marketplace to work, planning ahead for meals became a real challenge and hamburger became our national bird.

There's something about hamburger that's so . . . ground. It's like an old friend. I am never defeated by frozen hamburger like I am by a package of chops that are welded together or spareribs that wrap around a piece of frozen fat that is held captive until spring.

I never met a frozen turkey that was not capable of sinking the *Titanic.*

But hamburger is conquerable even at 6:30 when the big game starts at 7:30 and it's frozen like a rock. I know all of you have tried traditional ways to defrost hamburger, but have you considered some of the following new ones?

1. Tuck frozen hamburger under your armpit while setting the table.
2. Balance meat under your shower cap as you run through the hot water.
3. Put it in your dishwasher and run it through the dry cycle.
4. Have the children put it on top of the television when they first arrive home and begin playing video games.
5. Put it under the rear tire of your car and back up.

There are some people who put hamburger out on the countertop or sink before they go to work in the mornings. I don't know any of them personally.

Fruitcake—December 11, 1986

I never like to make generalities about people, but let's face it: People who love fruitcakes are "different."

In evangelism, they are to the right of Jerry Falwell and Pat Robertson. In fact, I wouldn't be surprised if fruitcake lovers founded the next major religion of the twentieth century.

I have never met a fruitcake baker in my life who didn't want to convert me to all that baked fruit. I can be standing in the baker's kitchen and announce without a trace of humor, "I do not like fruitcake. I have never liked fruitcake. I have sampled more than 10,000 species of fruitcake in my time, and it is my dream that I never have to sample it again," only to have someone put a slice in front of me and say, "Try it. This one is different."

Fruitcakes are not different. They all tend to be the same, each having an assortment of incompatible fruits and the distinction of weighing more than the stove they were cooked in. They defy all the culinary rules in the book. No one ever says, "This fruitcake is so light you don't know you're eating it." That is because the heavier the fruitcake, the better.

Another thing I hate about fruitcake lovers is they smile when their cake is rejected. I don't like people who do that. It's unnatural. I'd be more comfortable if they would just say, "Who asked you to eat this cake? It cost me forty-five bucks to make, and if it were up to me, I'd drop it on your ungrateful foot!" You can have respect for a person like that. But no, fruitcake lovers will stand by and watch you spit out the sample in your hand and say, "But isn't it moist?"

My mother is a fruitcake disciple. Every year since I've been old enough to hold a fork in my hand, she has tried to make a holiday conversion. Last Sunday, she opened her cake cover and there it was: 97 pounds of cooked fruit. "Doesn't that smell good?" she asked.

I said, "It smells like fruitcake."

She said, "I don't understand you. Your grandfather loved fruitcake."

"What has that got to do with me?"

"He loved you so. You were his favorite."

I watched her get out a small plate and knew what was coming. "The pineapple alone cost six dollars," she said.

"I hate pineapple, Mother."

"It's Julia Child's recipe, and you like Julia Child."

I was tired of fighting. I opened my mouth, and she put in a slice of fruitcake.

Put your hand on the fruitcake and say, "Hallelujah!"

Doggie Bags—August 25, 1987

I had dinner in a Chinese restaurant the other night, and when the waiter came to clear away the dishes I said, "Could you please put the rest of the almond chicken and the egg rolls in a doggie bag?"

He registered surprise.

"A doggie bag? What's a doggie bag?"

I explained to him a doggie bag was an American tradition where, when people ordered too much food, they took it home in boxes or bags to be put in the refrigerator, and when it was no longer recognizable or became restless, they threw it in the garbage.

Boxes he knew about, but he had never heard them called doggie bags before.

I told him that years ago people used to ask for the bones left on their plates so they could take them home to their dogs, but the dogs never saw them. The people either gnawed on them before going to bed or made soup out of them.

He was genuinely confused by this time. "This is an old American tradition?"

"The oldest," I said. "Bags stuffed with food were started by my family maybe a hundred years ago. If you'd go to one of my relatives for dinner, you never left empty-handed. My grandmother always baked extra yeast bread so everyone would have something to take home."

"So you enjoyed the bread in your own home?"

"Not really. Do you know how long it takes yeast bread to reach brick consistency? About three hours after baking. There were no preservatives then."

"So you threw it out?"

"Usually."

"And you carry on the tradition of doggie bags with your family?"

"I do indeed. I have three grown children who are not permitted to leave unless I send something home with them. They don't eat human, if you know what I mean. I send little leftover boxes with cold asparagus and lima beans in them. I pack macaroni and cheese and cabbage rolls in little foil containers where all they have to do is slide them in the oven. Sometimes I put leftover fruit salad in Dixie cups and cover them with aluminum foil, or I place leftover veal and chili in little storage containers. Oh, and jellies I have made with a cute little label that reads, *From Erma's kitchen. Made with love.* Believe me when I tell you an army of Tupperware marches out of my kitchen each week into my children's apartments."

"And what do they do with the doggie bags?"

"They put them on their refrigerator shelves, and when the food is no longer recognizable or gets restless, they throw it in the garbage."

"Maybe you should feed it to your dogs," he said.

What a weird suggestion.

Spices—July 26, 1988

Doris from Rochester, New York, writes:

"I've got my thirtieth wedding anniversary coming up in September, and I just used up my first box of bay leaves. The box has a price tag on it that says 15 cents. Am I alone?"

Pull up a couch, Doris. Of course you are not alone. You are a member of the largest cult of homemakers in the world, who hang onto everything in their kitchens—except their sanity.

If spices qualified as antiques, Sotheby's would be camping at my kitchen door.

I have a spice from Ceylon to sprinkle over my chilled melon, one from Jamaica for pickling, one from Sierra Leone for rhubarb, one from Spain for sweetbreads and one from Madagascar for winter squash. I have no idea what I'm doing with these spices, because I don't like any of the things you use them for.

But I know this is true: Once you get a spice in your home, you have it forever. Women never throw out spices.

There are several reasons for this. First, they smell so rotten to begin with that most of us have no idea when they go bad. Second, they don't take up much space, so we say, "What the heck." Homemakers also figure that one rainy day when they are trying out a new recipe and it calls for a quarter teaspoon of cardamom, they'll have it.

You couldn't get me to throw away my container of fennel. This probably seems like a shallow reason, but my husband alphabet-izes my spices, and it's the only *F* I have.

Men do not understand this attachment to spices.

One day, I asked my husband to put a small jar of mint in his vise and take the lid off with his pliers.

"When did you last use this?" he asked suspiciously.

"I've never used it," I said.

"How old is it?"

"What year did we move from Ohio?"

"You paid to have this transported from Ohio sixteen years ago? Why did you buy it in the first place?"

"It was on sale."

"But you hate mint."

"Maybe it will absorb some of the odor of the sauerkraut in the disposer. Get the lid off!"

If it makes you feel any better, Doris, I bought a small packet of saffron last week. Cost me an arm and a leg. Did you know it takes approximately 55,000 flowers to yield one pound of it? A pinch will flavor a whole pound of rice.

The Egyptians were buried with their spices. I know which one I'm taking with me when I go.

Older People Only Talk about Food—May 24, 1990

A thirtysomething reader posed an interesting question: "Why is it when speaking with older people about a trip or a vacation they've been on, I get an answer like this?

"Me: 'You were at Yellowstone last summer. How was it?'

"Them: 'Oh, it was wonderful! We had the best spaghetti I've ever tasted, just outside of Jackson Hole at a little restaurant.'"

The young woman observed that about 75 percent of the con-versation with older people is about food: where it is, how much it cost, how it tasted. She wondered if it was because they grew up in the Great Depression, when food was scarce and they had to eat the same thing all the time.

I think that's part of it. When I was attending college, my mother's letters read like a menu. She began with breakfast and outlined everything she had to eat for the entire week. Our phone conversations were always about the same thing: food. "What are you having for dinner? I'm heating up the leftover ham and frying some potatoes and having a little corn on the cob."

A few years ago, she and my dad took a cruise to Alaska. They took 125 slides. Only six had people in them. (Two of them were pastry chefs.) The other pictures were carved bits of ice, cheese displays, baskets of bread and flaming desserts.

I blamed the Depression years for having to clean up everything on my plate and eat up the black bananas before I could start on the yellow ones. We were told the heels of bread made your hair curly, and starving Armenians were waiting in line for those stinking brussels sprouts. Mom would spend a fortune on glass jars and lids to can a bag of free apples.

My theory is that, after a certain age, food is one of the few vices left that you can enjoy. The kids are gone and have their own lives. Your job is a memory. Physical activities are a real effort. A new car no longer gives you the kick it once did. Food is one of the few fantasies you can lust after and turn into reality. Food even replaces sex.

Our young friend said the weird part of her findings was that a couple of weeks ago a contemporary of hers went to a rock concert.

When asked how she liked it, the friend said, "Oh, it was great. You should have seen all the food we had before the concert—honey-baked ham, roast turkey, munchies. . . ."

I told my reader that her friend is older than she thinks.

Leftovers That Refuse to Die—December 17, 1991

My secretary and I are compiling a list of leftovers that not only refuse to die, they reproduce. Heading the list is her pasta salad. Out of a pound of macaroni, she fed a family of six for two meals, ate it for lunch every day for three weeks, and at that point still had more pasta salad than she originally made. She eventually buried it in the backyard.

Split-pea soup has a reproduction cycle. So does beef stew.

And I defy you to scoop out the last spoonful of fruit cocktail from a bowl. Every refrigerator in America has two tablespoons of fruit cocktail on a shelf somewhere, and the peach slices and brown bananas keep giving birth to more peach slices and more brown bananas.

Well, I've got a new immortal to add to the list. It's rice soup. It was a package deal, complete with spices and slivered almonds to give it a "nutty" taste.

All I had to do was sauté onions in butter and add them to the rice, along with 2½ cups of water. That was a Tuesday night, November 5, of this year.

Well, the water disappeared at the end of an hour and the rice seemed thick, so I added another couple of cups and continued cooking it.

Just before dinner, when I dipped in to serve it, it still seemed thick, so I added some more water.

We had a lot left over.

At lunch the next day, I added some more water to a bowl of it and nuked it in the microwave. Two nights later, I put some of it in the wok with some leftover pork.

When the weekend rolled around, I asked my husband if he wanted a rice sandwich. He said no.

I sent some of it home with the kids and put some in the bird feeders.

Every time I took the lid off the pot, there was still enough left to celebrate a Chinese New Year in Shanghai.

I patched plaster with it, mixed it with mulch and fertilized my roses, and gave myself a facial with it.

I was ready to freeze it last week and perhaps retard this senseless breeding, when it hit me.

I had stumbled upon the answer to one of the greatest dilemmas facing the planet today. I could feed the world on a pound of rice, an onion, a packet of spices and slivered almonds.

People have gotten the Nobel Prize for less.

Think about it. Rice exists in many climates, needs no refrigeration and has no natural enemies. All you do is add water—and water—and—water—and water. . . .

Leftover Halloween Candy—December 1, 1994

I polished off the last piece of Halloween candy today. Don't ask me why I have the need to tell you this, but there it is. For trick-or-treaters, my husband and I stocked 50 Hershey bars, 50 Nestlé snacks, and 50 Baby Ruths.

We had a total of three beggars. They were on the honor system. We held the basket out and let them choose. The little five-year-old was adorable. She delicately reached in and extracted a single candy bar. The kid behind her, who looked about eight, took three without batting an eye. And the oldest one, who probably had a mustache under his mask and drove the car, reached in with both pig hands and dragged out five or ten pieces. It was like one of those giant claws in a machine where you're trying to snare the diamond ring.

I had every intention of putting the leftover candy in the freezer, but my husband said, "Why? You'll just break a tooth or buy a chain saw." He thinks he's funny.

I buy candy only once a year. I know how I am. If it is around, I will not rest until every piece is gone.

I did not eat the Halloween candy indiscriminately. I used it as rewards.

I rewarded myself for remembering to take the chicken innards out of the freezer and deposit them in the trash can the night before garbage day. I got a candy for every right answer I got on *Jeopardy!* I got a treat for ironing the back of my husband's shirt and another for eating a two-day leftover.

One night just before dinner, my son dropped by in time to see me pop a Baby Ruth in my mouth.

"I thought you always told us candy would ruin our dinner."

"This is different. It's a reward."

"For what?" he asked.

"For having the strength to stop at one candy bar while I'm cooking."

"Come to think of it," he said, "all that Halloween candy we got that you stored in the freezer, we never saw again."

"I told you the ants got it."

"How could ants live in the freezer?"

"They dressed warm."

"I think you polished it off a piece at a time."

When he left, I was stressed from all the questions. A Hershey bar seemed to soothe me somehow.

Tooth Traps—June 4, 1995

This is one of those Jerry Seinfeld nothing topics that no one ever talks about.

Did you ever have a tooth that traps anything you put in your mouth? It can be in the smile zone or a molar in the back, but no matter what you chew, it ends up getting caught. I do not know anyone personally who can ignore this. Whatever it is must go.

If I am home alone and get a piece of grapefruit caught in my tooth, wouldn't you think I would walk to the bathroom and get a piece of dental floss? I am not challenged by that. Instead, I grab a card from my Rolodex and try sliding it between my teeth. It doesn't work.

Now I have a chunk of my gynecologist's phone number stuck in my tooth. I open my desk drawer and find a spool of pink thread. I snip off a long piece and wedge that in the tooth. It sticks there. Now I have a piece of pink thread dangling out of my mouth. I have one long fingernail that I grow for such a moment. It doesn't begin to budge all the litter trapped in the space.

The needlepoint needle doesn't loosen it. Neither does the letter opener. As a last resort I go for the floss. The space can take no more. Now the floss dangles next to the pink thread. I am going through life looking like a party favor.

I am angry at myself for not bringing out my big weapon to begin with—my tongue. Throughout the years, I have developed one of the strongest tongues in the world. It comes from sitting through dinners/concerts/movies/meetings and anywhere people frown on having you put your entire hand in your mouth to remove a foreign object from between your teeth. After years of probing and pushing, my tongue is not unlike that of the Budweiser frog who attaches his to a beer truck and yee-ha's his way down the highway.

I don't like to resort to the tongue. Everyone knows what you're doing. To begin with, you are so focused that your eyes glaze over, your mouth is set in a firm line and you have no idea what is going on around you. All you want to do is search and seize that piece of food from your tooth.

In many ways I'm lucky. The tooth that catches everything in my mouth is a molar. I've seen other people who get food trapped in their front teeth. A piece of spinach will not only stick there, it will cover the tooth like an ugly slipcover.

And if you think you can drop a napkin and force a piece of chicken out from between your teeth under the table, forget it.

I can say there is no sensation as euphoric as when the foreign object breaks loose. Yee-ha!

The Empty Nest

Daughter Returns to College—January 28, 1972

Our daughter has just returned to her college campus following three weeks of R and R at the Bombeck Hilton. She may be rested and rehabilitated, but we are beyond recovery.

As my husband and I walked through the gutted, bare rooms of our home, our footsteps echoed hollowly on the bare floors. Finally, my husband spoke. "It's incredible, isn't it? It took us twenty-two long married years to amass eight rooms of furniture, forty-three appliances, linens for five beds and an acceptable wardrobe and now . . . it's all gone."

I nodded. "And to think she condensed it all in two large suitcases and a zippered gym bag."

"I just don't believe it," he said, closing the doors on the bare linen closet. "The sheets, the towels, our electric blanket. All gone. Why don't you make us a cup of coffee?"

"Can you drink it out of an ashtray?"

"Forget it," he said. "I'm going to sit down and—"

"I wouldn't," I cautioned. "She took that small occasional chair you used to sit in."

"And the TV?" he gasped.

"The first to be packed, along with the transistor radio, the hair dryer, the makeup mirror, the iron, the electric skillet, your shaver and your parka jacket."

"And I suppose the phonograph is—"

I nodded, "College bound. Along with the typewriter, electric fan, space heater, bulletin board, label maker, bowling ball, popcorn popper and full set of encyclopedias."

"How will she lug all that stuff back to school?"

"I think she dismembered the bicycle and put it under her seat."

"What are we going to do?" he asked, looking at the barren rooms.

"If we looked better we might get on the *The Newlywed Game* and try to win a washer and dryer."

"I think we've got enough Green Stamps for—"

"Forget the Green Stamps," I said softly. "She took them."

"We could take a trip and—"

"If we still had luggage," I corrected.

"This is ridiculous," he snarled. "Why can't she go to college right here at home?"

"She wants to get away from materialism," I said.

Picking Up the Tennis Ball—July 24, 1975

There are few things in this world more satisfying than having your son teach you how to play tennis, unless it is having a semi-truck run over your foot.

It is almost as if he is paying you back for letting him fall off the dryer when he was a baby and you were bathing him . . . for putting him to bed on his fifth birthday when he threw ice cream into the fan . . . for bailing out of the car when he was 16 and you were teaching him how to drive. All the hostilities come out the moment you walk onto the court together.

"We're going to continue with our instruction on how to pick up the ball," he said.

"I know how to pick up the ball," I said.

"I've told you before, we do not pick up the ball like a gorilla going for a banana. There is the professional way and there are several approaches. You can use the western forehand grip, lean over gently and tap the ball with your racket until it bounces."

Several minutes later as I was on my knees pounding the racket into the optic yellow ball, he leaned over and said, "It is not a snake you are beating to death. It is a tennis ball. Let's try the ball-against-the-foot method."

I stood up exhausted. "How does that work again?"

"You grip your racket against the ball and firmly force it to the inside of your left foot. Bending your knee, you lift the ball to about six inches off the ground and drop it. When it bounces, you continue bouncing it with your entire racket until you can pluck it off the ground into your hand."

Gripping the racket, I forced the ball to the inside of my foot, where it rolled over the foot and toward the net. I cornered it and started inching the ball up my leg but lost my balance and fell into the net.

Approaching the ball once more, I accidentally kicked it with my foot and chased it in a crouched position to the corner of the court, slamming my body into the fence.

For the next 15 minutes, the elusive little ball moved all over the court like it had a motor in it.

Finally, I leaned over, grabbed it with my hand, placed it on my leg and supported it with the racket.

"Okay!" I shouted. "I picked up the ball."

"That'll be all for today," he said. "We'll spend a few more weeks on this before moving along to hitting the ball."

I put my arm over his shoulder. "Now, let me tell you how to pick up towels off the bathroom floor. You simply bend your body in the middle, grasp the towel firmly. . . . "

Empty Nest Overrated—October 1, 1978

All the child psychology books I've ever read take you down the yellow brick road past puberty, serious petting, into mature relationships and leave you.

But parenting isn't like that. There are 30 million parents out there with kids between the ages of 18 and 55 who dart in and out of their lives like a revolving door.

The empty nest syndrome is overrated. I have heard of some parents who moved during the night to another city (and left no forwarding address). Others have installed pay showers. Still another parent I know waited until her son got up one night to use the bathroom, then painted his room pink and rented it to a pocket computer salesman.

No parent likes to change locks, but the situation is definitely getting out of hand. Children simply aren't leaving the home after school anymore as they did in the sixties. When they do, they multiply and come back tenfold.

So how do you displace an aging teenager? It isn't easy. When our son's bedroom began to take on the appeal of a roadside zoo (complete with sawdust on the floor), we took action.

First, we set the table for two. This made him aware that he was not expected for dinner.

Second, we intercepted his mail, wrote *No such person at this address* and had it returned to the post office for forwarding.

We posted signs in the hallway reading, OCCUPANCY BY MORE THAN TWO IN THIS HOUSE IS A FIRE HAZARD.

We were considering telling him he would have to share his room with the family pet (and buying a wolf) when we came up with a daring but cruel idea. We stopped stocking the refrigerator.

If I live to be 100, I'll never forget the look of fear in that child's eyes, standing in front of the refrigerator door (the hairs in his nose becoming frosted) and saying, "Is that all there is?"

We never saw him again.

You hear a lot of dialogue on the death of the American family. Families aren't dying, they're merging into big conglomerates. Daughters and sons who are between roommates (legal and lethal) drift in and approach the desk like they're in a hotel, asking, "Is my old room still available?" Cribs and strollers appear with babies. Cars and special menus are requested.

I rechecked my child psychology book the other day for the answer and wondered, "Is there life after the index?"

Parents Covet Kids' Closets—August 9, 1979

I have always been led to believe that if you lose a daughter or son to an apartment/dormitory/barracks, you gain a closet.

An extra closet is a big thing with parents. Sometimes it makes the difference between sleeping with a set of golf clubs or eating dinner every night with a box of sewing scraps on your lap.

When our children were younger, sometimes my husband and I would sneak into their bedrooms as they slept. We would gaze at their closets as I squeezed his hand and smiled. "Just think, dear, one day all of that will be yours."

We fantasized about the time each of us would have a rod of our own for clothes . . . a shelf without Christmas decorations . . . floor space without boxes marked RAIN-SOAKED HALLOWEEN MASKS or EXPIRED WARRANTIES.

When the first child peeled off, we waved goodbye and ran to her closet. We couldn't get the door open. When we did, we couldn't get it closed. There were dolls, animal-shaped pillows, old records "that would one day be classics," traffic signs, posters and 15 or 20 boxes marked DO NOT TOUCH.

When the second child relocated, we spoke openly of the closet and what we would do when it was vacated. We soon lost hope when he wheeled a bicycle into our closet and said, "I don't have room to store it in my closet, and if I leave it out in the garage it'll get ripped off."

Today, I don't think anyone can touch us on closet occupancy. We've been running at capacity for nearly 30 years. We are storing composition books (lined and unlined), 2,080 friendship pictures, fuzzy dogs, rubber worms, graduation tassels, rugs from Disneyland, pennants, fins, sand-filled cameras, basketballs, kites, dog-eared letters, college catalogs, tennis trophies and license plates.

All I know is I'm sick of the battle. I'm sick of wearing clothes that look like they've been laminated, sick of having children come back to visit their drums, sick of falling over tennis rackets without string and jackets that don't fit anyone. Let the word go out: When I go . . . if I don't have a closet of my own . . . I'm not going.

"Not to Worry"—July 15, 1984

It was one of those days that a mother dreams about.

It was Saturday and I could sleep until I got a headache. The kids were grown and on their own. Nothing in the house leaked oil, dripped water, smoked when you plugged it in, made a funny sound or had a light burnt out. There were no deadlines, and the big insurance premium was paid. I did not have a thing in the world to worry about.

Then the phone rang.

It was one of my kids telling me she was driving to Las Vegas and not to worry. *Not to worry?* Now I had to devote at least five hours to wondering if the car would break down or if some crazy would cross the center line and run her off the road.

Suppose someone ripped off her credit cards and money. Five hours out of a perfectly good day sitting around waiting for a police officer to call and say, "I have someone here who wants to talk to you. Speak up. She's in traction."

Five hours of unrelenting fear. Would she reach over to change stations on the radio and hit a horse that ran out in front of the car? Would she drop into a roadside place for a hamburger and be dragged out on the road by a motorcycle gang who did wheelies around her? Would a sheriff running for governor pick her up for alleged speeding and accuse her of a crime for which he needed a suspect because he wanted national press coverage?

When the phone rang again, it was another child, who informed me he was going fishing in a rubber raft in the ocean.

"I hope you're not considering going this weekend," I said. "I'm already half crazy worrying about your sister driving to Las Vegas, which is going to take at least five hours of misery and mental anguish."

"We're only going to be out for about four hours."

I was going to wash my hair, but what's a mother to do? I canceled that in case a Soviet submarine surfaced just under their boat and dumped them into the Pacific. Or what if they caught a fish so gigantic it pulled their boat out into the open sea? Of course, there was always a strong possibility of Jaws III coming to the beach for the summer, or a tidal wave they didn't hear about because a rock station didn't carry the news.

By my calculations, I had 10 or 12 hours of worry ahead of me when I heard from my third child. "Don't tell me," I said. "You're climbing Mount Everest in tennis shoes just to punish your mother."

"Actually," he said, "I'm staying home this weekend."

I couldn't believe his insensitivity. Now I had to worry that he had no friends or social life. Unable to relate to anyone, he would become more and more withdrawn and finally trust no one. Eventually, he would pull his blinds and eat out of a saucepan on the stove. I would never go to his wedding, where everyone said, "She looks too young to be his mother." I would never dangle grandchildren on my knee, where people would say, "She looks too young to have grandchildren."

What are they trying to do to me?

My Son's Answering Machine—June 22, 1986

About three years ago, my son, who lives in another state, got an answering machine. At first I resented it. I knew as sure as God made little green apples the kid was lying in bed with the machine turned on, listening to me having an anxiety attack and loving it.

But after a while, the machine began to take on a human quality. It had such fine manners. It would say softly, "Hi, I'm not here right now, but if you would leave your name and your phone number, I'll get back to you as soon as I can. At the sound of the beep, you have ten seconds. Have a good day now." My son never would have said that!

Somehow I couldn't bring myself to say what I had called for. ("You bum! Is your arm broken? I have stretch marks around my knees and you don't have five minutes to talk to your mother!") So I ended up saying, "I know you're busy. I was just checking to see if you're alive. I hardly hurt at all today. You have a good day too."

Throughout the year, the machine and I continued to communicate on a regular basis. As I told my husband, "I've never had a relationship that was so satisfying. That little monkey was always there for me when I needed it. You know how you call some people and the phone rings and rings and rings . . . not this one. Why, even our son used to brush me off. Someone was always honking a horn or a buzzer was going off or his car was being stolen as we spoke. But not the machine."

On Christmas in '84 it actually played "Silent Night" for me and before the beep wished me a Merry Christmas. It meant the world to me. It was such a sweet, simple thing to do. No whining around about how the gift was in the mail or how the airlines were booked and he couldn't get home, just a sincere little electronic Christmas card.

Then one day, I think it was the spring of '85, I dialed the machine and heard it say, "You have reached 555-4455. I promise I'll return your call (God, I love integrity!). Got a little problem. The beep is broken, but if you'll just count to five and leave your name and number, I'll call you right back."

You'd have thought my son would have the decency to tell me the recorder was sick. I know him. He had probably abused it in some way, like dropping it from the stove or cutting off its current with its own cord. You know how kids are. They only think of themselves.

I called the recorder yesterday—just to chat—when a voice said, "Yeah?"

I said, "Who is this?"

The voice said, "It's your son." It had been three years since I had heard his voice. "How's it goin'? Are you there, Mom?"

I told him I was waiting for the beep. He said I just caught him on his way out.

I called the recorder a little later and we had a nice chat.

Remembering Children's Names and Ages—June 14, 1987

One of the things they never tell you about child raising is that for the rest of your life, at the drop of a hat, you are expected to know your child's name and how old he or she is.

Usually, you are given no chance to count on your fingers, make a phone call or dig up a certificate. Out of the clear blue sky, someone will ask, "How old is what's-his-name now?" and you're expected to spit it right out.

With the firstborn, it's a piece of cake. Everything is significant about the firstborn. But for the children who follow, most parents have to associate the year of their birth with something of major significance. I remember our second child was born the same year we paid off the freezer, and the third one came along the year Sara Lee came out with carrot cake. Or maybe it was the year we put a window fan in the attic. I get a little fuzzy on that one.

As far as I am concerned, their names are interchangeable. If I yell at the wrong one for something the other one is doing, they credit my account, and the next time they do something rotten, I blame their sibling for something they didn't do. It beats going through three or four names before I get the right one.

I suppose all of this belies the stereotype Hallmark mother, but give us a break. Mothers have to remember what foods each child likes or dislikes, who had roseola and mumps, which one is allergic to penicillin and hamster fur, who gets carsick, and who isn't kidding when he stands outside the bathroom door and tells you what's going to happen if he doesn't get in right away. And if they all have the same color hair, they tend to run together.

Middle names were always hard for me. Maybe if I used them more; but every time I enrolled the kids in a school, they were asked for the *full* name. To this day I cannot remember their confirmation names.

One of my sons, who is . . . let us just say he is older today than he was 10 years ago, accuses me of telling the wrong stories on the wrong kid. I thought he was the one who said cute things that I used to submit to *Reader's Digest*, but it turns out it was his brother. Whatever.

The other night I said to one of them, "Your birthday is coming up. Just think, you're going to be twenty-. . . . eight!"

"Nine," he said.

"Don't use that tone with me," I said.

"Mom, I was there."

"What do you think I did, phone it in? Don't you think I know how old my own child is?"

When he left the room, I said to my husband, "What's his name?"

Kids Show Up for Dinner—July 19, 1990

My husband said the other day, "We haven't seen our kids in a while."

"You want to see your kids?" I asked. "I can arrange it."

"You're not going to call and tell them we're changing the will again, are you? We've overdone that one."

"No, no. At least one of them will be here tonight for dinner. Trust me."

Sure enough. At 6 P.M. we heard a key in the door and our son walked in. My husband was astounded.

"How did you do that?" he asked.

"It's easy. I defrosted and cooked two thin pork chops for dinner."

That's the way it's been ever since they got their own apartments. I cook enough spaghetti to feed Sicily and no one shows. I nuke two small pieces of leftover pizza for dinner and they fly in from out of state.

How do they know I've cooked for two? It's one of the great mysteries of child raising. Kids were equipped with radar long before it went commercial. They knew when there were bananas hidden behind the popcorn popper in the pantry. They knew when there was a candy bar in the meat keeper in the refrigerator. It was not possible for a leftover piece of pie to survive a child in search of breakfast. When a dish rattled, they heard it, no matter where they were.

When you think about it, mothers set themselves up for it. We dedicated our lives to feeding our kids. Nobody went hungry. I fed a cold; I fed a fever. If an infant cried, I stuffed a bottle in her mouth. If a child fell off a bicycle, I promised him ice cream.

"You may not graduate? Have a piece of cake."

"Your car was totaled? Have you had lunch?"

"You're not overweight, you're too thin. Eat!"

We have created an image for ourselves of being able to feed a crowd on a pound of hamburger and bring forth food when the cupboards are bare. It has always been so. My grandmother would scurry when we pulled into the driveway. She'd open cans with one hand and set four more places at the table with the other. My mother did the same thing when five of us parked in front of the house at dinnertime.

Now that I think about it—maybe they just wanted to see us.

Parent–Child Bonding—January 13, 1991

When my children were born, bonding hadn't been invented yet. I was given a sedative just before the birth and didn't wake up until each kid was about two or three years old.

When my husband bought season tickets to the Phoenix Suns basketball games, we saw this as a time to bond with our children. With 40 home games to view, the combinations were without limit. He'd go with one son one night, and I'd go with my daughter the next home game. Then I'd go with another son, and he'd go with our daughter. This would be an opportunity to have social interaction with one another, find out how they felt about life, and form a covenant of feelings that sometimes get lost in the daily routine.

At the end of the first quarter in a game with the Chicago Bulls, I turned to my daughter to tell her how close I felt to her when I saw her leaning over the seat in front.

"What's the matter?" I asked.

"I lost an earring," she said. "I think it fell down that man's pants."

"I don't believe you," I said. "It's like going out with Peg Bundy on *Married with Children.*"

"Mom, I didn't do it on purpose," she said. "I'll know for sure when he stands up."

The man stood up to cheer and got a strange look on his face.

"Don't call me Mom," I whispered. "I don't know you."

My husband's experience wasn't exactly spiritual either. One of our sons complained that the seats were so far up he felt rain. My husband told him we were lucky to get them.

Right after the tip-off, he motioned to his dad to follow him to a closer section where there were vacant seats. His father said he couldn't do that because it was dishonest. So they sat apart.

When we tried to establish some kind of human relationship with our other son, we both had the same experience. He was like some wandering minstrel; he was never in his seat. If he wasn't standing in a line to buy soft drinks and tacos, he was going to the rest room or hanging out with friends. Once when he got back during the fourth quarter, I leaned over and said, "Daddy and I are glad you were born." He nodded silently and then asked, "Compared to what?"

When new parents talk about bonding, it sounds so warm and fuzzy. Maybe it works only when one party can't talk.

When Grown Kids Come to Visit—December 20, 1995

Have you heard about the minister who announced on Sunday that he was going to have a praise box for parishioners who would count their blessings and make a donation commensurate with their joy?

The next Sunday, an elderly lady came to the altar and said, "My praise is my children, who will be here this week for Christmas." She dropped a dollar in the collection box. The Sunday after that, she once again approached the altar and said, "Thank God they're gone," and dropped in $5.

We all love our children. We anticipate their return home for weeks. It will be like old times.

It is not like old times. We only think we are going to recapture the early years when they were children and we made the rules.

I never anticipated that I would have to pick them up at the airport. I've mentioned how we met our son at the gate with banners and balloons the first time he arrived home. The next year, we circled the airport, and when we saw him, we slowed down so he could grab onto the antenna and thread himself and his luggage through the window.

Last year, he called from a pay phone at the terminal and said, "Mom, who's going to pick me up?" I said, "Who is this?" He said, "It's your son." I said, "I have no son."

I don't know why I said that except I just lost it, thinking about going through the maze of Exit, Merge, Stay in Left Lane, Right Lane Must Turn Right, and Cars Left Unattended Will Be Towed Away.

In earlier days, I was a mother who made her kids pick up their rooms, make their own snacks and put their laundry in the utility room. Now when they come home, I put the rules aside. I am like a concierge looking for a big tip. I follow them around asking, "Are you hungry? Can I get you something? Do you have laundry?"

I eat when they want to eat, cook their favorite foods just before they tell me they are going out with friends and watch helplessly as they eat their way through a pound of baked ham at three in the afternoon.

On their visit, my life changes. I have no car. My washer is set at extra-large load and has two socks and a T-shirt in it. The phone rings constantly and is never for me.

At the end of their visits, we set aside a day, pack a lunch and head for the airport. It isn't until I return home that I sense how orderly my life has become. I enjoy the quiet. The TV tuner is rescued from the clothes hamper and is returned to its place on the coffee table. The empty milk and juice cartons are removed from the refrigerator. The wet towels are put in the washer. The bathroom is returned to health standards.

It is my world again. So why am I crying?

Special People

Grandma and Funerals—November 20, 1968

If I talk of my grandmother a lot it is because I spent a lot of time with her as a child.

I came into Grandma's life when she was going through her purple-hair syndrome. She was 55 (if you can believe a woman who lied on five birth certificates) but she felt and acted like 35.

We went everywhere together. On Mondays we played euchre at the Eagle's Hall; on Tuesdays we played euchre at the Knights of Columbus; on Wednesdays we went to a 50-50 dance; on Thursdays we ate in the dime store and went up and down Main Street making 50-cent payments on her credit purchases. And on Fridays we usually went to a funeral.

Grandma had an amazing number of friends who conveniently dropped out of sight on Fridays. Most of them were old euchre players who were mourned as if they ran the ship of state.

Grandma would always take the news of a death very hard with a gasp of, "My God! I don't have a thing to wear." Then we would run out and get a new hat, and we were off.

I never got used to funeral-home conversation. It was rather limited. First, Grandma would ask how the deceased felt on the day she died. They always said she felt wonderful, which seemed to please everyone. Then Grandma would remark on the crowd and how she hadn't seen so many people since the Turnip Festival at Haysburg.

Slowly, she would make her way through the flowers and finally arrive at the coffin.

"She looks just wonderful," said Grandma.

"You really think so?" asked the survivor.

"I certainly do. Last winter I thought she looked a little peaked, but today her color is so good. And the hair style is flattering."

Actually, she looked quite dead and a little pale, but Grandma never seemed to notice.

She would grasp the hand of the funeral director, pump it vigorously and say, "You've done a wonderful job. She looks so natural I half expect her to sit up and say hello." (You would think this would have delighted the funeral director, but he always looked a little uneasy.)

Then she would return to the survivor and smile. "I know this isn't important to you now, but she got 18 baskets, five vases, a spray and a nosegay. There are 105 names in the register. For a woman of her age that's quite a showing."

The relative would smile weakly while Grandma continued to compare her to last Friday's funeral. By the time we left, Grandma had them thinking the deceased would recover.

Outside in the fresh air I would ask Grandma, "Why do you keep saying how wonderful they look?"

Grandma looked annoyed. "She's got enough trouble dying. You want I should hurt her feelings by telling her she doesn't look well?"

Love Is a Grandparent—November 3, 1974

A preschooler who lives down the street was curious about grandparents. It occurred to me that, to a child, grandparents appear like an apparition with no explanation, no job description and few credentials. They just seem to go with the territory.

This column, then, is for the little folks who wonder what a grandparent is.

A grandparent can always be counted on to buy all your cookies, flower seeds, all-purpose greeting cards, transparent tape, paring knives, peanut brittle and ten chances on a pony. (Also a box of taffy when they have dentures.)

A grandparent helps you with the dishes when it is your night.

A grandparent will sit through a Greek comedy for three hours to watch her grandson and wonder how Aristophanes has time to write plays when he is married to Jackie Onassis.

A grandparent is the only baby-sitter who doesn't charge more after midnight—or anything before midnight.

A grandparent buys you gifts your mother says you don't need.

A grandparent arrives three hours early for your baptism, your graduation and your wedding because he or she wants a seat where he or she can see everything.

A grandparent pretends he doesn't know who you are on Halloween.

A grandparent loves you from when you're a bald baby to a bald father and all the hair in between.

A grandparent will put a sweater on you when she is cold, feed you when she is hungry and put you to bed when she is tired.

A grandparent will brag on you when you get a typing pin that 80 other girls got.

A grandparent will frame a picture of your hand that you traced and put it in her Mediterranean living room.

A grandparent will slip you money just before Mother's Day.

A grandparent will help you with your buttons, your zippers and your shoelaces and not be in any hurry for you to grow up.

When you're a baby, a grandparent will check to see if you are crying when you are sound asleep.

When a grandchild says, "Grandma, how come you didn't have any children?" a grandparent holds back the tears.

The Volunteer—June 24, 1975

I had a dream the other night that every volunteer in this country, disillusioned with the lack of compassion, had set sail for another country.

As I stood smiling on the pier, I shouted, "Goodbye, creamed chicken. Goodbye, phone committees. So long, Disease-of-the-Month. No more saving old egg cartons. No more getting out the vote. Au revoir, playground duty, bake sales and three-hour meetings."

As the boat got smaller and they could no longer hear my shouts, I reflected, "Serves them right. A bunch of yes people. All they had to do was to put their tongue firmly against the roof of their mouth and make an *O* sound. Nnnnnnnooooooo. Nnnnnnnooooooo. Nnoo. No! No! It would certainly have spared them a lot of grief. Oh, well, who needs them!"

The hospital was quiet as I passed it. Rooms were void of books, flowers and voices. The children's wing held no clowns, no laughter. The reception desk was vacant.

The home for the aged was like a tomb. The blind listened for a voice that never came. The infirm were imprisoned by wheels on a chair that never moved. Food grew cold on trays that would never reach the mouths of the hungry.

All the social agencies had closed their doors, unable to implement their programs of Scouting, recreation, drug control, Big Sisters, Big Brothers, YWCA, YMCA, the retarded, the crippled, the lonely and the abandoned.

The health agencies had signs in the window: "Cures for cancer, muscular dystrophy, birth defects, multiple sclerosis, emphysema, sickle cell anemia, kidney disorders, heart diseases, etc., have been canceled due to lack of interest."

The schools were strangely quiet with no field trips and no volunteer aides on the playground or in the classrooms . . . as were the colleges, where scholarships and financial support were no more.

The flowers on church altars withered and died. Children in day nurseries lifted their arms, but there was no one to hold them in love. Alcoholics cried out in despair, but no one answered, and the poor had no recourse for health care or legal aid.

But the saddest part of the journey was the symphony hall, which was dark and would remain that way. So were the museums, which had been built and stocked by volunteers with the art treasures of our times.

I fought in my sleep to regain a glimpse of the ship of volunteers just one more time. It was to be my last glimpse of civilization . . . as we were meant to be.

Mother Earned Her Wrinkles—February 8, 1976

According to her height and weight on the insurance charts, she should be a guard for the Lakers.

She has iron-starved blood, one shoulder is lower than the other, and she bites her fingernails.

She is the most beautiful woman I have ever seen. She should be. She's worked on that body and face for more than 60 years. The process for that kind of beauty can't be rushed.

The wrinkles in the face have been earned . . . one at a time. The stubborn one around the lips that deepened with every "No!" The thin ones on the forehead that mysteriously appeared when the first child was born.

The eyes are protected by glass now, but you can still see the perma-crinkles around them. Young eyes are darting and fleeting. These are mature eyes that reflect a lifetime. Eyes that have glistened with pride, filled with tears of sorrow, snapped in anger and burned from loss of sleep. They are now direct and penetrating and look at you when you speak.

The bulges are classics. They developed slowly from babies too sleepy to walk who had to be carried home from Grandma's, grocery bags lugged from the car, ashes carried out of the basement while her husband was at war. Now they are fed by a minimum of activity, a full refrigerator and TV bends.

The extra chin is custom-grown and takes years to perfect. Sometimes you can only see it from the side, but it's there. Pampered women don't have an extra chin. They cream them away or pat the muscles until they become firm. But this chin has always been there, supporting a nodding head that has slept in a chair all night . . . bent over knitting . . . praying.

The legs are still shapely, but the step is slower. They ran too often for the bus, stood a little too long when she clerked in a department store, got beat up while teaching her daughter how to ride a two-wheeler. They're purple at the back of the knees.

The hands? They're small and veined and have been dunked, dipped, shook, patted, wrung, caught in doors, splintered, dyed, bitten and blistered, but you can't help but be impressed when you see the ring finger that has shrunk from years of wearing the same wedding ring. It takes time—and much more—to diminish a finger.

I looked at Mother long and hard the other day and said, "Mom, I have never seen you so beautiful."

"I work at it," she snapped.

The Listener—February 26, 1977

It was one of those days when I wanted my own apartment— unlisted.

My son was telling me in complete detail about a movie he had just seen, punctuated by 3,000 *You knows.* My teeth were falling asleep.

There were three phone calls—strike that, three monologues that could have been answered by a recording. I fought the urge to say, "It's been nice listening to you."

In the cab from home to the airport, I got another assault on my ear, this time by a cabdriver who was rambling on about his son whom he supported in college and who was in his last year. He had put a P.S. on his letter. *I got married. Her name is Diane.* He asked me, "What do you think of that?" and proceeded to answer the question himself.

There were 30 whole beautiful minutes before my plane took off, time for me to be alone with my own thoughts, to open a book and let my mind wander. A voice next to me belonging to an elderly woman said, "I'll bet it's cold in Chicago."

Stone-faced, I answered, "It's likely."

"I haven't been to Chicago in nearly three years," she persisted. "My son lives there."

"That's nice," I said, my eyes intent on the book.

"My husband's body is on this plane. We've been married for fifty-three years. I don't drive, you know, and when he died a nun drove me from the hospital. We aren't even Catholic. The funeral director let me come to the airport with him."

I don't think I have ever detested myself more than I did at that moment. Another human being was screaming to be heard and in desperation had turned to a cold stranger who was more interested in a novel than the real-life drama at her elbow.

All she needed was a listener. No advice, wisdom, experience, money, assistance, expertise or even compassion, but just a minute or two to listen.

It seemed rather incongruous that in a society of supersophisticated communication, we often suffer from a shortage of listeners.

She talked steadily until we boarded the plane, then found her seat in another section. As I hung up my coat, I heard her plaintive voice say to her seat companion, "I'll bet it's cold in Chicago."

I prayed, "Please, God, let her listen."

Why am I telling you this? To make me feel better. It won't help, though.

Mothers of Disabled Children—May 11, 1980

Most women become mothers by accident, some by choice, a few by social pressures and a couple by habit.

This year, nearly 100,000 women will become mothers of handicapped children. Did you ever wonder how these mothers of handicapped children are chosen?

Somehow I visualize God hovering over Earth selecting His instruments for propagation with great care and deliberation. As He observes, He instructs His angels to make notes in a giant ledger.

"Armstrong, Beth: son; patron saint, Matthew. Forest, Marjorie: daughter; patron saint, Cecilia.

"Rudledge, Carrie: twins; patron saint . . . give her Gerard. He's used to profanity."

Finally, He passes a name to an angel and smiles. "Give her a blind child."

The angel is curious. "Why this one, God? She's so happy."

"Exactly," says God. "Could I give a child with a handicap to a mother who does not know laughter? That would be cruel."

"But has she patience?" asks the angel.

"I don't want to her to have too much patience, or she will drown in a sea of self-pity and despair. Once the shock and resentment wear off, she'll handle it."

"But, Lord, I don't think she even believes in you."

God smiles. "No matter. I can fix that. This one is perfect. She has just enough selfishness."

The angel gasps. "Selfishness? Is that a virtue?"

God nods. "If she can't separate herself from the child occasionally, she'll never survive. Yes, here is a woman whom I will bless with a child less than perfect. She doesn't realize it yet, but she is to be envied. She will never take for granted a spoken word. She will never consider a step ordinary. When her child says 'Momma' for the first time, she will be present at a miracle and know it! When she describes a tree or a sunset to her blind child, she will see it as few people ever see my creations.

"I will permit her to see clearly the things I see—ignorance, cruelty, prejudice—and allow her to rise above them. She will never be alone. I will be at her side every minute of every day of her life, because she is doing my work as surely as she is here by my side."

"And what about her patron saint?" asks the angel, pen poised in midair.

God smiles. "A mirror will suffice."

Heroes—August 2, 1981

Ironically, the two events happened within a day of one another.

On the first Saturday of last month, a 22-year-old U.S. tennis player hoisted a silver bowl over his head at Centre Court at Wimbledon.

The day before, five blind mountain climbers, a man with an artificial leg, an epileptic and two deaf adventurers stood atop the snowcapped summit of Mount Rainier.

It was a noisy victory for the tennis player, who shared it with thousands of fans, some of whom had slept on the sidewalks outside the club for six nights waiting for standing-room-only tickets.

It was a quiet victory for the climbers, who led their own cheering, punctuated by a shout from one of them that echoed on the winds: "There's one for the epileptics!"

The controversy that surrounded the tennis player's frequent outbursts of temper was justified by pressure. "It's not easy when it's a one-on-one situation. You have to prove yourself."

One man who climbed the mountain took 20 minutes to tie his own shoe.

There was a lot of rhetoric exchanged at Wimbledon regarding "bad calls."

At Mount Rainier they learned to live with life's bad calls a long time ago. The first man to reach the mountaintop tore up his artificial leg to get there.

Somehow, I see a parallel here that all Americans are going to have to come to grips with. In our search for heroes and heroines, we often lose our perspective.

We applaud beauty pageant winners; we ignore the woman without arms who paints pictures with a brush in her teeth. We extol the courage of a man who will sail over 10 cars on a motorcycle; we give no thought (or parking place) to the man who threads his way through life in a world of darkness or silence.

The care and feeding of heroes is solely in the hands of the public. Not all winners are heroes. Not all people with disabilities are heroes. "Hero" is a term that should be awarded to those who, given a set of circumstances, react with courage, dignity, decency and compassion—people who make us feel better for having seen or touched them.

I think the crowds went to the wrong summit and cheered the wrong champion.

Caregivers—November 26, 1991

Recently in a column I lamented the death of heroes. I was wrong. There isn't a scarcity of heroes. I was just looking for them in the wrong places.

I thought they hung out in sports arenas, great halls, battlefields or between the pages of adventure books.

I should have been looking for them in pharmacies, where they are waiting to have prescriptions filled; in hospital corridors, keeping vigil or collapsing wheelchairs and storing them in the trunks of cars. They are called nurturers—the well one in the family who takes care of the one with needs.

How many times have we passed by without seeing these nameless, faceless people who roll out of bed each day to serve? Most of them live in the shadow of those who are ill. They are not used to someone asking how they feel. If it should miraculously happen, they would probably feel guilty answering, "Fine."

Never underestimate what it takes to watch someone you love in pain. Nurturers face each day without benefit of numbing painkillers or anesthetics. They live in a world where personal feelings and duty clash. Those who have assumed the mantle of responsibility for another human being hate the word *hero*. They are doing what they want to do, must do and wouldn't want anyone else to do.

I have observed women who pay the bills, have the oil changed in the car, change furnace filters, negotiate for a new roof, turn over CDs and go crazy trying to keep pace with Medicare and Medicaid forms when their husbands are unable to do so.

I have seen men who bake pies, do the marketing, address Christmas cards, keep track of birthdays, water plants, scrub floors and go crazy trying to keep pace with Medicare and Medicaid forms when their wives are unable to do so.

And daily I watch grown children who run errands, make a million phone calls, take parents to appointments, drop off food, make sure their license plates are current, their lawns are cut and their walks cleared of snow and go crazy trying to keep pace with Medicare and Medicaid forms.

Today would be a good time to think about them. And when you see a nurturer, ask, "How you doin'?"

Mothers Who Have Lost a Child—May 14, 1995

If you're looking for an answer this Mother's Day on why God reclaimed your child, I don't know. I only know that thousands of mothers out there today desperately need an answer as to why they were permitted to go through the elation of carrying a child and then lose it to miscarriage, accident, violence, disease or drugs.

Motherhood isn't just a series of contractions, it's a state of mind. From the moment we know life is inside us, we feel a responsibility to protect and defend that human being. It's a promise we can't keep.

We beat ourselves to death over that pledge. "If I hadn't worked through the eighth month." "If I had taken him to the doctor when he had a fever." "If I hadn't let him use the car that night." "If I hadn't been so naive, I'd have noticed he was on drugs."

The longer I live, the more convinced I become that surviving changes us. After the bitterness, the anger, the guilt and the despair are tempered by time, we look at life differently.

While I was writing my book *I Want to Grow Hair, I Want to Grow Up, I Want to Go to Boise,* I talked with mothers who had lost a child to cancer. Every single one said death gave their lives new meaning and purpose. And who do you think prepared them for the rough, lonely road they had to travel? Their dying child. They pointed their mothers toward the future and told them to keep going. The children had already accepted what their mothers were fighting to reject.

The children in the bombed-out nursery in Oklahoma City have touched more lives than they will ever know. Workers who had probably given their kids a mechanical pat on the head without thinking that morning are making calls home during the day to their children to say, "I love you."

This may seem like a strange Mother's Day column on a day when joy and life abound for the millions of mothers throughout the country. But it's also a day of appreciation and respect. I can think of no mothers who deserve it more than those who had to give a child back.

In the face of adversity, we are not permitted to ask, "Why me?" You can ask, but you won't get an answer. Maybe you are the instrument who is left behind to perpetuate the life that was lost and appreciate the time you had with it.

The late Gilda Radner summed it up well: "I wanted a perfect ending. Now I've learned the hard way that some poems don't rhyme and some stories don't have a clear beginning, middle and end. Life is about not knowing, having to change, taking the moment and making the best of it, without knowing what is going to happen next. Delicious ambiguity."

Wish You Were Here
(Instead of Me)

Help Thy Neighbor—August 25, 1968

One of the finest traditions in America today is the camaraderie of neighbors who pitch in when one of them goes on vacation. These are the good Samaritans who take in animals, tend gardens, gather the mail and literally house sit while the family vacations in peace.

That's why I can't understand our neighbors Bob and Helen taking off the way they did in the middle of the night without so much as a simple goodbye, here's my door key or kiss my foot.

Heaven knows we've always tried to be good neighbors to Bob and Helen. We even kept their bird for them when they went to Florida. No one was more upset than we were when it died.

And the summer they asked us to pick their tomatoes and dispose of them. No one could have been more conscientious. We plucked them before they fell on the ground to rot and put them on their windowsills to ripen. I'm not Orville Freeman. How was I to know they were yellow tomatoes and were ripe when we picked them?

I don't understand it. I've always gathered their mail and saved it for them. Lucky I'm not a gossipy woman. I could not care less that the County Sanitary Department sent them a second billing or that Helen's brother, Stan, is trying to find work in St. Louis and will send for his family when he finds a place. Like I told Helen, "We at the card club contend if you get a bill from your gynecologist, that's your business . . . not ours."

One of the things we'll miss this year is straightening up little

Ralphie's paper route. It's like I told him, "There's only one way to deal with deadbeats. Sure you'll lose eight or nine customers by making them feel cheap, but in the long run you should be glad to be rid of them."

I can't believe Helen would leave without making some arrangements for her flowers. Like I told her the first year, "I'm no garden clubber, but I know about sunlight and water." I did the best I could. The year they went to Michigan, I lugged that rubber plant of theirs out on the patio every morning. The more water and sun I gave it, the more it drooped. Very frankly, I think it was Helen's fault for not telling me it was plastic.

It sure is strange not going over and turning on every light in the house at dusk or feeding leftovers to the tropical fish. They probably thought it would be too much for me. My goodness. What are neighbors for?

Men Never Ask Directions—August 24, 1969

An obstetrician once made the observation that male babies take longer to deliver. This bears out an old theory I have long held that, even at birth, men are reluctant to ask directions anywhere.

I can always tell when my husband is lost. At a crossroad he will take out a coin and mumble, "Heads right, tails left." Or he will snap on the car radio and yell, "Hold it down until I see where this station is originating from."

The way I figure it is it's a simple attack on male superiority.

"Are we lost?" I inquire.

"Certainly not," he says. "Why do you ask?"

"Because we are in a field of timothy, and a cow is nibbling away on the radio antenna."

"Give me the road map."

"Are you going to accuse me of moving the Mississippi River again?"

"Of course not. Ha! Those fools obviously just let 143 dangle out here in a cornfield. If you can't trust Triple A, I always say, who can you trust?"

"Here comes a farmer. Why don't you ask directions?"

"Because I am not lost. All I do is go back to where that hound dog was asleep in the road, pick up 17, and that will take us right back to the interstate."

"We've passed that hound dog so often now he thinks we're family."

"Look, don't worry about driving the car. You just keep the baby quiet and dry, see to it that little Charlie doesn't bleed all over the seat covers and Eloise doesn't get sick again and the two boys don't fall out of the car fighting over who sits next to the window, and entertain them with some kind of a fun game. In other words, sit back and enjoy yourself."

"We've been driving for hours. Why don't we stop and ask directions at a service station?"

"Because I am not lost."

"Why are you so stubborn? What would happen if you stopped and asked directions? Would your beard stop growing? Would your voice become high-pitched? You don't need a wife and family with you. You need Lowell Thomas and a Boy Scout patrol."

"Will you stop acting like a fishwife and quiet those kids down? One has his wet nose on the back of my neck."

"It isn't a kid. It's a lost cow."

The Last Family Vacation—June 1972

When you talk about it in years to come, you will refer to it as "The Last Family Vacation."

It will start out like a score of other family vacations. One kid will yell because he has to sit on the hard hump in the middle of the seat, another will sulk for 300 miles because he can't hear the radio, and another will hang his feet out the window because his legs are cramped. (When did they grow so tall?)

There will still be the perennial recording of "When we gonna eat?" (muted because their mouths are full of food). And you'll ask, "Anyone for a hamburger? A salad? A hot dog?" (Did it always cost $20 to buy them lunch?)

Boredom hangs like a thick fog over the entire backseat.

"Hey, kids," you say. "Look at the colors in that mountain."

"Gross."

"Would you believe that sunset? It's like a painting."

"Gross."

"Hey, group, Daddy and I are going to chip in and buy you all a new word when we stop."

"Gross."

(When did the excitement of a mountain give way to *Mad* magazine?)

At the beach, you begin to suspect things are changing when you and Daddy are the only two splashing around in the water. One child is in a phone booth making plans to split. Another has found a girl and is trying to palm himself off as an orphan. And the other is going through Daddy's trousers getting the car keys. (When did they stop talking to us?)

Going home, it is like old times. They are excited at the idea of going swimming with a friend, making it in time for a party, and bolting to their rooms to turn up the stereo until their ears shrivel.

As you unload the car, there is a silence. Without saying a word, everyone seems to know what the silence means. It is a memorial to the last family vacation.

It will never be the same again. The wet diapers in the plastic bags under your feet, the soggy cookies, strains of "This Old Man He Played One," burying your feet in the sand, cries of "He's hitting," the cold caves, the burnt hot dogs, the camper that leaked, the giggles at bedtime, the Laundromats . . . and the wonderful, warm feeling that a woman feels when she sees her family tucked in at night.

It is the end of an era—and the beginning of a new one.

You might allow yourself the luxury of a tear, or you might say to yourself, half in anger, "God! Why did I spend every summer vacation yelling, 'Don't throw rocks in the water!' and 'Don't sit on the seats!'"

Parking the Family Trailer—June 1972

There is nothing in this world any more appealing than an ad for a camping trailer. It pictures a hysterical family of four grouped around a fire on a deserted beach. The kids are carrying wood and playing Frisbee. The family dog is chasing the family rabbit (in jest, not lust). And Daddy (looking like Mark Trail) is whittling the heads of four presidents out of an old tree trunk.

Well, I am here to tell you that the family who camps together gets cramps together.

We have been camping for seven years and have yet to have an evening where we all go to bed speaking to one another. The problem has remained the same for the past seven years: parking the trailer.

Some trailer parks have pull-in parking spaces. This is for marriages that cannot stand too much strain. For the rest of us there is the trailer park where you have to back in the trailer, being careful to line up evenly with the picnic table and the water and sewer hookups.

To assist my husband with this task, there are two large mirrors on either side of the car, three children, one adult (a high school graduate) and a barking dog. Before I record our dialogue, I will only comment that, "You never know what you have married until you have seen him back up a twenty-four-foot travel trailer into a spot between two trees."

Helpers: "Turn your wheels."

Husband: "Which way?"

Helpers: "That way."

Husband: "Which way is *that* way? I don't have eyes in the back of my head. You have to say right or left."

Helpers: "Right . . . no, left . . . no, right."

Husband: "Make up your mind. And which wheels right, the car or the trailer?"

Helpers: "Back up. Now stop. Stop! *Stop!* Why didn't you stop?"

Husband: "I couldn't hear you in all this rain with the dog barking."

Helpers: "It isn't raining. You hit the water connection. When we motion like this—"

Husband: "I'll pull up and back in again. Now, for crying out loud, guide me." (Helpers wave madly.) "Why are you directing me in this way?"

Helpers: "We weren't. We were just waving to our neighbors."

Husband: "It's a crummy time to get friendly. Why don't you wait till I'm parked?"

Helpers: "We'd better be friendly now. You just backed into their tent. You know, the trouble with you. . . ."

We should have learned something from the pioneers. They had the entire West to park in, and they pulled their wagons into a circle.

Showing Slides of Vacation—February 26, 1974

We have just been on vacation and returned with a total of 610 slides of our trip.

I cannot tell you how invaluable these 610 slides have been to us.

I can walk on a crowded bus solid with bodies and announce, "I have 610 slides to show," and within seconds I have my choice of any seat on the bus.

In the middle of being mugged I can say to my assailant, "I have 610 slides to show you when you are finished," and he will drop my handbag and disappear faster than I can say "Turn off the lights."

I would make a conservative claim that if I took these 610 slides to a war no one would show up.

Actually, it was by sheer chance that we stumbled onto this secret weapon that could be an answer to overpopulation. We invited a group of our dearest friends over one evening for dinner, and after coffee my husband said, "Speaking of antelope, we have some really great shots of antelope that we took on our vacation. Get the light, Erma."

Before I could reach the switch, one guest said his malaria was returning, his wife feigned false labor (she wasn't even pregnant), another couple decided to try a trial separation beginning at that moment, and one woman thought she heard her mother calling. (Her mother had been dead for eight years.) My husband and I both concurred. "Who needs friends?"

We invited our minister to the house, figuring he was a man of God and welcomed suffering, but when we mentioned our 610 slides, he confessed he had always been afraid of the dark, especially when the only light was that of a slide projector, and left. As we saw him to the door my husband observed, "Who needs a minister who has it in for antelope?"

We didn't tell Mother about the slides until she was settled comfortably in a deep chair. "Now we have a treat for you," we said. "We are going to contribute to your knowledge of the antelope."

She fought desperately to get out of the chair and said, "I gave at the office."

So who needs a mother?

My husband doused the lights and began to show the slides. I watched 386 slides of antelope rumps before I slipped quietly out of the room. So who needs a marriage?

Continental Breakfast—August 17, 1975

This year millions of Americans are busing their way through Europe on package tours that offer scenic grandeur at budget prices. My husband and I just whipped through nine countries in 21 days. (OK, so I looked down to change the film in my camera and missed Italy.)

How are they able to offer this bargain to travelers, you ask? Simple. The Continental Breakfast.

To the non-traveler, I must explain that the Continental Breakfast consists of a paper napkin, a knife, fork and spoon for which you have no use, a cup and saucer, a pot of coffee or tea, and a container of marmalade dated PLEASE USE BEFORE JULY, 1936. Finally, two four-letter words that have come to strike terror in the hearts of travelers everywhere: *hard roll.*

The Continental Breakfast (literal translation: Keep Out of Reach of Children) has a gradual but unmistakable effect on people who eat it for a period of 10 days or more.

For the first several days, partakers of the hard roll will pretend it is just the thing they need—the Famine Is Fun number. Women will pinch their waists and say, "I've been eating too much on this trip. A light breakfast is just what I need."

The truth is, the hard roll is not designed to take off weight. Even though eaten in small pieces, once in the body it will form again into its original ball and build a hard wall across the hips and the stomach. After the eleventh day, the hard rolls make you mean.

We had our first hard roll in Ireland on July 1.

By July 15, the group was irritable and noncommunicative. On the seventeenth, while in Venice, my husband, in a fit of violence, grabbed a hard roll, carved his initials in it, WLB 1975, and sent it back to the kitchen.

By the nineteenth day, the prospect of a hard roll for breakfast forced some travelers to remain in their beds with their faces turned to the wall. Others used the hard roll to pry their luggage open, prop open their doors or rub stubborn stains from their shirt collars.

On the twenty-first day, we looked at our last Continental Breakfast in Paris. My husband ran his fingers across a roll that was initialed "WLB 1975."

"It's just a coincidence, isn't it?" he asked.

Some things, it's best not to know.

Elusive Rest Area—July 11, 1976

Last summer, when our family took to the highways, we noted that every 15 miles or so there was an exit on the freeway marked REST AREA. As we whizzed by, we saw happy families at play. Daddy was making yummies over a grill, the kids were tossing a Frisbee, Mother was moving a picnic table that was chained to the ground to the shade, and the dog was holding his stomach with laughter.

"We could do that," I said enviously. "It wouldn't take much to toss a cooler, a bag of charcoal and a few folding chairs in the backseat. We could stretch our legs, use the facilities, get a cold drink of water, and Daddy could read one of those big maps framed in glass to find out where we are."

This year, everyone forgot but me. When we packed the car, I announced, "No more driving for days to find a restaurant where grease is the beverage. This year, it's rest areas for the Bombecks."

We were on the road only 15 minutes when we saw our first rest area. "Want to stop?" asked my husband.

"No need." I smiled confidently. "There'll be another one in thirty miles."

I was right; 30 miles later was another rest area. Another 30 miles, we saw a third. Then lunchtime came and we never saw another one.

At two o'clock, the children became restless. One started to kick the back of the seat in protest. "Sit back and put your seat belt on," I commanded.

"I ate it," came the reply.

At 2:30, one child with his nose pressed against the window shouted, "Rest area spotted at nine o'clock!" We swiveled around and said numbly, "Rest area acknowledged . . . negative . . . on wrong side of turnpike."

At three o'clock, our stomachs were singing as a group. We were irritable, listless and one of the kids had raw hamburger breath, but I couldn't prove it.

"Check the road map," said my husband. "Isn't that a rest area marked with a little tepee? Don't you see it?"

"No. It's my saliva," I said.

By four o'clock we could stand it no longer. My husband pulled over to a soft shoulder under a sign that read NO PARKING ANYTIME. Here, we ripped through plastic with our teeth, ate cold wieners, and watched tomatoes drip off our elbows while we were blown off our feet by passing traffic.

We weren't on our way 15 minutes when we saw a sign: REST AREA.

I knew without looking that there would be one every 30 miles from here on in.

Seeing America by Headlights—September 16, 1980

It's been explained to me a thousand times, and I still don't understand it.

Why is it that men embarking on a fun-filled, pleasure-seeking, leisure-paced vacation feel obliged to start at four in the morning?

I ask you, what good are breathtaking colors of the Smoky Mountains in the dark? How can I feel the pulse and excitement of New York City when David Hartman going to work and a passed-out wino are the only things on the street? What good is a vacation if you can't keep awake through lunch?

We were the first family ever to "See America First" by headlights. Every morning before hitting the road, the alarm would go off in the middle of the night. Picking my way through the darkness, I'd guide arms and legs through clothes. It was like threading a needle with wet spaghetti. As the kids continued to sleep, I'd walk them to the car and arrange them in the backseat. I'd wait until the motor was running and we were ready to leave before I did my last dastardly deed on those still sleeping: flush!

My children never awoke asking "Where are we?" It was always "What time is it?" They could never play games other children played, like Count the Chevys or Out-of-State-License-Plate Rummy. There weren't any other cars on the road.

We'd sit there like zombies, listening to the hog and grain markets on the car radio, trying to figure out which meal we would spoil if we ate a candy bar.

Once as we stopped at a roadside park for a potty break and I hooked my sweater over the hood ornament to keep from falling, a station wagon pulled in with another family. They looked terrible. The kids stumbled along with blankets dragging on the ground, their hair uncombed, their eyes puffy and glazed. The woman and I didn't say anything at first. Our eyes met in that rare moment of understanding without words. Finally she said, "Would you have married him if you had known he was nocturnal?"

A few weeks ago on vacation, the alarm went off at 3:30 A.M. as my husband whipped out of bed and began to dress.

"Why are you doing this?" I mumbled.

"I've told you before, the children travel better by night when they can sleep."

"We don't have children with us."

"There's no traffic on the road and I can make better time."

"We're flying."

"If we start early, we can stop early and be sure of getting a hotel room."

"We're going home."

"I'm basically sadistic."

Now that makes sense!

Eleven-Piece Vacation Wardrobe—July 21, 1981

The ad said if I bought an 11-piece coordinated vacation wardrobe, I could make 135 clothes combinations and exist for three weeks living out of one suitcase.

The coordinated ensemble included a basic dress, reversible skirt, slacks, blouse, jacket, shorts, T-shirt, vest, two scarves and a cap with a bill.

I will not bore you with all 135 combinations, only the interesting ones.

Three days out, I outgrew my slacks.

Four days out, I ripped the breast pocket on the jacket and could wear it only when my arms were folded or if I used one of the scarves as a sling and pretended I had a broken arm.

Five days out, the blouse did not dry and the scarf faded over it, forcing me to wear it with the darts facing backward.

The T-shirt shrunk on the sixth day and I found that by buying another cap with a bill and joining the two caps with a scarf, I had an interesting bra in which to play tennis.

The skirt was getting on everyone's nerves, and one night as it stood in the corner of my room, I noticed it still had my body molded in it. The next day I turned it around, put my blouse on the outside and told everyone I was expecting in four months.

Mercifully, on the eleventh day the hem dropped out of the dress, giving me a new look for evenings.

The ugly oil spot on the reversible skirt penetrated both sides on the fourteenth day, giving me a choice of wearing my handbag on my left side or my right.

The vest was the only clean thing in my suitcase by the seventeenth day, but I didn't know what to do with it. When my blouse was ordered off the sightseeing bus by a vote of 43-0, I wore it sleeveless with pins holding it together.

By the twentieth day, nothing mattered anymore. I wore the scarf with the oil-stained skirt, the slacks with the broken zipper with the two caps with a bill, the dress with the torn jacket, the T-shirt with the shorts. On the last night, there was a masquerade party. I went as myself and won first prize.

When I arrived home, there was one scarf that had been soaked in perfume that leaked. The fashion coordinator had thought of everything. All I had to do was to light a match, ignite it and, in time, forget all 11 pieces.

Traveling with Tripod—July 27, 1982

For those of you who think pictures grow on postcards, I will explain that a tripod is a three-legged stand that supports a camera so it will remain perfectly still.

When fully extended, a tripod will stand waist-high and weigh in at five or six pounds.

Every year, five million amateur camera enthusiasts leave home without one. My husband is not one of them.

For eight years he has dragged that tripod along on our vacation. He has yet to use it. So what good is it, you ask? For starters, it smashes down my dresses so that whatever I wear to dinner, someone will look at the permanent indentation and remark, "Oh, I see you own a tripod."

When you run your suitcase through security, bells will chime, buzzers will beep and you have to ask them when was the last time Great Britain was attacked by tripods.

It gives young cabbies and bellhops their first American hernia. Oh, and once when the towel bars were full of laundry, I hung a few socks on it to dry.

Mostly it makes my husband feel like Ansel Adams.

I know now I should never have married an amateur photographer, but when you're 35 and not moving, you panic. My life has been a series of "Would you hold this lens?" "Stand still, I'm losing my light" and, "So the bus left without us. There's always another one."

Blessed are the women who marry a man who photographs the Grand Canyon from a moving car through the windshield with an Instamatic. They don't know how lucky they are.

My husband's version of the tripod is quite different from mine. He will tell you about the hummingbird he saw with crossed eyes, the sun setting over the Kremlin that looked like a hammer and sickle and the dramatic picture of the men on Easter Island facing away from the sea. What he won't tell you is that his tripod was in the suitcase in the hotel room all the time.

We didn't take the tripod this year. I said it was either it or me. He thought about it for a week before leaving it behind. The guide at Christ the Redeemer statue in Rio said, "I assume all you serious photographers have a tripod."

I knew what I had to do: drop to all fours, balance a camera on my head and remain still for as long as it took.

Alaska Cruise and Smoked Salmon—April 21, 1987

Last spring, my husband looked up from the travel section of the newspaper and said, "Have you ever thought of what it would be like to catch and smoke your own salmon?"

"I think of nothing else," I said.

"Think of the money you could save by doing it yourself and eliminating all those middlemen. And look at all the fun you could have in the process."

The next sound I heard struck terror in my heart. Jack the Clipper was ripping out the story in those little zigzag cuts that meant he was going to put it in his billfold for future reference.

In June, he booked passage on a ship for the two of us to cruise the Bering Sea off the coast of Alaska in search of bargain salmon loaves, salmon steaks and pâté. The cost of the cruise was excessive, but as he pointed out, "Salmon don't swim by your front door."

Since we live in a desert climate, both of us had to buy a warm wardrobe for salmon searching, consisting of windbreakers, parkas, knee-length boots and extra rain gear.

The first several days were the fun ones, when I threw up every minute I was awake. Then it went downhill. We boarded little Zodiacs and sat in the rain for hours at a time. The monotony was broken only when one man got a hook caught in his lip, and when I thought a plane was landing in the boat . . . and it turned out to be a mosquito.

On the next-to-last day, we caught 45 pounds of salmon. They were expensive to air-freight home, but as my husband said, "Those little babies will pay for themselves in pure pleasure."

Their arrival necessitated giving away less exotic fare in our freezer like chicken, roasts and steaks. What with the holidays, we didn't have time to fiddle with the salmon, but soon after the New Year, we purchased an electric smoker that we discovered was missing two wing nuts. The assembly instructions were written in Swedish.

Last week, my husband decided the time was perfect to smoke our own salmon and have that fun he talked about. He was going to serve our guests smoked salmon on little crackers. He went out once for salt for the brine, made another trip for the wood chips and still another for bags to hang the salmon in to dry.

When he plugged in the smoker, the fuse blew. He put the smoker in his workroom for a higher voltage plug, and the smoke alarm went off. By the time our guests arrived, the process hadn't even begun. I put out a bowl of nuts.

At three in the morning, the salmon was ready. We figured it cost $3,095 an ounce.

Gold costs $405 an ounce.

Who wants to be worth their weight in salmon?

The Holidays

Children of Christmas—December 25, 1969

There is nothing sadder in this world than to awake Christmas morning and not be a child.

Not to feel the cold on your bare feet as you rush to the Christmas tree in the living room. Not to have your eyes sparkle at the wonderment of discovery. Not to rip the ribbons off the shiny boxes with such abandon.

What happened? When did the cold bare feet give way to reason and a pair of sensible bedroom slippers? When did the sparkle and the wonderment give way to the depression of a long day? When did a box with a shiny ribbon mean an item on the charge. A child of Christmas doesn't have to be a toddler or a teen. A child of Christmas is anyone who believes that kings have birthdays.

The Christmases you loved so well are gone. What happened? Maybe they diminished the year you decided to have your Christmas cards printed to send to 1500 of your "closest friends and dearest obligations." You got too busy to sign your own name. Maybe it was the year you discovered the traditional Christmas tree was a fire hazard, and the needles had to be vacuumed every three hours, and you traded its holiday aroma for a silver one that revolved, changed colors, played "Silent Night" and snowed on itself.

Or the year it got to be too much trouble to sit around the table and put popcorn and cranberries on a string. Possibly you lost your childhood the year you solved your gift problems neatly and coldly with a checkbook.

Think about it. It might have been the year you were too rushed to bake cookies and resorted to slice-and-bake with no nonsense. Who needs a bowl to clean? Or lick?

Most likely it was the year you were so efficient in paying back all your party obligations. A wonderful little caterer did it for you for $3 per person.

Children of Christmas are givers. That's what the day is for. They give thanks, love, gratitude, joy and themselves to one another. It doesn't necessarily mean you have to have children around a tree. It's rather like lighting a candle you've been saving, caroling when your feet are cold, building a fire in a clean grate, grinding tinsel deep into the rug, licking frosting off a beater, giving something you made yourself. It's laughter, being with people you like and at some time falling to your knees and saying, "Thank you for coming to my Birthday party."

How sad indeed to awake on Christmas and not be a child. Time, self-pity, apathy, bitterness and exhaustion can take the Christmas out of the child, but you cannot take the child out of Christmas.

Kids Are Sick . . . It Must Be Christmas—December 18, 1970

The other day Bruce complained, "My head hurts and my nose is stuffy."

"Ridiculous," I said. "It's too early. Christmas is a week away."

Normal people can always predict when the holidays are near at hand. There is an air of excitement, the smell of evergreens, the ringing of bells, the singing of carols. There is a saying at our house: "We got measles. It must be Christmas."

Down at the Laundromat, I am known as Typhoid Mary. "What are you having this year for Christmas?" they ask as I sort my clothes.

"Well, I've got one exposure to chicken pox, one who has had mumps only on his left side, and two just throw up to keep things interesting."

It's never serious enough to be an emotional drag, but I've forgotten what real Christmases are like. I cornered my friend Donna Robust and begged, "Tell me again about Christmas at your house."

"Well," said Donna, "on Christmas morning I get up first and—"

"Start going through the yellow pages to find a drugstore open," I said, my eyes glistening.

"No, no"—she laughed—"I turn on all the lights around the Christmas tree. Then I ring the sleigh bells and—"

"I know, I know," I said excitedly, "it's pill time. You give one a spoon of Coke syrup, another an aspirin and the baby a suppository for nausea."

She shook her head. "I summon them all around the tree to open up their presents. Then, after breakfast, we all get dressed—"

"Can you imagine that?" I sighed. "Everybody dressed!"

"Then we go to church, and that afternoon we have fifteen or twenty people in for Christmas dinner."

"Once I saw my dad on Christmas. He slid two batteries under the door for a robot monster that didn't include them."

"I bet that was nice," she said.

"Oh, and another time the doctor dropped by to check on us and brought in a bit of snow on his boots. The kids went wild."

"Maybe this year things will be different," said Donna, patting my hand.

"Maybe so." I sighed. "But tell me again about how you all get dressed and go out. . . ."

Family Christmas Newsletter—December 9, 1971

I regard the family Christmas newsletter with a mixture of nausea and jealousy—nausea because I could never abide by anyone organized enough to chronicle a year of activities; jealous because our family never does anything that I can talk about on a religious holiday.

For years I have been assaulted with Frieda and Fred's camping adventures, Marcia and Willard's bright children (their three-year-old has a hit record) and Ginny and Jesse's kitchen table version of "The Night Before Christmas."

"You know something?" I announced at dinner the other night. "We're a pretty exciting family. This year, instead of the usual traditional Christmas card, why don't we make up a newsletter?"

"What would we say on it?" asked a son.

"What everyone else says. We could put down all the interesting things we did last year. For instance, you kids tell me anything you did in school that was memorable." Silence. "This is no time for modesty. Just spit out any award or recognition you received throughout the school year."

Finally, after five minutes, one son said, "I passed my eye examination."

"See?" I said excitedly. "I knew if we just thought about it a bit— now, where have we been that's exciting?"

"We got lost that Sunday and went by the Industrial School where you told us one of your uncles made license plates."

"I don't think our Christmas list wants to read about that," I said. "Let's see, have I been anyplace?"

"You went to that Sarah Coventry jewelry party last spring."

"How about that?" I said excitedly. "Now, keep going. Anyone get promoted? Married? Divorced? Hospitalized? Retired? Give birth?" Silence.

"Anyone say anything clever last year? How about the year before that? Did anyone compose a song? Write a letter? Belch after dinner?" Silence.

"Anyone protest anything? Stop biting their nails? Scrape a chair in the Christian Science reading room? Get up in the morning before ten?" Silence.

"Anyone lick a stamp? Kick the dog? Wash their gym suit? Sit up straight in class? Replace a lightbulb? Breathe in and out?"

They all sat there silently contemplating their year. Finally, I brought out a box of Christmas cards.

"What are you doing? We thought you were going to send out a family newsletter for Christmas."

"No sense antagonizing the poor devils who sit around and do nothing all year."

Christmas Chimes—December 23, 1976

Everything is in readiness.

The tree is trimmed. The cards taped to the door frame. The boxes stacked in glittering disarray under the tree.

Why don't I hear chimes?

Remember the small boy who made the chimes ring in a fictional story years ago? As the legend went, the chimes would not ring unless a gift of love was placed on the altar. Kings and men of great wealth placed untold jewels there, but year after year the church remained silent.

Then one Christmas Eve, a small child in a tattered coat made his way down the aisle, and without anyone noticing he took off his coat and placed it on the altar. The chimes rang out joyously throughout the land to mark the unselfish giving of a small boy.

I used to hear chimes.

I heard them the year one of my sons gave me a tattered piece of construction paper on which he had crayoned two hands folded in prayer and a moving message, OH COME HOLY SPIT!.

I heard them the year I got a shoe box that contained two baseball cards and the gum was still with them.

I heard them the Christmas they all got together and cleaned the garage.

They're gone, aren't they? The years of the lace doilies fashioned into snowflakes . . . the hands traced in plaster of paris . . . the Christmas trees of pipe cleaners . . . the thread spools that held small candles. They're gone.

The chubby hands that clumsily used up $2 worth of paper to wrap a cork coaster are sophisticated enough to take a number and have the gift wrapped professionally.

The childish decision of when to break the ceramic piggy bank with a hammer to spring the 59 cents is now resolved by a credit card.

The muted thump of pajama-covered feet padding down the stairs to tuck her homemade crumb scrapers beneath the tree has given way to pantyhose and fashion boots to the knee.

It'll be a good Christmas. We'll eat too much. Make a mess in the living room. Throw the warranties into the fire by mistake. Drive the dog crazy taping bows to his tail. Return cookies to the plate with a bite out of them. Listen to Christmas music.

But Lord . . . what I would give to bend low and receive a gift of toothpicks and library paste and hear the chimes just one more time!

Son Home for the Holidays?—January 2, 1977

"Wasn't it wonderful having our son home for the holidays?" I asked my husband.

"It certainly was," he smiled wistfully.

"I didn't realize we'd miss him so much. He's grown taller, hasn't he?"

"And looks a little too thin? I suppose a mother would notice those things before a father, wouldn't she?"

"How's he doing in school?" I asked. "He'd talk those things over with a father, wouldn't he?"

"Not really. He has matured quite a bit, though, hasn't he?"

"A father would observe that right off the bat."

"If you want to know the truth," said my husband, "I never set eyes on the kid the entire three weeks he was home."

"You're kidding!" I gasped.

"No. I thought I saw the back of his head once as he was backing the car out of the driveway, but I couldn't be sure. How's he doing?"

"I never saw him either."

"He *was* here, wasn't he?" asked my husband.

"Oh, yes, I'm sure of that. I could see him mounded in the center of the bed. He'd get up around the crack of noon and take a shower, and once I handed him the phone through the door."

"You actually saw him?"

"It was steamy, but I'm pretty sure it was him."

"Wait a minute," said my husband. "Does he have a gray sweater with three stripes on the sleeve? I think I saw him one night holding both refrigerator doors wide open like he was welcoming a convention."

"That's wasn't our son; that was Mark."

"I wish I had known that. I apologized to him for not spending more time with him."

"It's a natural mistake. He was here the entire Christmas vacation. Wait a minute. There's the phone."

"Who was it?" asked my husband later.

"Mark's mother. She wanted to know how her son looked and if he needed anything."

"Any news of our son?"

"He's fine and says he doesn't know if he can get home for spring vacation or not."

"How will we know for sure?" shrugged my husband.

"Just feel the hood of the car."

Halloween Challenges "No Talent" Mother—October 30, 1979

I never approach Halloween that I don't remember my first brush with discrimination.

I've never told you this before, but I was the first "no-talent" mother to integrate a neighborhood of mothers who were art school graduates. When I looked at the house, the real estate agent tried to warn me. He said, "See that mailbox next door to you? The one with the flowers and butterflies hand-painted? Mrs. Walters did that freehand."

A bit farther down the street he pointed to another house and said, "Isn't that a clever play area with the Peter Pan motif? Mrs. Tierney did that. She's very handy. In fact, all the women in this neighborhood can make anything out of nothing."

I was undaunted. You can't keep a person out of a neighborhood just because she doesn't have imagination. When they knew me, they'd learn to love me and to accept me for what I am.

I was wrong.

Their cakes at the bake sale made mine look like sliced bread. Their garbage cans were hand-painted with cartoons and cute sayings. Their hedges were clipped and shaped to look like farm animals. Their hand-smocked yokes for their daughters' dresses were everywhere, and macramé hung from every porch.

They turned old discards into museum pieces, decoupaged until they fainted, and looked the other way the Christmas I bent a coat hanger, twisted nose tissue over it and called it a wreath.

But it was Halloween that did me in, that single day when your children turn to you for imagination and creativity, the one day of the year when you must transcend fantasy.

There was something about the hand-carved pumpkin in the

window across the street I couldn't put my fingers on. Then I realized it had capped teeth.

The porch on the other side of us had a replica of Ray Bolger right out of *The Wizard of Oz*. When the doorbell rang I was greeted by a parade of monsters, pirates, queens, animals, ballerinas and spaceships right out of the wax museum. My daughter came home in tears when everyone wanted to know what she was doing running around the street with a grocery bag on her head.

I learned a lesson that night. You may exist in a clever neighborhood, but you can't be happy there. They'd have to bus me in to get me back.

Grandfather's Solitude—December 25, 1979

I have always directed my Christmas column toward families who are caught up in a tinsel marathon of tree trimming, stocking stuffing, music making, dog barking and children squealing.

They're so busy that sometimes I get only a glance before the garbage is wrapped in me. Occasionally, someone puts me on the back porch to catch the slush from boots. If I'm lucky I escape the licking flames when I get thrown into the fireplace with discarded wrappings and warranties.

So I've decided to write to all of you today who have the time to read me: those who have just moved to an area and haven't made new friends . . . those who are alone because they can't afford the trip home . . . those whose families have been splintered by distance or disinterest. And you are alone.

Let me tell you about my grandfather. He lived by himself in a little trailer in southwest Ohio until he died a few years ago. I always felt sorry for him when I visited at Christmas because he only had about five cards on top of the TV set, two or three packages at the most to open, and a pitiful artificial tree with a single strand of lights that bubbled like they were going to boil over.

You would have thought those pathetic trappings were straight from the Sistine Chapel.

He'd pick up each card, trace the scene with his fingers and marvel, "This is pretty enough to put in a frame." Then he'd recite the message inside, which he had memorized.

The boxes were another delight. He'd shake them and make a guess as to what they held and place them gently under the tree. Then he'd prime you for that big moment when he said, "I'm going to light the tree for you!" My sewing machine had a bigger light.

The year before he died, when he spent Christmas in the hospital, he raved the entire visiting period over a favor on his dinner tray: a Styrofoam Santa Claus with a red gumdrop hat held on by a toothpick.

Every Christmas since then, I have had to ask myself: Can I quote a single line from the stack of cards I receive? Can I visit without keeping an eye on my watch? Can I become childlike with excitement over a box that obviously holds a handkerchief? Can I live with my solitude without self-pity?

God help me. I think my grandfather felt sorry for me.

No One Diets on Thanksgiving—November 26, 1981

Sometimes I feel the real meaning of Thanksgiving is lost in a flurry of turkey, prayers and homecomings.

What we're really talking about is a wonderful day set aside on the fourth Thursday of November when no one diets. I mean, why else would they call it Thanksgiving?

It's pig-out time throughout the land. No sauces made from blue milk. No pies constructed with sugar substitutes. No potatoes baked with the nutritional value still in the skins. No tradeoffs for the next five weeks for a spoonful of dressing. It's elastic waistband time, when you not only plan on eating everything in sight but usually exceed your own expectations.

I have come to await Thanksgiving Day like a child with her nose pressed against the cold window awaiting the arrival of Santa Claus. It's the only day of the year I set my alarm. This morning, I will get up at dawn and have my turkey-preparation breakfast. This is followed by my turkey-in-the-oven formal breakfast with the family.

The third breakfast I will combine with snacks and tasting sessions with the cranberries, carrot-cabbage salad, pumpkin chiffon pies, relish plate, vegetable casserole and dressing.

By three or four in the afternoon, my fourth breakfast will consist of crackers and cheese, canapés and hors d'oeuvres of varying sizes and consistencies, as I certainly do not want to ruin my dinner.

Around five or six, dinner will be served, at which time I will announce that I have had nothing to eat since breakfast. (Dieters are always managing the truth. It's their way.)

After dinner, I will offer to clean out the roaster, only to chip the turkey skin out of the grease and pop it in my mouth before anyone notices. Every bowl I return to the refrigerator as leftovers will also be sampled.

Around 11 tonight, I will sneak out and put together a dressing sandwich, my last official sin before saying goodbye to the day. As a dieter, I have had my day of liberation.

If the president ever put Thanksgiving on a Monday, I don't like to think what dieters would do to him.

"Love Is" List for a Gusto Husband—February 14, 1982

Some women married sentimentality.

Every Valentine's Day these women get a $1.50 card at their plate with a heart on it and a present expensive enough to be called in on the charge card.

I married gusto.

At the birth of our first child, my husband leaned over, punched me on the arm and said, "Way to go, kid."

If you're going to live with gusto, you have to look for the little expressions of love that come each day. The following is a Valentine's Day message for such a man. If you are a gusto husband, clip it out, mount it on a lacy doily and kiss your wife when you give it to her. It might save your marriage for another 15 minutes.

LOVE

Love is climbing out of a warm bed at night and checking to see if all the doors are locked when you think you hear something.

Love is giving you the pizza with the two slices of pepperoni on it when I love pepperoni.

Love is acting excited over a $72 needlepoint canvas you bought when we both know you haven't finished the quilt, the pillow top, the kitchen curtains and the latch-hook rug.

Love is being mad at the kids at the same time you're mad at them.

Love is moving the car seat up as far as it will go when I get out, so you don't have to do it.

Love is painting a room together and letting you have the roller once in a while while I do the windowpanes.

Love is never remembering what birthday you're celebrating.

Love is learning how to make coffee and where the cups are.

Love is pretending to be jealous of your old boyfriend who became a priest.

Love is never going on a diet when you're fat.

Love is giving you the women's section of the paper to read first when the sports news is in the same section.

Love is refraining from telling you how the thermostat works.

Love is a lot of little things that add up to caring. It doesn't always add up to three little words. Sometimes, it adds up to six: I got your tank filled today.

Happy Valentine's Day!

Thanksgiving and Families—November 25, 1982

This is the day of families.

The patriarch who smokes big black cigars that stink up the house for three months.

The kids who don't even say hello but start pounding on the piano with their fists until conversation is no longer possible.

The couple who always pull up in a new car, even though you know they have only about $2 in their pockets and are afraid to answer their own phone.

The dominant in-law who arrives just when you sit down to eat and leaves right after dessert is served.

The one who works like a field hand from the moment she arrives until the last dish is put away.

The uncle who teases the dog.

The one who never forgets to say grace.

The short one who volunteers to sit on the piano bench and whose head is three inches above the table.

The son who always comes in with a buzz on, keeps on drinking and tells everyone he was "overserved."

The kid who refuses to eat in the kitchen with the other children and ends up sitting on Mama's lap at the table.

What has brought all of them together? Does anyone remember anymore?

When you think of it, what is a family? A psychological study that got out of hand? A genetic blind date? A group of people related by bad debts? The results of a steering committee that didn't meet regularly?

Actually, family members are mirrors of every facet of your life. They know you better than anyone in the world and are willing to overlook and forget. They've seen you at your best and your worst. Often, they're colossal bores. They've told the same stories a hundred times, but sometimes the familiarity is like an old bathrobe, too old to brag about in public, but too good to discard yet.

Like it or not, you're bound to them by your history.

I think about families a lot at Thanksgiving, even more so than at Christmas. Maybe it's because Thanksgiving offers no incentive for being together except that elusive, mysterious tie that binds us together.

All I know is, I would kill to see my grandfather smoking those stinking cigars, my uncle teasing that poor dog, my mom bustling around the kitchen helping Grandma, and me banging that piano with my fists just one more time.

Memory Tree—December 22, 1983

We call our Christmas tree a memory tree. Each and every ornament on it has a special meaning to someone in our family, and every year we unwrap them one by one and together gather these precious moments around us like spirited fireflies.

As we lovingly placed each bauble on the tree recently, we could again remember.

"Look at this," I said, holding a miniature pie tin with a picture of the Christ child done in crayons with the message OH, COME HOLY SPIT on it. "How old was Andy when he did this? Three? Four?"

"He was fifteen years old, Mom. He didn't spell *spirit* until the year he learned how to drive."

"And look at this dear little snowman with the crocheted hat and scarf. I made that when I was in the hospital with Matt."

"You bought that at a half-price sale at Penney's after Christmas. I was with you. Besides, you don't crochet."

"No matter," I said. "Oh, and look at this little Mexican hat with *Feliz Navidad.* Call your father. This will stir up a lot of memories for him."

My husband appeared.

"I won't say anything," I teased. "Just tell me what this reminds you of."

He looked blank.

"Mazatlán, 1976. Remember, I wanted something for my memory tree?"

"That's right," he said. "And you had the green apple two-step so bad you couldn't get out of bed."

"I got that Mexican hat at a restaurant in LA," my son said. "It used to have a swizzle stick on it."

As I rummaged through the tissue, I carefully unwrapped a little rag doll. "Get Betsy," I shouted. "She'll never believe this."

"That's cute," she said. "Where did you get it?"

"Surely you jest," I said. "Why, that's one of the first dolls I bought you."

"Couldn't be. It has all the eyes, and there's no fear on its face. All of mine ran away from home."

It took me a couple of hours to put on the little sleds, the mice dressed in red, the bread-dough figures and the wreaths made of leaves and berries and to recall the stories behind each and every one.

Memories: They can't take that away from me.

Or can they?

Christmas Newsletter Winner—December 12, 1985

Twenty years ago I publicly passed sentence on Christmas news-letters. It was a terrible way to enter the joyous season of Christmas to learn that other people's children were "sleeping dry" at age three months and that Ed and Margaret got 18 miles to the gallon out of their camper on the way to Raw Sewage Lake. I found these photocopied diaries impersonal and boring, and if their poodle was depressed following her hysterectomy, I really didn't care.

Most letter writers would begin with January and stop off at every month to share some accomplishment. Some of them would include pictures of the family so dark and blotched they looked like Rorschach tests. Some of them set down their achievements in po-etry form.

Every year I get hundreds of newsletters from people who want to convert me or prove to me that people enjoy hearing what their family has done in the past year. Every year I save one to run on the following year in observance of this joyous holiday. The following newsletter, in its original form, ran for two and a half pages. It is trimmed (and the names changed) in the name of mercy and mental health.

WISHING YOU GOD'S RICHEST BLESSINGS THIS CHRISTMAS
Dear Friends and Relatives:

On June 15, Madge went home to be with the Lord. As we were eating supper, she began to shake, and I put my arms around her. She stiffened out and I believe she died in my arms, but the hospital said no, it was a few hours later.

In July, Aunt Ceil somewhat reluctantly left her home on Grimes Avenue to live in an apartment with my folks. How-ever, it was short-lived as Mom passed away two weeks later.

The week Dad moved out she had a bad spell and a stroke. I might mention that Margaret had a heart attack just prior to Aunt Ceil's stroke.

Stuart and Sarah were married in September and Dad de-cided he'd move into Stuart's room. We have lost several rel-atives and friends this year. During the summer it seemed like every week someone close passed away. Martin said he spent his whole vacation going to funerals and was glad to go back to work.

Wishing you all a blessed Christmas and a glorious New Year.

That is the winner of last year's competition for "Joy to the World." It tops the one the year before where there was a picture of an elderly family member with breathing tubes in his nose.

I beg all of you newsletter writers. Don't try to cheer me up this year. I can't stand it.

Undecorating the Christmas Tree—January 1, 1987

You say you've had enough people around to last you a lifetime?

You say if you don't get some time to yourself you may start braiding your hair and humming?

You'd like to clear everyone out of the house and be able to have some quiet time alone?

Read my lips and slowly repeat after me: "I am going to take the Christmas tree down." You will only have to say it once and feet will scurry, doors will slam, car motors will turn over. In 30 seconds you'll feel like the last person on Earth.

No one loves a Christmas tree on January 1. The wonderful, soft branches that the family couldn't wait to get inside to smell have turned into rapiers that jab you. The wonderful blinking lights that Daddy arranged by branch and color have knotted themselves hopelessly around crumbling brownery and have to be severed with a bread knife. The stockings that hung by the chimney with care are hanging out of sofa cushions, and they smell like clam dip. And the angel that everyone fought to put on top of the tree can only be removed with an extension ladder that is in the garage, and no one can remember how to fit it through the door.

Next to the presidency, detrimming a tree has to be the loneliest job in the world. It has fallen to women for centuries and is considered a skill only they can do, like replacing the roll on the toilet tissue spindle, painting baseboards, holding a wet washcloth for a child who is throwing up or taking out a splinter with a needle.

How to undecorate the tree is my business. There's no one around to give advice, so I do it my way. I take the end of a rope of gold tinsel and give it a jerk. The tree spins around, and I clean the whole thing off in eight seconds. I eat the candy canes as I go along. Better me than the mice. I never bother with sheets to catch all the dry needles. I just vacuum them up until the sweeper smokes. Then I empty it and start all over again. The balls near the bottom I catch in a box, and the ones near the top I shake off and sometimes catch in midair.

If this creates wear and tear on the ornaments, tough. Next time around, my husband can marry a tall girl who plays basketball.

Any gift left under the tree legally reverts to the person who untrims the tree. This includes money left on branches and magazine subscriptions.

In nearly 38 years, you'd think someone would be curious enough to ask what happened to that large tree that was in the living room last week. No one ever does. Somewhere between Arizona's first down on Michigan's 15-yard line, Christmas '86 passed into history.

"Equal" Christmas Gifts—December 22, 1994

I tallied up the price of my gifts to the children the other day and realized one is $2 short of the amount I spent on the other two.

There are those who will say, Christmas isn't about money. It's about little tokens of love and giving and sharing.

I say to you, You've been reading too many Hallmark cards.

It's a stupid thing I'm doing. I know that. Ask me why I look both ways before I cross a one-way street. I don't know. I just do it.

But I know for a fact that children are born with microchips in their brains that record and store the exact day their brothers and sisters got their first bicycle/watch/car. If you miss doing the same for one child within that time frame, that can mean only one thing: You love his brother better than you love him.

Every child in the family vies for the attention of his parents. Some will get it by sticking two carrots in their nostrils at the table. Others will make all A's. Another will speak only two words to you a year. But they're all in the race.

My husband says the kids have outgrown the Christmas tabulating routine. I don't want to take the chance. "It's just going to be stocking stuffers," I said.

When I went to buy a $2 gift for the one on the short end, I found I had to pay $10 for an address book. That made the other two $8 short. In buying a fanny pack for my daughter, I had to pay $12 for it. That meant my first son was now $12 short and his brother $4 light.

That wasn't right. So I charged the malls again.

I'm at the stage now that if I buy a candy cane for one, a postage stamp for the other and a stick of gum for the third, I'm paid up on my affection for another year.

I know in my heart they're all grown-up adults and don't even think about such things at Christmas, but years ago when they were small, I told my son the poignant story of a town's quest to make the chimes ring in the old church.

The townspeople were told that when someone put a gift of value and sacrifice on the altar, it would happen. One by one they offered gold and valuables. The church bells remained silent. Then a little waif took off his coat, which was his only protection against the cold, and placed it on the altar. It was the only thing he had. The chimes rang gloriously.

My son turned to me and asked, "What did his brother give?"

The Gang's All Here

Entertaining—November 18, 1965

Some naive book publisher has just sent me an advance copy of a new book called *Company's Coming.*

It's a beautiful white ledger that tells me the secret to gracious entertaining is planning, organization and relaxation. In the back of the book is an index card for frequent guests, listing their food preferences, allergies, children's names, what they were served the last time they were guests and what the hostess wore. This may be "utterly utt" for the woman who takes her entertaining seriously, but, my friend, you are dealing with the Tugboat Annie of Lower Suburbia!

There is only one reason uppermost in our minds when we stage a party—it's an incentive to clean and patch up the house.

When we reach a point where we can no longer dig out, we simply announce, "Let's give a party." My husband knocks out a wall or two, gives the baseboard that long-promised second coat, changes the furnace filter, replaces lightbulbs where there has been no light for five years, squirts glazing compound into holes and wall cracks, and hot mops the driveway.

The children are in charge of scouting the sandbox and toy chests for good silverware, hauling away the debris under their beds, disposing of a garage full of bottles and returning the library books.

I have my own busywork. I discard all the jelly glasses and replace them with matched crystal, exchange all the dead house plants for new ones from the nursery and, of course, plan a menu and guest list.

This I try to keep simple (the guests, not the menu). I always invite a few live ones, like the man who has it on good authority that Santa Claus is a subversive and a rebellious neighbor who is advancing a theory that the local PTA is a private-key Bunny Club with a good "cover."

The afternoon of the party goes like clockwork. The kids eat all the olives and leave bite marks in the canapés. I trim these back to their original shape with a pair of sharp scissors (which my son announces he cut his toenails with the night before). Someone always remembers to close the draft in the fireplace. This is a must at our parties. We build a roaring fire and then herd our guests into the cold street to watch the fire trucks provide an evening of entertainment.

Another tradition at our parties is the wet picture frame. We always manage to paint or varnish one at the eleventh hour, and invariably a guest becomes stuck to it. (They are cut away with the same scissors used for the toenails and canapés.)

The evening of the party, however, is perfection itself. As I take the key off my belt to unlock the hall bath (which has been off limits since the previous Tuesday), I smile easily and ask, "Where are the kids?"

"I mailed them to my mother in Orlando," says my husband.

"Good thinking." I sigh, relaxing in a chair . . . just like the book says.

Mouse in the Pump Organ—January 13, 1971

We've never given a party in our lives that something (or someone) didn't crawl inside our house and die.

It's the price you pay for rustic, rural living.

In my mind, I visualize a group of mice meeting in a cornfield and one of them says to the other, "Bufford, you don't look too good."

"Oh, I'll be all right," says Bufford. "It's just a head cold."

"Nevertheless," says the leader, "why don't you check in at Bombeck's wall?"

The night of our last party, Bufford didn't make it to the wall. He staggered into our old pump organ and kicked off.

My husband came into the house, sank to his knees and gasped, "Not again! Where this time?"

"In the pump organ," I said.

"Can't we get rid of the odor?"

"Only if you want to paint the living room."

"We mustn't panic," he said, patting his wrists with a deodorizer wick. "We're just going to have to make sure that no one plays the organ tonight." We both nodded.

The party was in high gear when Max Marx sat down at the organ. I grabbed a can of deodorizer and followed him.

"What are you doing?" he asked, annoyed.

I turned the deodorizer on myself. "It's Skinny Dip," I said feebly, "to make me irresistible."

I watched in horror as he pulled out the stops on the organ and started to pump. As the bellows wheezed in and out, spreading misery through the house, three women fainted and one man put out his pipe.

"I say," he said, pausing, "do you have a dog?"

"We have three of them, but they're outside."

He began to play again, then stopped and sniffed. "Is someone in the apartment cooking sauerkraut or making sulfur with a junior chemistry set?"

"We don't live in an apartment."

"Is someone wearing old gym shoes?" he asked.

His wife came over at the moment and leaned over his shoulder. "Max, your music stinks."

"Is that it?" he said, and moved on to the kitchen for a stronger drink.

My Husband Builds a Fire—December 1971

There are elements of human nature I will never understand.

A careless camper will flip a match during a rainstorm, and seconds later the entire forest will be in flames.

We will give a party and my husband will "lay a fire" using 30 pounds of paper, a mound of brittle kindling and a seasoned log with a guarantee stapled on the side. Within minutes, an entire party will be driven into the streets by smoke.

He's the only man I know who had a fireplace with a gas lighter go out on him.

"Why don't you forget the fire tonight?" I said, collaring him before a party.

"Nonsense," he said, "I've got the secret. I just have to use more paper and get it started early. That's the secret. Start it early and get a bed of hot coals. Then just feed it logs all night."

At 6:30 P.M., he burned the evening paper, which I had not read.

At 6:35, he emptied three trash cans into the fireplace and created another small flame.

At 7:05, he emerged from the garage with a wagon full of papers I had been saving for the last three months for the Boy Scout paper drive.

The guests began to arrive.

At 7:45, he burned all the calendars in the house, plus five napkins that he was able to snatch away from guests.

At 7:50, he frantically tore the plastic bags off the dry cleaning in the hall closet and burned a drawer full of brown-paper grocery bags I save for garbage.

At 8:05, with the living room snowing with flying fragments of soot, he began emptying shoe boxes and wedging them under the log.

At 9:00 he was reduced to lighting unpaid bills with a match and throwing them in on the smoldering log. I collared him. "Look, Smokey Bear, will you forget about the lousy fire and pay some attention to your guests?"

"I almost got it," he said feverishly. "Just a few more pieces of paper." He ran to the cedar chest and emerged with the baby books, our wedding pictures and our marriage license.

At 1 A.M. he grabbed me by the shoulder. "It's going," he said. "It's really blazing. Remember those cereal boxes with only a little cereal left? I threw it away and the boxes did it!"

"Wonderful," I said, pulling the covers around my neck. "Now will you put it out and come to bed? We've got a big day ahead of us tomorrow. I am having you committed."

"Come Casual"—April 1975

I wish to heaven Emily Post would spell out what "come casual" to a party means.

Casual in my dictionary reads, "A thing that is accidental. Not planned or sought." When I go to a party casual that's exactly what I am, an unplanned, unsought accident.

My husband's idea of casual is going to bed without a necktie. If he would back me up in whatever style I chose, it wouldn't be so bad. But it never fails. We never match. I emerge from the closet where I am dressing and look at him for the first time.

"What are you doing?" I shout. "You look like the groom on top of a wedding cake."

"What are you supposed to be?" he grimaces. "Hansel or Gretel?"

"Look," I said. "The hostess made a big point of telling me to 'Come super casual.'"

"That doesn't mean wearing a gym suit with a whistle around your neck."

"This is not a gym suit. Why don't you at least take off your tie?"

"I'll take off my tie if you wear a skirt."

"I got it. You change to a sport shirt and I'll put on slacks."

"I've got a better idea. You wear a dress and I'll wear a sport coat."

I retire to the closet again and come out a few minutes later in a sleeveless basic black and heels.

In the meantime, he has changed to a pair of baggy pants and a sweatshirt.

"She said casual, not destitute," I said.

"Then why are you dressed up like a dining room hostess? I am going back and change."

After several trips to the closet, I finally decide on my original outfit and he goes back to his original selection.

At the party it becomes obvious that no one knew what "casual" meant. All the women are formally attired, as are all the men.

As I pass by a group, I hear my dapper husband explain, "I just picked Erma up at the gym and she didn't have time to change."

Boy, is he going to get a "casual" punch in the mouth on the way home!

Party Hostess Loneliest Person in the World—September 1975

A line in a sermon got me to thinking the other week. It posed the question, "Whom do you consider the loneliest person in the world?"

The candidates began to fill my mind like a free lunch at a bar. Unquestionably they were:

The man with 800 slides of his vacation.

A kid at camp with measles.

An obscene phone caller who has only one dime.

The owner of a Laundromat in a nudist colony.

The vice president of anything.

The woman who bleaches her hair at home.

Chaperones on a field trip to Passion Park.

Then it hit me. Maybe I don't speak for anyone else, but for me the loneliest moment in my life is when I have a living room full of guests and I am in the kitchen checking on a new recipe: Chicken Wonderment.

There is no other moment to match it.

The guests have been smiling for two and half hours and are so bored they're discussing their dental appointments . . . the snacks, so colorful and appetizing when the guests arrived, now have the appeal of a cage that hasn't been cleaned in a while . . . and everyone is anxiously facing the kitchen as if anticipating the Second Coming.

In the kitchen I approach the oven like a pitcher going to the mound in the bottom of the ninth with men on first and third and the count three balls and two strikes.

I am alone. I summon my best friend, Mayva, who says, "You'd better snap it up. They're starting to organize rescue parties."

I am alone. My husband, without a hint of compassion, says, "For crying out loud . . . another twenty minutes and I can't guarantee the safety of our parakeet."

I am alone. I summon God and He puts me on hold.

Loneliness. It's that moment when you take the lid off the roaster and the sour cream that was supposed to thicken into a rich sauce didn't. And the chicken that was supposed to cook to plump tenderness is as hard as Billie Jean King's thigh. And the peas have drowned in their own butter and are lying in the pan like the creek dried up . . . and the rolls spill over their pans and are heading for the other wall, and the candles have reached the end of their wicks and are sputtering in their own wax.

The guests have stopped talking now to conserve energy. That's loneliness.

College Reunion—November 3, 1977

I never go to a college reunion that I don't come away feeling sorry for all those paunchy, balding jocks trying to hang onto youth.

I feel sorry for the men too.

Mayva and I always sit together. We seem to be the only two in the class who have fought the battle of middle age and won.

"How do we do it?" I whispered, watching the class of '49 dance away in merciful darkness. "I feel like Marie Osmond at a Prune Festival."

"I know what you're saying," said Mayva. "Look at Ginger Horwich. Can you believe she's wearing glasses this thick? Blind as a bat."

"Where?" I asked, digging in my purse and holding my bifocals to my nose like a lorgnette.

"And what about Marci Miller? Who is she fooling with that caftan?"

"Mayva, as I have always said, 'You show me a woman in a caftan, and I'll show you a lot of fat that doesn't fit.' Incidentally, isn't that caftan a lot like yours?"

"No," said Mayva irritably, "mine has no waist. Oh, my goodness, would you look at who just came in: Mary Moosebaum, with hair as white as the driven snow. Who does she remind you of?"

"Thomas Edison."

"Exactly. Of course, we shouldn't laugh. Someday our hair will start to turn and we'll no longer be—"

"Henna number four. Hey, look at the next table. It's the class success, Barbara Judson, our newly elected senator. They're sure making a big fuss over her, but I respect her. If you have to work to make ends meet, you have to work. Besides, it might lead to something big. At least she's not like Paula Pringle."

"That vicious old broad," said Mayva. "Never has a kind word to say about anyone. I'm going over and tell her how much I've missed her."

As Mayva left the table, I couldn't help remarking to my husband, "Mayva looks old. Wonder how long it will take me to start showing my age?"

Trip to the Rest Room—October 25, 1979

We were eating in a Spanish restaurant the other night when my friend and I excused ourselves and went to the rest room.

Since both of us are farsighted, she arrived at the first door, pressed her nose two inches from it, and with her hands traced the outline of what she thought to be a hooped skirt.

It turned out to be the cape of a bullfighter, and we found ourselves in the men's room. The two of us hid in a booth until it was prudent to come out.

Naturally, we do not consider ourselves authorities on men's rooms, but since few women have visited this last bastion of male dominance, we made some observations on the subject.

Men go to the rest room alone. I don't know why they do this, but I have yet to see a man stand up in a room, announce where he is going and ask if any other man at the table would like to go with him. With women it's a social outing, something you share. My husband calls it the ark connection. Women go into the rest room two-by-two and come out the same way.

Men whistle. Without fail, every man who came into the rest room whistled and didn't stop until he left. Women, on the other hand, never whistle. They talk. There is everything to talk about: Why there are no towels. Why there is no soap. Why the hand blower doesn't work. Why there is a toll charge for using the bathroom. I have established more meaningful relationships from holding the door of a pay booth open than you can imagine. In fact, a lot of us still correspond.

Men return from the facilities and seem embarrassed to discuss where they've been. They never hear any gossip. Never see any celebrities. Never find out if the fish on the menu is frozen or that the blond waitress is married to the drummer, who is jealous.

To women, a rest room is an adventure. Where men instinctively check out the location before they sit down, women buzz around asking the bartender, the cashier or the maître d' and end up wandering around the kitchen, going through the doors that lead to the parking lot and giggling in a dark corridor about whether or not a unicorn is male or female.

I don't know how to explain any of this. Maybe women just don't get out a lot.

Pepper Mill Experience—December 18, 1983

It's hard to go to a restaurant anymore and not go through the Black Pepper Experience.

For some reason, pepper has gone from a table staple to wine status. Restaurants will serve no pepper before its time.

It's a ceremony comparable to the presentation of Eliza Doolittle to society.

First, a waiter will poise over you with a pepper mill the size of a piano leg (the bigger the pepper mill, the larger the check). Then he will sing out, "Pepper?" All conversation comes to a halt. For reasons that no one can explain, it's something you have to think about.

As long as people have been stalking me with a pepper mill, you would think I would have made up my mind as to whether I want more. I never do. For a moment, I ponder. Then I clear my throat and say, "Yes." He watches my hand, waiting for me to orchestrate how much and the precise moment to stop.

Now here's the weird part. Not one grain of pepper comes out of the mill. In fact, no one has ever seen pepper come out of the mill.

If it did, wouldn't the entire table be sneezing?

The Pepper Experience is nothing more than a ritual without meaning, like watching the first piece of luggage come off a carousel in airport baggage. Ever see anyone claim it? Of course you don't. Because it doesn't belong to anyone, that's why. It's just an exercise to give you hope that more luggage is on the way.

Maybe it's the same with pepper. People need little visits from their waiter occasionally to know that he is still with you and has not left town for the weekend. They need to know that he loves you and cares about you and wants to be by your side.

Let the word go out: People do not need help with their pepper! For most of us, it's something we can handle. If you waiters want to make yourselves useful, hold a flashlight while we read the menus, assist with easy financing when we pick up the bill for a party of eight or help us as we valiantly try to rescue a square of frozen butter from the ice age.

Help us dispose of our aluminum foil from our baked potato before we eat half of it; remind us to retrieve our knife from the salad plate before it goes back to the kitchen, leaving us defenseless for the meat course; and deliver us from air conditioners over our table that blow out our only source of heat—a candle.

I'm a college graduate. I can operate my own pepper mill. Why doesn't it twist? What's wrong with it? There's nothing coming out of it. Maybe I'm twisting it the wrong way.

I heard somewhere that pepper causes bad skin.

Grandma's Grudges—May 1, 1984

This is the first family reunion our family has planned since Grandma died. Frankly, it's going to be the biggest mess in the world. Grandma was the only one who kept track of who was speaking to whom . . . and why.

Grandma was an apostle of grudges. She believed if you paid attention and kept a firm grip on things, you could go to a funeral and the deceased would know you were only there because you shared the same mother and father. You could fall into disfavor with Grandma for a number of reasons. Each carried its own grudge sentence.

"You didn't answer your phone when I called because you knew it was me" (four years).

"You never paid me the three dollars when we went in on flowers for Margaret's funeral" (18 years).

"I was the last one to hear you were expecting" (two years).

"When you looked through my photo albums, my picture of Dad was there. When you left, it was gone" (25 years).

"You know!" (This was the dreaded grudge that lasted for life.)

I remember going to one reunion where you needed a program to know which side of the picnic table to sit on. I approached Marie, one of my cousins, and said, "Are we speaking to each other this year?"

"I don't think so," she said.

"Why?"

"I never thanked your mother for the pen and pencil set the year I graduated."

"How old are you now, Marie?"

"I'm forty-seven, but I'm gonna write her tonight."

I felt my grandmother looking at me.

"I'll check in with you next year," I said.

My grandma was really a nice lady. There wasn't anything she wouldn't do for you, but she had a sense of justice that when you had been wronged, you had to make it right. I once asked her what it would take to get my Aunt Jeanette to be welcome in her house. (Grandma sent home a loaf of freshly baked bread with her once, and she never returned the pan.) Grandma thought a bit and said, "Grovel. She would have to grovel."

The other day my mother got a thank-you note for a pen and pencil set. "Who's Marie?" she asked.

"She's the one at the reunion who grabbed the picnic table in the shade for her family."

Grandma would have sentenced her to 10 years for that!

Houseguests—August 6, 1985

My mom has a plaque just inside her front door that reads, *If we get to drinking Sunday afternoon and start insisting that you stay over until Tuesday, please remember we don't mean it.*

My mother likes houseguests as well as the next one, but let's be realistic. Houseguests should be regarded as perishables. Leave them out too long, and they go bad.

It is rare when you can unite in holy wedlock two families in one house any longer than 48 hours without the hostess attacking her welcome mat with a steak knife. Some families eat at 4:30 in the afternoon. Others fall right out of the happy hour into bed.

Some guests consider a picnic in the park as a forced death march while others, if allowed to sit around and watch TV for more than an hour, whine, "We can do this at home. We want to see something!" It's a game.

Take Len and Bernadine. Take their children Puberty and Sissy. Take their dog, Carl. Please.

We could hardly wait until they came for a visit. Hadn't seen them in six years. You forget a lot in six years.

We forgot that Bernadine was a vegetarian but was allergic to 18 vegetables and nine fruits.

We forgot that when Len snored, cattle became restless 40 miles away.

Somehow, we had forgotten that Puberty was lightfingered, so you had to hide your purse in the vegetable crisper in the refrigerator.

There were a lot of little things: the fact that Sissy could bounce a ball against your bedroom window at six in the morning 5,786 times without missing.

We had forgotten that Len and Bernadine each smoked three packs of cigarettes a day and kept assuring us we would get hit by a beer truck driven by the surgeon general before the smoke got us.

It had slipped my mind that Bernadine never touched a dish, because "I don't know where they belong," nor a washer, because "I don't want to break it," or came into the kitchen, because "I don't want to get in your way."

It's the sandlot game. If you are hospitable, you can't seem to get a hit. You get walked a lot. You strike out a lot. You sit on the bench helplessly and let it all happen.

And then, on the last day of their visit, Len and Bernadine said, "You know, you should get a booster for your hot water. We've been taking cold showers since we got here."

They had forgotten something too. They had forgotten that my husband in his infinite wisdom had installed the hot water spigot on the cold water and the cold water spigot on the hot water.

Visitors: 138. Home: 1.

Restaurant Conversation—October 20, 1985

The other day I was trying to remember when restaurants were places where you sat down, ordered, ate, talked to one another and left. There were no introductions, no social amenities and no monologues. Oh, occasionally a group of waiters and waitresses would hoist a cupcake with a sparkler on it and sing "Happy Birthday," but it was no big deal.

The other night we drove into the restaurant parking lot, and the valet opened the doors and said, "My name is Hal and I'll keep an eye on your car. Have a good dinner."

I said, "Thank you, Hal. I'm Erma and this is my husband, Bill, and our friends, Dick and Bernice."

Inside, after we were seated, a young woman appeared and said, "Good evening. My name is Wendy, and I'm your cocktail waitress. What could I get you this evening?"

I introduced all of us again and we ordered something from the bar.

My husband leaned over and said, "So Dick, what's happening?"

A waiter brought a basket of bread to our table and said, "Good evening, folks. I'm Brick, and these are our special toasted garlic rounds with just a hint of Parmesan and fresh parsley. If you need more, yell. Enjoy."

"Thanks, Brick," my husband said. "So, what's happening, Dick?"

Another waiter appeared and said, "Hello, I'm Stud, and I'll be your waiter for this evening. I'd like to interrupt just a minute to tell you about our specials for this evening. The chef has prepared *osso buco*. This is made with knuckle of veal, garlic, chicken sauce, white wine, tomato paste and anchovy fillets finely chopped.

"The catch of the day is smoked cod's roe, which the chef makes into *tarama salata* smothered with black olives, heavy cream, lemon and olive oil. The soup of the day is everyone's favorite, watercress and apple, with just a pinch of curry. I'll give you a minute to decide."

Numbly, we looked at one another. His monologue had lasted longer than most marriages.

"So, Dick, what's happening with you?" my husband began.

Wendy reappeared and said, "Refills anyone?"

We shook our head.

Stud followed her to the table and said, "Are we ready to order now?"

No sooner had Dick and Bernice agreed to share a salad when a table appeared and Stud narrated the drama of the birth of Caesar salad like a midwife.

Meanwhile, Frank (the chef) appeared with a naked fish, which he stuck under my nose for approval. (Thank God I didn't order the strangled duck!) After the salad came another table with flames leaping off it, and Stud electrified us with his commentary on sauce for the Moroccan meatballs.

Arthur appeared with a key around his neck and a book that weighed 36 pounds and introduced himself as our wine steward. I introduced him to Bill, Dick and Bernice.

When we got into the car, my husband said, "I'd like to get together again and get to know you."

"Thanks," Hal said.

"I was talking to Dick and Bernice," my husband said.

Hors d'Oeuvres—December 5, 1985

About 20 years ago, my husband and I were invited to an open house for about 200 people. As open houses go, there was nothing really significant about it. We didn't meet anyone we later married, and no one fell in the punch bowl.

However, we did discover something on that day we would remember the rest of our lives: Hors d'oeuvres do not flush. We would have to think of some other way to get rid of them.

The problem with these before-dinner snacks is that there is no way of knowing what you are about to eat until it is in your mouth. Then it is too late. They do not break down by chewing. Sometimes swallowing does it. Sometimes not. Heaven only knows what is heaped on those little crackers and dry triangles of toast.

In the beginning, a hostess set out a dish of nuts to stave off hunger. Then someone found a cute cracker and arranged it on a plate. The next hostess decided a cracker looked naked and put a slice of cheese on it. From that came the dips.

I made a promise to myself never to eat anything that was navy blue or khaki green or excited the dog when it hit the floor. When a hostess dumped a package of dry onion-soup mix into some sour cream, I knew it was a threat to every rule I had made.

I'm a social outcast at dips. Some people instinctively know the stress factor involved in how much a chip can hold. I never know that. When it breaks, my hand is thrust into the bowl, and all night I have a white residue of garlic and sour cream under my fingernails.

What really frosts me is that a hostess will never reveal what she is serving on her hors d'oeuvres. "What's this little brown thing on top?" I ask. "What do you think it is?" she chirps.

I then get 20 questions to come up with the answer. "Is it living or dead? Is it American? Is it in politics or the arts? Would I be likely to find it in my house? Is it bigger than a breadbox? Is it considered to be a gourmet treat in this country but bait everywhere else? Does it run under a rock whenever there are bathers nearby? Did it look like this when it was young?"

I have never objected to a little mystery in cooking, but things have gotten out of hand. I have a whole season of hors d'oeuvres ahead of me, two months of strange little lumps of unidentifiable things being snatched from freezers and popped into microwaves to challenge my mind. Let us pray someone starts building a better hors d'oeuvre . . . or a better toilet. It doesn't matter which comes first.

Family Goodbyes—July 28, 1994

When I married into my husband's family, I was surprised when we spent an evening with them, said goodbye, got into the car and left.

Saying goodbye in my family is not so simple. I leave with a watermelon balanced between my knees, leftover meatloaf for my lunch the next day, bags of homemade noodles, a "start" off a vine from the backyard, and a pie pan being returned from the pie I sent home with them. Sometimes I get an ugly piece of furniture they were going to throw away anyway.

My late sister was the worst. She'd start stacking things up on the kitchen counter while you were there. The longer you visited, the less counter space there was. She gave you beans she had canned, potholders she had sewn and a bucket of fresh cherries as parting gifts. If she had bought two pounds of bacon on sale, she felt obliged to give you one. "I got a bag of homemade frozen turtle soup for you," she said.

"I hated turtle soup last year, I hate it this year and I will still hate it next year," I reminded her. "Too bad," she said. "You're not going home empty-handed."

This practice is an enigma to my husband.

The only explanation I can think of is that I come from a line of Ohio farmers. They were rural people who shared their harvest with anyone who came to the door. When they moved to the cities, they brought the practice with them.

Our tools and personal things are so inbred at this point, we don't know whom they belong to. We borrow maternity clothes, cars that have big trunks, paintbrushes, dishes, grills, lawn furniture, card tables, folding chairs and cots. For a period of 15 years, one set of luggage went back and forth and did more traveling than Charles Kuralt. We never wanted to know where it had been.

I read stories of what I can do with my leftover turkey and sweet potatoes after the holidays. I never have any leftovers. Everything gets parceled out in plastic bags and goes to new owners.

There is a downside to this game of musical food, clothes and household belongings.

The other night after dinner at Mother's, I was laden with a box of wild rice that she bought without her glasses, an unbaked pie crust that was about to expire, and candy bars left over from Halloween. "Wait a minute," she said. "I've been meaning to give you this dress. I hated it from the moment I bought it. It never fit right, and it's not my color."

"I bought that dress," I said, "and gave it to you."

Our eyes met. She smiled and said, "I'll send it home with your cousin Dede with a nice pie."

Planning Birthday Celebrations—November 8, 1994

I like to get together with my family and bond as well as the next person, but getting all of us together at one time anymore is like Dole and Clinton doing lunch.

It was always a tradition that the family celebrate one another's birthdays. If the birthday is in April, I begin calling the family in December. "Don't forget April twenty-seventh," I remind them.

"Well, you can't have a celebration on the twenty-seventh. That falls on Wednesday. It's got to be early on the weekend of the twenty-third or late on the thirtieth.

"I pick late on the thirtieth," says the sibling who shops in a car-wash for a gift on his way to the celebration, waits for the first gift to be opened, snatches the paper and runs to the bathroom to wrap it.

In February, I call them all again.

"I can't do it either of those weekends. I have plans," says another one.

"I told you to protect that date."

"What date? It wasn't firm."

"I'm taking my car in on the twenty-sixth. It may not be finished in time."

"What's wrong with May seventh?" says another voice.

"Totally wrong. I don't get paid until the fifteenth."

"Is anyone busy the second week of May?"

"I'm helping a friend move. She has a piano."

"OK," I say, "June fourteenth."

"That's my birthday," says my daughter. "I don't want to share a birthday. The next thing you know, we'll be having one of those Reverend Moon mass weddings for seven hundred people. We'll just line up and pass out birthday cards."

"Wait a minute," I said. "Let's get one birthday settled at a time. We're working on April twenty-seventh. Are you available in July?"

"No!"

"August?"

"Too hot."

"September?"

"That's my birthday," said another son, "and we haven't celebrated it from last year. It's still on hold."

"Anyone who sends each member of the family a subscription to *TV Guide*—and we never see it—deserves to be on hold."

"Why don't we just do it October sixth?"

"I can't make it. I'll be out of town."

"Who cares?"

"It's my birthday!"

Of Missing Socks, Promiscuous Hangers and Other Unexplained Phenomena

Socks Lost in Washer—May 28, 1969

Don't tell me about the scientific advances of the twentieth century.

So men are planning a trip to the moon. So computers run every large industry in America. So body organs are being transplanted like perennials.

Big deal! You show me a washer that will launder a pair of socks and return them to you as a pair, and I'll light a firecracker.

I never had what you would call a good relationship with washers. They hate me. They either froth at the lid, walk across the utility room or just plain quit. But mostly they have a sock deficiency that defies reason.

Men don't understand this. They are too rational. My washer repairman leads the list.

"If your socks don't come out even, lady, that means you didn't put them in even," he said flatly.

I looked at him closely. (How can you trust a repairman who looks like Barnabas on *Dark Shadows?*) "I remembered distinctly gathering them two by two. Believe me, Noah didn't do a more complete job. I took two black ones from my son's sleeping feet, a red pair from the tennis bag, a stiff pair from his ceiling, a mud-caked pair from the glove compartment of the car and a moldy pair from two boots. You can see for yourself I have only one of each. The mates have disappeared."

"You've got a pale blue pair that match," he said.

"Of course we've got a pale blue pair, you cluck. We hate the pale blue pair. They come out of the washer even when we don't put them in. This washer is just plain insolent. Don't you understand that?"

"I mean no disrespect, lady," he stammered, "but you aren't a tippler, are you?"

"I think inside this washer is a little trap door that pulls in one sock from each pair and holds it captive. Somewhere in this machine lies a secret treasure house of mismated socks."

"Maybe just a little cold one to get you through your ironing?"

"If we could just find it, do you know what that would mean?"

"Get hold of yourself, lady, they're probably clogging up the pump. I'll take a look."

Exactly $12.50 later, the repairman shook his head. "The pump is clean. Tell you what. Why don't you put the socks in a little bag and—"

"I have put them in a little bag by twos, and you know what? When I take the little bag out, every snap is in place and still there is one sock missing from every pair. I tell you I can't go on much longer like this. Not knowing where the next sock will disappear. Having the children go around with one foot bandaged all the time. What's a mother to do?"

"For starters, lady, I'd keep the bleach away from my nose. And if that didn't work, maybe you and your friend could get on the *Ed Sullivan Show*."

I told you they didn't understand.

Girdles—May 18, 1970

This generation must be doing something right. I read in the paper last week where a girdle factory shut down due to lack of sales.

I regard the obituary of a girdle factory with mixed emotion. It's like having your mother-in-law move out because you have snakes in your basement. There is something good to be said for girdles. Maybe I'll remember what it is before I finish this column.

The problem with girdles is that they are designed under the law of redistribution. They really don't contain the flab; they merely reappropriate it. For example, when I put on a girdle, three things happen immediately; my stomach goes flat, my chin doubles, and my knees inflate. So I always say, "What does it profiteth a woman to have a flat stomach if her tongue is swollen and discolored?"

I have had some miserable experiences with girdles. One was with a miracle garment that I bought while carrying one of the children. It was expensive and rather complicated and came with some rather explicit instructions.

I read: "Welcome to the Constrictor 747. The Constrictor 747 is mechanically engineered to take inches off your waist and hips. When laced and hooped properly it will perform for 18 hours without adjustment. Before wearing, please familiarize yourself with the two pressure exits located over each kidney. In the unlikely event oxygen is required, the stays will open and automatically eject an oxygen mask. Please extinguish all fire material and place the mask over your face and mouth and breathe normally."

The Constrictor 747 was a great disappointment to me. I was wearing it one afternoon when a friend saw me and asked, "When is your baby due?"

"I had it two weeks ago," I said, and went home to give the Constrictor 747 a decent burial.

After that, I stuck with a little cheapie . . . a model called the Little Nothing Tourniquet. It was reinforced over the tummy, the hips, the rib cage, the legs, the seat and sometimes the ankle. But it did the job. You may have seen it. When I started wearing short skirts, everybody saw it. It cut me just above the knees. One day my daughter said, "Gee, Mom, haven't you heard? This is the era where you let it all hang out." And that, my friend, is what is closing girdle factories.

I promised you I'd remember something good about girdles. I just thought of it. The other day a friend asked me, "When are you expecting?"

"I had the baby 11 years ago," I said, and went home to dig out my Little Nothing Tourniquet.

Creeping Underwear—December 1972

We have virtually erased bad breath in this country, stamped out dandruff and done away with burning, itchy feet, but we have been unable to conquer one of society's most dreaded diseases: Creeping Underwear.

Everyone talks about Creeping Underwear, but no one does anything about it. Technical research has put powdered orange juice on the moon, yet on Earth we are still plagued with pantyhose that won't stay up, slips that won't stay down and girdles that should contain a label, HAZARDOUS TO YOUR HEALTH.

To suggest that Creeping Underwear changes a person's personality is the understatement of the decade. The other night I went to a movie, a fully confident, well-adjusted, stable human being. Two hours later, I was a totally different person.

My slip had crept to my waistline to form a solid inner tube that added about 15 pounds to my form. My girdle, in a series of slow maneuvers, had reached several plateaus during the evening. First, it slid to my waist. Upon finding this area was already occupied by a slip, it moved upward, cutting my chest in half, and gradually moved upward to where it pinched my neck and caused my head to grow two inches taller.

The pantyhose were quite another story. They kept sliding down until I realized halfway through the movie that I was sitting on the label in the waistband and that if I dared stand up the crotch would bind my ankles together.

I tried to adjust these garments in a way so as not to call attention, but every time I bent my elbow two straps slid onto my shoulder and bound my arms like a straitjacket.

My husband was the first to notice the change in my personality. "What are you doing sitting under the seat in a fetal position?" he asked. "Are you trying to tell me you do not like the movie?"

"I am suffering from Creeping Underwear," I whispered.

"You should have taken a couple of aspirin before you left the house," he snarled. "Now, get up here and sit up straight in your seat."

He didn't understand. They rarely do. Nearly 98.2 percent of all the victims of Creeping Underwear are women. As I sat there I looked under the seat next to me and saw another woman in a fetal position. "What are you doing down here?" I asked.

She sighed. "I crossed my leg and was flogged to death by a loose supporter."

"Do you think they'll ever find a cure?" I asked hopelessly.

"I hope so," she said. "Your tongue is beginning to swell."

Socks Still Lost in Washer—April 1, 1973

I haven't said anything lately about my washer that eats socks. To tell you the truth, I've been afraid to. After my last column on it, several things transpired.

First a half-crazed woman in Minneapolis sent me 36 single socks left in her washer in the hopes of finding a match in my washer.

Then an inventor from Cleveland sent me little chains to bind two socks together while being laundered. The chains disappeared after the first rinse.

And I was approached by a national health organization to pose with my head caught in a washer lid as their poster child.

I figured if I didn't shut up about it, they'd take away my cuticle scissors and the strings in my tennis shoes. This is not to say I don't think about it a lot (as I go through the house humming and strewing rose petals over the living room).

I think about it every time my husband has to wear a cast on one foot because he has no sock to match the one he is wearing. I think about it when I put six all-black socks in the washer and *still* end up with one black sock. I think about it when my kids leave the house every morning looking like they are going to a freshman initiation.

Last week, I looked at my washer and was saying, "Why are you doing this to me?" when my husband came in.

"Who are you talking to?"

"No one," I said quickly.

"You aren't hearing those little sock voices from the washer again saying 'Help me!' are you?"

I shook my head. As he started to leave, my eye caught something hanging out from under his coat. It looked like the mate to his new gray socks.

"Where did you get this?" I demanded.

"Darned if I know," he said. "I felt something in my underwear the other day, checked it, and it was a tennis sock from the boys. Must be static electricity. The girls in the office picked a knee sock and a footlet off my sweater yesterday."

I looked him in the eyes. He had the same look on his face that Charles Boyer had when he was driving Ingrid Bergman crazy in *Gaslight*.

"Why?" I asked hysterically. "Why would you let me believe that my socks have been going to that big utility room in the sky? Why would you let me paint anklets on the kids when you're running around with their socks in your underwear? Why . . . oh, good grief!"

"What's the matter?" he asked.

"This isn't your new gray sock. I've never seen it before."

"Want to check in with Minneapolis?" he asked hesitantly.

Pantskirt in the Rest Room—September 1973

Dear Mother:

I am writing you from a rest room in a restaurant just outside the city. While I am drying out, this seems as good a time as any to thank you for the pantskirt you made for me from a new pattern that requires no zipper and a minimum of sewing. What will they think of next?

When I first received it, I must admit it looked like a slipcover for a pyramid. But after I figured it out, it really looked neat and I decided to wear it out to dinner this evening.

Shortly after we ordered, I excused myself to come to the powder room. I untied the belt of the pantskirt and voilà! the entire garment slid off me and under the door like a coral snake in pursuit.

As I leaned over to retrieve the skirt, the bodysuit I was wearing gave way, rolled up on me like a broken blind and cut off the air to my windpipe.

This would have been a humorous situation had I not (a) peeked under the door and seen someone dragging my pantskirt in her heel toward the door, (b) become so hysterical I dropped my contact lens down the commode, and (c) sprung a run in my pantyhose.

I peeked through the crack in the door and said, "Pardon me, madam, but you are walking on my pantskirt." The poor woman was terrified. Her eyes searched upward, looking for the voice from nowhere.

"Where are you, dear?" she asked, holding up the garment and starting to walk away from me.

"No, no," I shouted, cracking my head on the purse shelf. "Here. Over here!" She slid it under the door, looked around suspiciously and left.

Meanwhile, back in the booth, I began to pull myself together. First, I shinnied out of the pantyhose, then coaxed the bodysuit down. I started to assemble the pajamas on me. I snapped them around the waist, took the rest of the material and heaved it between my legs and into the commode, where it proceeded to sink.

I have been in the rest room for nearly 35 minutes now while a steady stream of tourists have filed by to look at me, a nearly blind person with a cut on her head, hanging limp over the sink while the hand blower is trained on her backside.

I've been thinking, Mother. In the time it took me to come to the ladies' room, Detroit has turned out 1,372 cars . . . and they think that's a big production!

Coat Hangers—September 18, 1984

With sexual promiscuity running rampant, I could not believe a letter I received from a woman this week who said she could not get her coat hangers to reproduce.

"I know how much success you've had and wondered how you did it," she said. "I've tried everything from hanging Burt Reynolds on the wall to spraying sexy perfume to hanging a nightie from Frederick's of Hollywood on a hanger. Nothing. Since you are obviously a sex therapist for inanimate objects, maybe you can tell me your secret. The future of my closet hangs on your answer."

Good grief! Didn't your mother tell you anything?

Sexually active coat hangers are at their peak when they are in a small closet. The smaller the closet, the better. We once lived in an apartment with a closet so small it couldn't support a rod . . . just two nails. Within a week (the shortest gestation in the history of coat hangers) we had 37 of those little suckers.

Don't look for fertility among satin-covered hangers or sturdy metal skirt hangers with the clamps. The rich hangers that can afford to produce never do. It's the lower economic hangers (like the wire ones that bend over double when you put a silk blouse on them) that are bearing.

The ones that do best in my closet are the ones with no visible means of support, the ones with the top made out of piano wire and the bottom of rolled-up cardboard. I call them one-night stands. They're totally useless, but who has the heart to throw them out?

Hangers left in cars do well, especially the ones that take lodging under the brake pedal or hook over the seat belt and flap out the window.

You have to know that hangers in captivity never reproduce. You know, the ones that are welded to the rod in posh hotels. I don't know how it works, but I think they're neutered when they affix them so you can slide them out of the groove, put your jacket on them and fit them back into the slot.

Some people have tried to trick hangers into reproducing by installing hooks and putting as many as 26 garments on the doorknob. Most coat hangers are too smart for that.

If you're looking for a hanger orgy, just open your closet and announce, "I'm moving next week." You'll get a population explosion you won't believe.

I've told you all I know. The rest you'll have to get from the gutter.

No Luck with Pantyhose—November 10, 1985

Every time there is an unpleasant act of personal violation committed upon innocent people in this country, six groups rush forward to shoulder blame for it. Yet every day across this nation, women pull on pantyhose fresh from the package, and before they can say "Give me something for the pain," a run races from crotch to toe.

Not only does no one come forward to take responsibility, no one cares. And what do women do? Like a bunch of wimps, we cut our losses.

I have a drawerful of pantyhose with runs that stop at the knee. I wear these with slacks. In another stack are pairs missing an entire foot. These I wear with boots. In yet another mound are the ones that look like lace curtains. I wear these when I'm around the relatives who said I'd never amount to anything anyway.

For more than 20 years, the nylon stocking industry has been answerable to no one. You buy a car that does not run, you take it back. You buy a bathing suit that fades, you return it. You buy a chicken you can't eat, you get your money back.

All you have to do is to look at that shriveled piece of nylon (with a waistband so small you'd have to force it around a doorknob) to know it has not been tested. I've seen car doors tested for endurance and waistbands of men's underwear that are pulled and tugged to make sure they perform in the marketplace. Where is the guarantee that I will get even one wearing out of a pair of pantyhose?

Since I work in my home, I go to the office in bare legs every day, but when I travel I take six or seven pairs in the original packages. On the last trip, I lost four in the first week. I get better odds at a nickel machine in Las Vegas.

As nearly as I can figure, pantyhose fall under acts-of-God provisions that apply when no one can control the outcome, so no one pays. But the only way I can buy that rationale is if my pantyhose drowned during a flood or I left them on the clothesline during a tornado.

I have never had much luck with socks or hose. For 30 years I battled the case of the missing socks in the washer and dryer, which necessitated my kids wearing a fake cast on one leg and spurred my attempt to launch a New York Sock Exchange, where women from all over the world would send their single socks for a match.

I don't know what the answer is. I buy the industrial strength wide load size for a woman 6-foot-10 or over. I wash them by hand and try not to climb stairs or sit when I am wearing them.

The other day I put on a new pair of tights for aerobics. They cost $6. A large hole erupted at my knee. I am going to wear them until someone steps forward and takes responsibility for the deed. I am not vindictive, but if they are caught, they will be punished. They will be forced to walk in my pantyhose for an entire week.

Crockpot Sock—March 20, 1990

For as long as there have been washers and dryers, women have been plagued by the Bermuda Sock Triangle. For every pair of socks put into the laundry, only one is returned.

In the sixties, I got a grant from the Mental Health Association to find out where all these socks were going. I talked with mothers who put casts on their children's legs, bought black stockings for everyone in the house—and to one woman who told her husband she was conducting a test to see if his "green" leg was less tired than his "navy" one at the end of the day.

We bounced around a lot of theories. Some thought socks were victims of a great cosmic force that demanded one be sacrificed like a virgin maiden. Others thought lost socks were reincarnated and appeared in your dryer as bras and panties you had never seen before. The defection theory was suggested for "socks who wanted to get out of the pressure of living in Boston."

They were just speculations. The only person who had a reasonable solution was a man who bought two dozen pairs of new socks each year, tore them apart and threw out one sock from each pair to save his wife the trouble of losing them.

Me? I just caved in and told my kids the other sock went to live with Jesus. They seemed to accept that.

The other day, I received a package from a woman in Plymouth, Maryland. "I know you have given up on the missing socks," she wrote, "but I just thought you'd be interested to know where one of ours went—one that had been missing a month or two.

"On Christmas Eve, I was preparing clam chowder in my Crockpot for company dinner. There was a strange odor in my kitchen all afternoon—not at all Christmasy, like evergreen or bayberry candles, but rather putrid. I knew I wasn't the world's best cook, but I wasn't that bad, either.

"When it was time to serve dinner, we found a sock half melted between the pot and the crockery. I thought of you that evening and wanted you to have it."

A charred-black, brittle piece of fabric fell out of the package. I didn't want to look at it. I promised myself 15 years ago that if I didn't stop writing about missing socks, I would end up on the pages of the *National Enquirer* next to a spaceship that gave birth. But I couldn't resist. I held the burnt sock up to a light and . . . here's the scary part . . . I have the mate to it.

I don't want to talk about this anymore.

The Restless Car—October 1, 1995

When you suggest to someone that your automobile reparks itself when you're in the supermarket, he looks at you as though you've just told Phil Donahue an alien from a UFO impregnated you with twins.

But it happens. The part about the restless car, that is.

The first 20 minutes when I wander hopelessly up and down three lanes with a carry-out boy who is maturing before my eyes, I want to turn to him and announce, Someone stole my car.

But I've done that before, and you get a reputation. (When I said that, and after we finally stumbled onto it, the carry-out boy snorted, "So this is the car you thought someone wanted to steal?")

There was a time when I thought I was the only one who parked my car in a spot, made note of where I left it and proceeded to shop. But I was wrong.

Shoppers who try to find their lost cars all have a way of dealing with it.

The mumblers are the ones pushing their own carts and carrying on a conversation with themselves. "It has to be here. I remember I was going against the one-way arrow and had to take up two spaces, and the sun was coming in my windshield, so I had to be facing east."

The fakers are the people who pretend they know where their car is. They walk in and out of the rows, confidently pushing their carts to the end of each lane. They remain cool.

When they finally spot it in another lot, they whisper, "You little imp. Mother doesn't like it when you play games with her—especially when her ice cream is melting."

The climbers don't mess around. They shinny up the nearest pole or climb atop a van and scope the entire area. When they spot their car, they pursue on foot, only to find it has moved again.

No one has ever actually seen a driverless car finding a new spot in the parking lot. Well, I've never seen Elvis at Wal-Mart, but I know he's there.

One rainy afternoon in one of those spiral parking garages that has the lighting of a mortuary, a car drove past me in the darkness. You can say the driver was picking something up off the floor, but I say some poor woman who left her car on E Level, Green Concourse, in Slot 27 will go nuts trying to find it.

The Catchall Drawer

Talent—June 6, 1966

The sermon today is talent. It is dedicated to the woman who believes that when talent was passed out, she was on her knees scraping no-crumble cookies out of the carpet.

When I was five I thought talent was winning $3 for singing the "The Music Goes Round and Round." When I was 15, I was sure it was Dorothy Thompson covering a war. When I was 25, I knew it had to be anything that wasn't sticky and didn't smell like formula, and I didn't care so much what it was but what it wasn't.

I knew it wasn't setting three clean children out on the curb five days a week. It wasn't breaking out in a rash because you baked the best chocolate cupcakes on your block. And I hope there was more to it than being able to bring an African violet to full bloom.

Occasionally, when I was gagged by routine, had little outside stimulation and took an overdose of self-pity pills, I would suffer a self-confidence breakdown. I couldn't be like the optimist who was given a barnful of fertilizer for a present and ran happily through it, shouting, "I know there's a pony here somewhere!" No, I wanted a talent you could immortalize in cement.

It occurred to me I didn't know what to look for, so I began to isolate the talents I most admired in my friends. Oddly enough, they weren't the flashy, glamorous skills at all that are usually associated with talent.

I envied the talent to laugh and regroup your wits when the kids ate the bridge snacks. The self-confidence it takes to walk across a stage and not look back to see if your slip is hanging out. The talent to bear your neighbor's pain and problems when you're filled up to the eyeballs with your own.

The talent of charity when the rest of the room drops the ax on a woman's reputation and you have the courage to stand up to them alone. The talent of patience it takes to live each same, routine day and add a personal spark to it. The talent it takes to hope and put aside your own personal dreams of achieving until your commitments to everyone else have been fulfilled.

And the big one, the talent to recognize what you have going for you and to use it to its fullest.

Someone said talent is measured by the legacies you leave. How many of you will leave rare paintings, great books or moving symphonies? For that matter, how many of you will leave an organization that will proclaim in its minutes that you will be missed . . . a stranger whom you took under your wing at a PTA meeting who can't remember your name but who will never forget you . . . a small twig in the garden that you pointed skyward . . . a child who has known your love and will pass it on to generations to come?

Hey, you, scraping cookies out of the carpet. You were there when talent was passed out. He just had to bend down a bit to give it to you. Don't return it to Him unused.

Even Charity Has Its Bounds—January 2, 1967

A note in a church bulletin in Iowa reaffirmed what I have always known—even charity has its bounds.

It read: "Clothing collection for the needy people of the world. Bring them to school. The clothing must be usable. *Not wanted: handbags, girdles, high-heel shoes.* Give these to the Salvation Army."

I didn't check with the Salvation Army to see if they were so crazy for them either, but I did check with a missionary in a native village called Pwatanya to see what effect some of our western apparel has on primitive people.

"Actually," said the white-haired missionary, "handbags are quite sought after. The men prop them open with sticks and use them as traps for small animals. It's not uncommon to see the men with four or five handbags slung over their shoulders, looking much I suppose like your western women after they've emerged victorious from an end-of-the-month clearance.

"The high-heeled shoes were a curious item at first. The natives tried sticking them through their noses as ornaments. Then they figured out, by attaching them to long poles, they made very good spears.

"Finally (remember, we're quite primitive here), someone suggested putting them on the feet of those being punished for some crime and have them actually walk around the compound in them. Our crime rate has diminished drastically.

"As for the personal apparel, some of it is quite perplexing to receive. Not long ago, we received an item that was labeled a Living Bra. Not having any instructions, we tried feeding it a thick broth called Lumba, and Pongow, a sort of a bread meal, but the poor thing must have died en route. It's a pity.

"We never really found out what it was supposed to do. We gave it a Christian burial.

"As for girdles, we did have a few *Liberty* magazines that some church sent to keep us current, and there were ads in there showing these garments being worn about the middle. A few of our men tried them on, were immediately gouged and threw them off shouting, 'Evil spirits!'

"For months, the natives shunned them. Then one day a small child kicked at one and a stay flipped out and hit him in the eye. Natives are strange people. They rationalized it was punishing the child for disobeying its parent in going near it in the first place. The girdle received status. It was restored, propped up in a bamboo chair, garnished with palm leaves and today is head of the tribe."

Moral of the story: Be kind to your girdle. It may be someone's leader.

Time—November 17, 1971

Time.

It hangs heavy for the bored, eludes the busy, flies by for the young and runs out for the aged.

Time. We talk about it like it's a manufactured commodity that some can afford, others can't, some can reproduce, others waste.

We crave it. We curse it. We kill it. We abuse it.

Is it a friend? Or an enemy?

I suspect we know very little about it. To know it at all and its potential, perhaps we should view it through a child's eyes.

- "When I was young, Daddy was going to throw me up in the air and catch me and I would giggle until I couldn't giggle anymore, but he had to change the furnace filter, and there wasn't time."

- "When I was young, Mama was going to read me a story and I was going to turn the pages and pretend I could read, but she had to wax the bathroom, and there wasn't time."

- "When I was young, Daddy was going to come to school and watch me in a play. I was the fourth wise man (in case one of the three got sick), but he had an appointment to have his car tuned up and it took longer than he thought, and there wasn't time."

- "When I was young, Mama was going to listen to me read my essay on 'What I Want to Be When I Grow Up,' but she was in the middle of the Monday night movie and Gregory Peck was always one of her favorites, and there wasn't time."

- "When I was older, Dad and I were going fishing one weekend, just the two of us, and we were going to pitch a tent and fry fish with the heads on them like they do in the flashlight ads, but at the last minute he had to fertilize the grass, and there wasn't time."

- "When I was older, the whole family was always going to pose together for our Christmas card, but my brother had ball practice, my sister had her hair up, Dad was watching the Colts and Mom had to wax the bathroom, and there wasn't time."

- "When I grew up and left home to be married, I was going to sit down with Mom and Dad and tell them I loved them and I would miss them. But Hank (he was my best man and a real clown) was honking the horn in front of the house, so there wasn't time."

Women Are Financial Giants—February 19, 1980

Women have known for years that they are the financial giants of this country. They regulate the economy, control the purchasing power and establish guidelines for spending.

You want to know how we know it? Because someone told us.

If I seem underwhelmed about the distinction, it's because I just broke my own record for writing the smallest check ever recorded in the *Guinness Book of World Records*—seven cents. This marvel occurred at one of those self-service gas stations. In trying to force a leaded nozzle into an unleaded gas tank, I inadvertently spilled a little gasoline on my shoe.

Realizing my error, I quickly changed to the unleaded nozzle and got exactly what I had cash for—$6.32. When I went to pay the girl behind the glass she said, "You owe seven cents on pump No. 34."

I said, "I didn't put that gas in my car."

She looked up tiredly and asked, "What did you do with it?"

"I poured it on my foot."

"Why would you do that?"

"I meant to pour the unleaded."

"On your foot?"

"In the car."

"That'll be seven cents."

I whipped out my charge card.

"You want to charge seven cents?"

"Of course not," I snapped. "I also want to get a windshield wiper, a whoopee cushion for the front seat and a traffic-light dog that lights up for my rearview window when I hit the brakes."

"We only sell gas. Besides, we don't take credit cards. That'll be seven cents cash."

"I have tons of money at home," I said.

She looked at me, and I realized I was not exactly dressed for success. "Then I'll write you a check," I said.

Seconds later, I ripped it out of the checkbook and gave it to her (with two IDs), and she said, "Aren't you going to record it?"

My cheeks burned with humiliation as I jotted it down. I said, "Did you know that women control 85 percent of the nation's wealth and that if we ever quit buying this nation would come to its knees by noon?"

She snapped her gum. "It must be lonely at the top."

Junk Drawers—January 17, 1984

The organized people of this world, all six of them, who insist that everything has a place are really out of it!

Everything does *not* have a place, which is precisely why catchall or junk drawers are born. They are as vital a part of the American scene as electricity or indoor plumbing.

They are like compost heaps: The older and the higher they are, the better and richer they become.

I entered marriage quite deprived. I not only did not have a button box, I did not even have the makings of a decent catchall drawer. Within six months, I had one of the finest in the neighborhood. The secret?

First, you start with a large drawer, usually in the kitchen, in which a bottle of glue or nail polish has spilled in the bottom. This is what makes the expired coupons and old rubber bands stick together, making a firm bed for the rest of the junk you are going to add.

Near the back should be the things you need the most: a hammer, screwdriver, ice scraper for removing snow from the car windows, chewing gum, new fuses, appliance warranties and emergency phone numbers.

I like to store hibachi sticks and a broken ruler so that every time the drawer is opened they catch, and you can't open the drawer anymore, nor can you close it.

Toward the front are the floating candlewicks, floral wire, a half deck of cards, a box of sparklers and a spool of chartreuse thread with a needle that draws blood every time you open the drawer.

Catchall drawers must be maintained. That means every time you go by one, you must open it and shove something in: an old cork, a knotted shoelace, a cat caller, a packet of airline almonds, an unidentified key or a death notice of someone you do not know. It all adds to the mystery.

Catchall drawers are not confined to the home. One of the best monuments to clutter I ever saw in my life was the middle desk drawer of a schoolteacher. When she finally got it opened, it was like an active volcano. Everything in it was restless and moved slowly and rhythmically. She threw in a used corn pad, slammed the drawer shut quickly and said, "You have to keep feeding it."

Mousetraps are overrated for getting people to beat a path to your door. If you have a good catchall drawer, you can write your own ticket.

Box Savers—December 20, 1984

This is the time of year when the box savers of the world have their finest hour.

You know who they are. They're the ones who squirrel away every box and carton they ever receive and bestow the gift of immortality upon it.

There is something arrogant about people who save boxes. They remind me of the sanctimonious people who always have their ticket and the right change at the parking garage, or whose car is always in gear when the traffic light changes.

The carton queen in our family is my mother. There is nothing you can name that she does not have an empty box for. Want to wrap a piano? Go to Mother's. Want to surprise someone with a load of firewood? Mother has the carton for it. Buying a goalpost for your grandson? Mother can wrap it.

Box savers are not only arrogant about their habit, they are downright evangelistic. I remember the first time I gave my mother a pair of earrings wrapped in a rectal thermometer box. I thought she'd be choked up that I found a box with cotton. Instead, she gave me the God-knows-I-did-the-best-I-could look and said, "Why didn't you come to me for a box?"

I've watched her at birthday celebrations and Christmases. She is like a minesweeper. No sooner is the paper off the present than she is winding the ribbon around her fingers and smoothing the creases out of the wrapping paper. As soon as the recipient holds the gift up for everyone to see, the box disappears to be recycled. It will appear again for the next 35 years . . . somewhere . . . holding something.

This week when I discovered a jogging suit would not fit into a shoe box, I did something I do not take lightly. I went to Mother's for a box.

She flipped on the light in her closet, and I thought, If Tutankh-amen's mother had a tomb, this would have been it. I had never seen such a box glut. There were boxes in boxes, boxes for folding chairs, lampshades, tubes for posters and cartons for mattresses. There were boxes singed with black where she had pulled them from the fire.

She turned to me. "What are you putting in this box? Where are you sending it? How much did the item cost? Is there a chance you can get it back after it's used? How important is it to you?"

"I'm not adopting it, Mother, I'm only borrowing it."

"You're the one who makes fun of me every year for saving boxes, aren't you, missy?"

"That's true, Mother, but you know what a rotten person I am."

"You don't treat boxes nicely. I saw you jam an afghan in one one year, and it broke down the sides."

"Mother! I'm begging!"

She handed me a box off the shelf. "Tell me what time it is to be opened, and I'll be there."

I'm-Not-Going Syndrome—October 28, 1986

I'm at the age of my life where every time I buy something of any value, I have visions of my kids marking it down to $2 at a garage sale. I don't know if that kind of anxiety has a name or not, but for the sake of reference I'll call it the "I'm-Not-Going Syndrome."

Sometimes I wake up at night in a cold sweat just thinking that my cup and saucer collection will fall into the hands of someone furnishing a summer cabin who doesn't mind dishes that don't match. A friend who is older and wiser than I suggested I start early to find homes for all my treasures and not leave my legacies to chance.

I got out my 17-year-old mink stole the other day and came to a decision. I was going to spread joy while I was still alive to see the excitement on the face of my daughter when I gave it to her. When she came to dinner, I unzipped the plastic garment bag and said, "Do you know what this is?"

She put on her glasses and came in for a closer look. "Help me," she said.

"Christmas. Severely depressed. Family. Daddy. Surprise."

She shook her head excitedly. "Daddy killed this and we ate it for Christmas dinner."

"It was my first mink coat," I said. "And it's yours."

I placed it around her shoulders. She was speechless.

There are so many priceless bits of memorabilia in my possession, I hardly know where to begin. I want to be fair. There's a glass lid that belonged to a cast-iron skillet given to me by my grandmother. The skillet's lost, but the lid doesn't have a crack in it. No sense having some attorney rip it off. I offered it to the child who would take care of it. Each one humbly refused it. Those little monkeys always surprise you.

So far, I've dispersed a hand-blown glass sea urchin I bought at Disneyland, a coconut shell necklace from Hawaii and a book of Emerson's essays that looks real old, plus a piece of sheet music with a picture of Martha Raye before she had dentures, and Christmas ornaments that we had on our first tree.

Every time I part with my class ring or a clothespin painted like a pig that holds a recipe, a little of me dies with it. The other day when my son was visiting, I placed a box before him and smiled. "We only have our todays."

"Is this another living bequest?" he asked.

"This is the rug I hand-hooked for your nursery. Remember the little sailboat and the seagulls?"

"I remember," he said solemnly.

"Remember that it took your mother twelve years to finish it at an expense of $140 . . . $90 in yarn alone."

Last night I saw the rug in his apartment. It was lining the dog bed.

I tell you, I'm not going until all this is settled!

Fashion Trends Pioneer—October 11, 1987

We visited friends recently, and their kids marched in dutifully to say hello.

Their son was wearing a pair of faded jeans that looked like they had been rescued from a coral reef. His shirt was frayed, and there was a hole in the elbow. His small sister was wearing jeans so thin her knees showed through. They were stuffed in a pair of high-top gym shoes without laces. She topped it with a jacket three sizes too big and tattered at the cuffs. If it hadn't been for the two quartz watches on their arms, they could have passed for a couple of Waltons.

I whispered to my husband, "How can they afford to dress their kids like that? Ed doesn't make that kind of money. Those outfits must have set him back a couple of hundred dollars."

My husband looked at me with disbelief. "Our kids dress like that."

"Yes, but that is because you have a clever wife," I countered. "I don't follow trends. I create them. Who do you think invented acid-bleached and stone-washed jeans? *Moi*, that's who. Every major fashion breakthrough in the last twenty years started in my utility room.

"Take pastel shirts for men. I had no idea I was charting a new course in fashion history the day I put all of your shirts in the wash with a new set of red towels. No one expected to see a high school principal roam the halls in pink shirts week after week, but within a year, if you remember, manufacturers were bringing out shirts in shades of pink, blue and yellow, and you know the rest.

"Some trends surprise even me. Like the Monday morning our son got up late and we had been out late Sunday and I didn't have a chance to iron his shirt and the bus was honking the horn and he tore out of the house wearing the top to his ski pajamas. Well, the next thing you know the entire *Star Trek* crew on the *Enterprise* was wearing pajama tops, and the rest is history.

"I don't purposely set out to change the destiny of style. It just happens. I'll be honest with you. The day I inadvertently knocked over a bottle of bleach and it snaked across my best blouse, I never dreamt that I had invented tie-dye. And who would have believed that story of the pure silk blouse with the dry-clean-only label on it that I stupidly put into the washer? When it came out limp and wrinkled, I called it 'raw silk' and now everyone is buying it."

"I had no idea all those fashion trends were yours," my husband said, as he lifted his pant leg. "Are you telling me it's only a matter of time before everyone in the country will be wearing one black sock and one burgundy?"

"Trust me," I said. "Any day now Neiman and Marcus will both be wearing them."

Shoulder Pads—December 1, 1988

It's not as if I don't already have enough lumps on my body to keep track of. Now I've got shoulder pads.

Why did I think that after a couple of seasons they'd go away? Every time I bought a blouse or a dress, the first thing I did was rip out the shoulder pads. The minute I did that, I was punished. The shoulders dropped, making my chest look like I was backing out of a room. The sleeves covered my hands, and the hems dragged on the floor. I couldn't walk into a room where people didn't look at me and ask, "What happened?"

Shoulder pads were designed using the same principle as fun-house mirrors: Make the top of you look wide, and in contrast the bottom of you will look small. This is true, but I always feel as if I'm Scarlett O'Hara wearing the draperies with the rods still in them.

For some strange reason, I never throw the shoulder pads away. They're like those subscription cards that fall out of magazines. I save them and hate myself for not being able to throw them away. When my discarded pads spilled out of two drawers and threatened to take over my bedroom, I finally admitted to myself that they were here to stay.

Now I play a little game called the Shoulder Pad Chase (suitable for ages 15–79, one player at a time, batteries not included). You are standing around at a party making conversation when you feel your entire left shoulder slump forward. You cast your eyes downward to see a chest that gives new meaning to the phrase "peaks and valleys." You are a victim of a wandering shoulder pad. Your mission is to get it back on the shoulder where it belongs without attracting attention.

There are ways. There's the Fake Cough, where you throw your head forward, at the same time jerking your left shoulder back, hoping the pad will balance on your shoulder once again.

There's the Bumping into the Wall Ploy, where you pass by the corner of a wall to reposition the pad. A riskier way is Shock Reaction, where you grab your throat in horror at what is being said, and in a movement that is faster than the speed of light, slip your hand inside your dress and hike the shoulder pad back to its original position. When I see someone staring at my bulges, I usually say lamely, "I retain water."

All this is reminiscent of the old joke in which a woman used to store two nose tissues in her bra, and one night when she was fishing around and got caught, she said, "Funny, I had two of them when I came here."

Some people have it down to a science. As my husband watched a pro football game the other night, 22 men came out on the field in shoulder pads that would have thrown Donna Karan into shock. The pads never moved! I think they were implants.

Comfortable Shoes—September 14, 1989

Attention, Sisters of America! I want you to hear it from me first. I have just sold out. On my feet are a pair of running shoes that cost more than the monthly payment on our first house—and I don't even run. Nor do I intend to.

All the reasons I wore heels no longer exist for me. Forget the fat ankles. Forget about looking tall. Forget about trying to entwine one leg around the other like poison oak climbing a tree trunk just to look sexy. I'm going to be com . . . comfor . . . I can't say the word yet, but it will come.

I am like the kid at a college commencement I addressed last year who approached the platform on crutches. As soon as they gave him his degree, he threw the crutches into the air and shouted, "I can walk!"

I have left that majority of women who vow to wear uncomfortable shoes because they look good. The transformation takes a bit of getting used to.

My husband said the other day, "What's wrong with you?"

"Nothing," I said. "I'm not wearing heels, and I'm shorter."

"Shorter! You could walk under the coffee table. I thought short women were supposed to wear heels to make them look taller."

"Woody Allen wears sneakers, and no one worries about his height," I said.

"That's because men never play the game women play," he countered.

Unknowingly, he had put his finger on the problem. Men have always dressed com . . . comfor . . . it'll come. Think about it. Would a man wear anything with a zipper he couldn't reach? Of course not. Unlike women, they never get married because they can't dress themselves.

You don't see a man sitting around all night in pain because a label (made out of a double-edged razor blade) is digging into his neck every time he moves his head. Only women do that. Men have labels that are unflappable.

And more important, you don't see a man fishing around the floor of a theater with his feet to find his shoes so he can get them back on before the lights come up.

Yes sirree. You can snicker at my sneakers all you want, but I feel good about myself. I feel secure enough not to care about what other people think, but about how I feel. I'm not afraid to make fashion history.

Tomorrow is the test. I'm going outside in them.

Seize the Moment—June 25, 1991

I have a friend who lives by a three-word philosophy: Seize the moment. Just possibly, she may be the wisest woman on this planet. Too many people put off something that brings them joy just because they haven't thought about it, don't have it on their schedule, didn't know it was coming or are too rigid to depart from their routine.

I got to thinking one day about all those women on the *Titanic* who passed up dessert at dinner that fateful night in an effort to cut back. From then on, I've tried to be a little more flexible.

How many women out there will eat at home because their husband didn't suggest going out to dinner until *after* something had been thawed? Does the word "refrigeration" mean nothing to you?

How often have your kids dropped in to talk and sat in silence while you watched *Jeopardy!* on television?

I cannot count the times I called my sister and said, "How about going to lunch in a half hour?" She would gasp and stammer, "I can't." Check one: "I have clothes on the line." "My hair is dirty." "I wish I had known yesterday." "I had a late breakfast." "It looks like rain." And my personal favorite: "It's Monday."

She died a few years ago. We never did have lunch together.

Because Americans cram so much into their lives, we tend to schedule our headaches. We live on a sparse diet of promises we make to ourselves when all the conditions are perfect. We'll go back and visit the grandparents—when we get Stevie toilet-trained. We'll entertain—when we replace the living-room carpet. We'll go on a second honeymoon—when we get two more kids out of college.

Life has a way of accelerating as we get older. The days get shorter, and the list of promises to ourselves gets longer. One morning, we awaken, and all we have to show for our lives is a litany of "I'm going to," "I plan on" and "Someday, when things are settled down a bit."

When anyone calls my "seize the moment" friend, she is open to adventure and available for trips. She keeps an open mind on new ideas. Her enthusiasm for life is contagious. You talk with her for five minutes, and you're ready to trade your bad feet for a pair of Rollerblades and skip an elevator for a bungee cord.

My lips have not touched ice cream in 10 years. I love ice cream. It's just that I might as well apply it directly to my hips with a spatula and eliminate the digestive process.

The other day, I stopped the car and bought a triple-decker. If my car had hit an iceberg on the way home, I would have died happy.

Brain Capacity Is Limited—July 4, 1993

I don't pretend to know how the human mind works. My theory is that brain capacity is limited. You can store just so many phone listings, addresses, credit card numbers, names of former classmates, allergies and the date and year you bought the sofa, and you go on overload. You have to get rid of one statistic before you can add a new one.

Whenever anyone tries to tell me something, I weigh the odds. Is that something I will ever need to know again unless I am chosen to appear on *Jeopardy?* Can I use it to impress someone? Or in a week, will anyone care?

My husband seems to have a lot of useless information rattling around in his head, things that when he works them into a conversation cause people to stare at him like he's overmedicated. He files away every fact he reads in his brain.

I, on the other hand, never remember the ages of our children. They're always changing anyway. I don't clutter up my mind with recipes, the dates of my surgeries, the names of people who spell my name with an *I*.

There was a time when I stored the spelling of a lot of words. I've stopped doing that too. What's the point of knowing how to spell "inauguration" when you only use it every four years?

I never record the addresses of our kids in ink in the Rolodex, let alone commit them to memory. They move too often and I'd go crazy reprogramming my brain.

I don't need to know my ring size, license numbers, the words to the old school fight song or how much pressure I use in my tires.

It's not important for me to retain how many years Burt and Loni were married or the names of all the Jacksons/Osmonds/Seven Dwarfs.

The point is, you can't go around year after year stuffing information into your brain that you rarely use. That's why, from time to time, I clean house. I get rid of all those excess dates and phone numbers. I may get halfway through a book before I realize I've already read it or watch a TV show that I have seen before, but in the long run I actually save a lot of time.

When you get right down to it, there are only three things worth remembering: your Social Security number, the formula for your hair dye and how many hours you were in labor with your children.

Let's Face It, Not All Ruts Need Repair—April 17, 1996
(The last column Erma wrote)

Well, Betty Crocker has had her eighth face-lift, and I'm sitting here looking like a car backed over my face.

I'm not alone. There's an army of women like me who talk about cosmetic surgery, but our philosophy prevails: No guts to live with the ruts.

They shouldn't call it "elective surgery." That makes it too easy for women to get out of it. If they labeled it "Body 911," they would put another spin on it.

Frankly, I didn't think Betty was all that shallow. She's not a model on a runway for crying out loud. She's selling cake mix.

Did Uncle Ben hit 45 and go out and buy a rug? Did Colonel Sanders lose the glasses and get contacts? Did Ben Franklin feel the need for an earring in his ear?

Someone observed Betty looks like a working woman. Is that redundant or what! Besides, what does a working woman look like? Can you tell she's wearing damp pantyhose just by looking?

I can look on my shelves and figure out how old my pancake flour is by the shape of Aunt Jemima's face. She gets younger every year.

Why is there a need for these mythical characters to have cosmetic surgery? It's like putting Mickey Mouse through puberty when he doesn't have to.

It's bad enough when real people keep going back for repairs.

When *The Thorn Birds* miniseries first aired on television, Richard Chamberlain was believable as a young, handsome priest, although his face was as smooth as a baby's behind. Several years later in *Thorn Birds II*, his skin was as glassy as a frozen pond at midnight. If repairs continue, by *Thorn Birds III* he will not be able to frown, laugh, cry or make the sign of the cross without pulling something.

Realistically, everyone grows old, but some characters don't have to mess with the aging process. Miss Piggy doesn't need a nose job. Barbie doesn't need liposuction.

I belong to the Mother Teresa school of skin care. So I didn't moisturize enough. My deeds will be measured not by my youthful appearance, but by the concern lines on my forehead, the laugh lines around my mouth and the chins from seeing what can be done for those smaller than me or who have fallen.

As for Betty Crocker, she is fooling no one with that collarless blouse and youthful smile. She's pushing 106!

Tributes

Sister Agnes Immaculata S.N.D.N., from a letter to the family

I wish to assure you of my deep and prayerful sympathy in the loss you have sustained in the death of your beloved wife and mother, Erma. Now in my 99th year, as I look back over the years, I consider it a priceless privilege to have known Erma personally. As Dean of Women at the University of Dayton, I was associated with Erma for some years during the 1940s.

How the angels must have smiled as she entered Paradise!

I assure you of my continuing prayers for you and your family. May God's special blessings be yours always.

Norma Born, from her tribute at the memorial service

This is a pretty intimidating assemblage for someone who is terrified of public speaking, but I have to try to do this—for Erma and for myself.

The author of this poem is unknown and can't sue me for copyright infringement—I hope—so I've taken the liberty of changing the original gender. It's titled "The Measure of a Woman."

Not—"How did she die?" But—"How did she live?"
Not—"What did she gain? But —"What did she give?"
These are the units to measure the worth
Of a woman as a woman, regardless of birth.
Not—"What was her station?" But—"Had she a heart?"
And—"How did she play her God-given part?"
Was she ever ready with a word of good cheer,
To bring back a smile, to banish a tear?
Not—"What was her shrine?" Nor—"What was her creed?"
But—"Had she befriended those really in need?"
Not—"What was her way?"
But—"How many were sorry when she passed away?"
For she left a good name that will remain always.

Art Buchwald, The Washington Post, *April 23, 1996*

I lost a dear friend yesterday. Her name was Erma Bombeck. And over the years she made people laugh and think through her columns and books and on television.

She died because of complications from a kidney transplant that somehow failed. But possibly the real reason was that Erma waited a very, very long time for a kidney. She refused to "jump the line" to get one before her turn. That tells you most of what you need to know about her.

Erma was such a wonderful friend and her humor transcended what she did for a living. When we got on the phone we made fun of everything. Erma hated phonies of all kinds, and you could tell this from her writing. She knew that 95 percent of the awards she received were because the organization wanted a free speaker. She loved the people who loved her column and had no use for editors who cut it to squeeze in a snow shovel ad.

One of my favorite stories about Erma was when she was invited to a dinner at Dinah Shore's house and Dinah sat her next to Cary Grant. Cary knew Erma's column and Erma was walking on air. On the way back to the hotel I accused Erma of putting her room key under Cary's plate. Instead of denying it, she answered mischievously, "So what?"

We corresponded regularly over the years through an organization called "The American Academy of Humor Columnists." It was pure invention and lacked any hint of legitimacy beyond the name. Several of us, including Russell Baker, Calvin Trillin, Art Hoppe and Andy Rooney, felt that since every profession has an academy, we should have one as well. We never had a meeting, but the mail among members—who came to include Dave Barry and Mark Russell—was enormous. And all of it non-PC and irreverent.

We told Erma she was the only woman being considered for membership, but before accepting her we asked her to write a letter outlining the contribution she could make. She replied that she was the best coffee maker in the world and would be great at cleaning up after the meeting. As a woman, she promised she would never speak if a male member of the academy wished to speak first, and while she made more money than the rest of us, she offered to dress down whenever we got together.

When a friend passes away, there are certain things you remember vividly. The thing I remember most about Erma is her laugh—it had a wonderful, joyful ring. She loved to laugh, and laugh a lot. Even when she didn't think something was funny, she *pretended*, just so you wouldn't feel so bad.

Erma's gift to the country was a gift of humor. Her columns invited people in. The only person she ever made fun of was herself. She met readers where they live—their tract houses, their car pools, their kids' band concerts and PTA meetings. Her columns struck a chord. I bet they were clipped from the paper and stuck to more refrigerator doors than those of any other columnist in history.

Toward the end, she even found humor in illness, laughing, I imagine, even when she didn't really think it was funny.

No other person could do it in quite the way she did.

I am also certain she would not appreciate an appreciation. She would prefer we all send money to the Kidney Foundation. She and I talked about how we wanted to be remembered by the media after we were gone. Erma said, "Why can't my work stand by itself?"

It will, Erma. It will.

The Most Reverend Thomas J. O'Brien, Bishop of Phoenix,
Celebrant at the Funeral Mass, April 29, 1996

If there was ever a person who I would like to have return from the dead, I suppose it would be Erma. God knows what she would write about—and I don't know if God would be happy with that either.

Marla Adelman, from a letter to the family

I admired Erma for her ability to tune in on all aspects of life so acutely and communicate her thoughts and feelings so well, with such a profound impact on so many people's lives. She had an uncanny ability to make such great laughter. She made me feel so much less alone. She inspired people to have greater strength, endurance, awareness, sensitivity and, most importantly, a sense of humanity which I find missing in so many people today. She inspired determination to pursue what you truly believe in and perseverance in spite of all life's obstacles.

We must all keep in mind that when a loved one has passed away, they will return in our dreams to comfort us, and wonderful memories of Erma will live on in our minds for sure, especially as we read and reread all her great works and well put words. Erma's talent, intelligence, and wit can be matched by no one. Now, we'll all have to work a little harder to poke fun at ourselves and look for the humor in life to keep us going during difficult times, perhaps trying to imagine what Erma would have said about things. I intend to catch up on reading every one of Erma's books. I hope I can look forward to perhaps seeing all her columns published into volumes of books some day, and maybe seeing a movie or documentary of her life story.

Robert A. Kelly, from a letter to the family

I am only one of the many readers that loved Erma and were touched by her columns. I wish I knew her better because she was one of God's better creations.

Erma wrote a column many many years ago that had to do with God giving a mother a handicapped child. As it happens, our daughter recovered from a cerebral hemorrhage in 1977, and it left her with mental and physical handicaps. Whenever I reread that column, I get tears in my eyes and a big lump in my throat because it was so touching.

There will never be another Erma Bombeck, nor will there be another Michelangelo or a Rembrandt. I would be joyful just to know that I had shared the life of someone like that. God has blessed you greatly.

By Liz Carpenter, Austin American-Statesman, *April 23, 1996*

Erma Bombeck's laughter will always ring out for me from a hundred places where we traveled together for more than five years fighting to get the Equal Rights Amendment passed. We lost (for now) but what a great trouper she was for the cause.

She would recite the proposed amendment to the U.S. Constitution—"Equality of rights under the law should not be denied or abridged on account of sex"—and then add with a grin, "Look, ladies, those 16 little words simply mean one size fits all."

We traveled every weekend to one or several of the 16 states yet to ratify the amendment and called on governors and legislators. We went by bus, motor home, plane and, occasionally, by foot and on bended knees. Once in Florida as we boarded a "see through" helicopter, Erma leaned over and whispered, "I wish we'd worn better underwear."

In Little Rock, Arkansas, after a long day of speeches, we headed by car through a rainstorm to a late dinner. As we searched for the designated landmark—a red mailbox—I rolled the window down and stuck my head into the driving rain. "Watch those two-dollar permanents," Erma yelled. "They frizz."

Around the fire at our host's home, I asked the group assembled, "Why do we do this? After all, Erma, you could be playing tennis in Scottsdale."

She replied, "Because when my children ask me, 'What did you do in the war for the equality of women, Mom?' I don't want to have to say, 'I gave at the office.'"

What an asset she was. Women poured out to see her and cheer her—white-collar and blue-collar women who knew her through her columns because she shared the problems of dishwashers and clothes dryers. When we found ourselves short of money, she was there to auction off anything in sight—including her husband's socks and boxers.

Erma and I became such allies that our friendship took us on a Greek vacation. At a restaurant, I'll never forget the look on her face when the waiter brought her a stack of dishes to toss and break in the custom of the country. With each shattering sound, Erma cast eyes to heaven and exclaimed, "God forgive me."

Erma was a practicing friend. I had written a piece for *Texas Monthly* called "The Silver Lining" which I sent to her. She called to say, "That's a book, Liz. I'm calling my agent, Aaron Priest." In two days he was in Austin demanding an outline, and in another month he had auctioned the book for the most money I ever made at one time.

The last time I saw her, she had invited me to Phoenix to speak at a luncheon to raise money for her favorite cause, the Arizona Kidney Foundation. She came to the event despite her growing health problems. When she walked in with her mother, her husband and family, the room of more than 1,000 people stood and cheered.

The last few years, Erma has kept laughing and writing despite a run of bad luck: a mastectomy that prevented her from getting a kidney several years ago, a fall on her shoulder recently, and the long wait for the phone call telling her that a kidney was available. For someone who gave so much laughter, it doesn't seem fair that so many bad things could happen to a person so kind and good.

Erma was with me a few days after I became a substitute mother at 70. She looked at me in astonishment and said, "Liz, don't you know teenagers are hazardous to your health? If it is adventure you want, why don't you go to Mt. Rushmore, attach a bungee cord to Lincoln's wart and jump."

That's the way she faced whatever life handed her, and I suspect, knowing her deep faith in God, she is at peace with this Last Great Adventure.

Farewell, my friend.

The Catholic Sun, *editorial, May 2, 1996*

Erma Bombeck made people laugh. Never in a mean-spirited way. Never resorting to crudeness or profanity. She had us laugh by allowing us to look at the lighter side of everyday life and seeing it's not as bad as we thought it was. . . .

That's the public side of Erma, the side printed in hundreds of newspapers across the country. We all got to know Erma Bombeck through her columns and books.

On the more private side, when she was struck by kidney illness five years ago, Erma got on the waiting list for a kidney, and, just like everyone else, she waited. At first she kept her illness private, but when the news leaked out, she became a public advocate for the cause of all those seriously ill. Even in her difficult times, she helped others and cheered them on.

While conventional wisdom these days says that celebrities like Larry Hagman or Mickey Mantle get pushed to the top of the list,

Erma's case proved what organ donor organizations have been saying all along: the system is fair; there is no favoritism.

Erma's turn came, finally, just a few weeks ago, but it was not soon enough. There is, tragically, a nationwide shortage of organs to be donated. For many people like Erma Bombeck, the body can't keep fighting long enough to wait for an organ to become available because not enough people have signed up to donate their organs upon their death. A critical shortage of organs exists, according to the executive director of the United Network for Organ Sharing. Approximately 45,000 people are waiting for organ transplants. More than 3,400 died last year while waiting for a suitable organ. But you can help change that.

If something Erma wrote ever made you laugh, or cry, or think, you can repay her in some small way for the way she touched your life. You can commit today to become an organ donor.

Erma Bombeck gave us the gift of laughter. We can give others the gift of life—so that they too can live and love and laugh. Sign up today.

By Kevin Cuneo, Erie (PA) Times, *April 25, 1996*

I suspect that Bombeck's column, *At Wit's End,* which has appeared in our newspaper since the late 1960s, was an acquired taste for some men. It was for me. Her stories about family life, including toddler mishaps, surly teenagers and adventures at the supermarket, seemed stupendously mundane to a know-it-all kid fresh out of college.

Fortunately, an assignment in the spring of 1977, I think it was, to cover a local appearance by Bombeck helped open my eyes. She turned out to be a person of great warmth, insight and humor.

It took about thirty seconds for Bombeck to size me up. "Let me guess," she said. "Rather than covering my visit tonight, you'd rather be out exposing crooked politicians and all the vast corruption in Erie." She said this with a smile. Was it that obvious? . . .

Newspaper columns, however insightful or enjoyable, are but

temporary delights. As much as you like the best of columnists, their prose is disposable. And once the writer is gone, their work is generally forgotten as well.

Sad as it seems, that may eventually be Erma Bombeck's fate. Except, that is, for one column she wrote for Mother's Day a few years ago. It's entitled *No More Oatmeal Cookie Kisses,* and it cuts right to the heart of every mother who's ever dreamed of the day when the kids are finally all grown up and out of the house. My wife gets about halfway through the column every time before the tears start welling up and the sobbing begins. I, on the other hand, never read it because a grown man should not be seen crying in public.

I told you this woman could write.

Betty Cohen, from a letter to the family

Erma Bombeck will be sorely missed by legions of people and for many reasons.

My special reason is that when she wrote *I Want to Grow Hair, I Want to Go to Boise* and subsequently appeared on the *Phil Donahue Show* with children who had survived cancer, my grandson, Aaron Alvidrez, was among those children, the only boy in the group. He thinks Erma was the absolute "greatest"—and she was.

I can't write any words that will make you feel better but you can take solace in the fact that God has another lovely angel in heaven and she will make all of them laugh.

Lynn Colwell, from a letter to the family

I don't know whether you remember meeting me. I'm the person who wrote the book for young people about Erma.

Erma made a stronger impression on me than anyone I've ever met outside of my family and several lifelong friends. She was everything I aspired to be.

Erma not only made me laugh, she gave me guidance and support. The few hours I spent with her changed my life in terms of how I thought about myself. There are two things that I found extraordinary about her. First, that with all her success, she didn't seem to have one iota of ego and second, that writing was work for her, just as it is for me.

Phil Donahue, from his tribute at the memorial service

In 1961 in Centerville, Ohio, on Cushwa Drive, I lived diagonally across the street from the Bombecks. We were all thirtysomething and were making about $15,000 a year, and after you paid the pediatrician you still had a little walking-around money. We all had stairstep kids, and most of us were Catholic. And the most fun that was to be had on Cushwa Drive in Centerville—where, incidentally, there are some places where the grass is greener than at other places—the most fun you could have was at the Bombecks. Erma would not let you fail. No matter what the joke may have been, she was the most generous audience—then and now and forever.

She was working for the *Kettering-Oakwood Times*—if you can call an occasional column working. We would entertain each other in our homes. We all had the same house. It was a plat house— $15,500—three bedrooms, two bathrooms and the fireplace was $700 extra.

Everybody had Early American decor. I had an American eagle from Sears over the fireplace—not brass, black (they were cheaper). The Bombecks had beams in the ceiling. I mean real wood Early American beams, perfectly mitered. You kept looking for Martha Washington. Bill Bombeck made those beams all by himself. I envied those beams so much. It explains why my relationship with Bill throughout my adult life has been so difficult.

The spirit of those times has lived in the work of Erma Bombeck ever since 1961, and that is a remarkable thing when you realize what's happened to us since then. We were everything our parents prayed that we would be, our parents sacrificed for us, and by 1961 we had achieved more than they had ever dreamed. We were making more money than they had ever made. And then somebody killed our president and we lost a war and the Japanese took over automotive engineering and a president resigned in disgrace and we looked up to discover that we were prepared for a world that never materialized. But while cities were burning and all this was happening to us, there was one constant in our culture and it was Erma Bombeck. Her spirit never flagged. Her humor never waned. Her light shone out from millions of refrigerator doors, just one of the many venues Erma found herself in, and allowed her work to reach the hearts of countless readers around the world.

She became a historic figure of publishing and newspapering. It is not so much that she was the best; she was the *only*. There is no other time when the phrase is more appropriate to say than now: We shall never see her likes again. We shall never know again her brilliance, her insight, and especially her generosity. She is the modern Catholic woman. She is the married-once, faithful wife, who got more fun out of writing about infidelity than would be approved by the early Church, and she was without pretense. She was real and she brought us all down to earth—gently, generously, and with brilliant humor. She is a twentieth-century political figure, and when the scholars gather hundreds of years from now to learn about us, they can't know it all if they don't read Erma.

For all these reasons, I feel so blessed to have known this woman who made me a better person—not an easy task. I am so, so, grateful to her. I join you in mourning her passing, but she will live. She will live forever.

By Pat Murphy, Tribune Newspapers (Arizona), *April 24, 1996*

Erma Bombeck made us love her because of her willingness to poke fun at herself, to expose her personal sense of insecurity. . . . But there was more to Erma Bombeck and her infectious wit, something deeper about her character that makes her unforgettable. . . .

Erma Bombeck was a model of charity. She endorsed and supported every good cause, speaking in behalf of it, sharing her resources.

Erma Bombeck was a model of humility. She was a Phoenix homemaker shopping in our neighborhood supermarkets, never dressing or acting with pretense, pausing to laugh with an admiring stranger in the canned vegetable aisle, never ducking a fan wanting to shake her hand, always finding time to dash off a handwritten note.

Erma Bombeck was a model of family. She was the adoring mother of successful children, proud wife of an educator, loving daughter of a mother who inspired her.

And finally, Erma Bombeck was a model of the American dream. She was an Ohio homemaker who rose out of utter obscurity to the pinnacles of fame and fortune, without ever losing respect for her humble roots.

The finest tribute to Erma Bombeck is that millions "knew" her almost as a next-door neighbor or favorite aunt, but had only met her through her columns and books.

Ellen Goodman, The Boston Globe, *April 25, 1996*

It was 1970, and I was a twenty-something reporter in a rented car looking for a hill in Bellbrook, Ohio. My editor had sent me out to interview Erma Bombeck, this housewife-humorist, this anti-Heloise, this funny lady of the home pages.

The forty-something Bombeck had given me these directions: "You head for Ohio and turn left. You take another left at the traffic light. You go down the road until you come to mailbox 3875, only the 7 is missing. Then go to the top of the hill."

A New Englander looking for a hill in Ohio, I passed the RFD mailbox three times before I figured it out and turned up the five-degree incline to the rambling white farmhouse. There at the top—the top?—was a pond with large ducks and two dogs named Kate and Harry.

These were the first words that Erma Bombeck said to me: "Come in, come in. Harry, you stay out there, you've got bad breath. Please don't look at the mess, they're tearing apart the kitchen and there's this brown dust that settles every day all over the house. You must be hungry, but the hamburger is absolutely refusing to defrost. Take your coat off."

It was vintage Erma Bombeck, the same in person and in print. She was the mistress of controlled chaos, the head of the house of absurdity. She was a warm and generous woman whose body gave out so much sooner than her spirit.

On that distant March day, over bologna sandwiches and Bugles, over coffee from a percolator that sounded like John Henry's sledgehammer, she talked about mothering and loneliness, about deadline humor and deadly seriousness.

It was the height of the Vietnam War, and some reporter had asked how she was going to observe the day of protest. "I told them I had three weeks of laundry I was going to do." Now she worried. "Am I just sitting here writing a funny column while Rome burns?"

It was the beginning, too, of the women's movement and she said, "I had a member of the Women's Liberation Movement write to me and say, *Lady, you are the problem.*"

Erma Bombeck, the problem? I wonder now if that young feminist thought, after the revolution, that washing machines would stop eating socks as a gesture of solidarity? Or that husbands should stop watching football?

Erma Fiste, daughter of a teenage mother, was a reporter in the 1950s when newspaper women were few and far between. Later she would write that as a young mother at home in suburbia with three children, "I hid my dreams in the back of my mind—it was the only safe place in the house. From time to time I would get them out and play with them, not daring to reveal them to anyone else because they were fragile and might get broken."

She began to work again from home in 1964, just one year after Betty Friedan's book was criticized as the ranting of a neurotic and probably frigid woman. Bombeck's column was pegged, or dismissed, as "housewife humor." But it was, in its own way, wonderfully, deliciously subversive.

When she started, suburban housewives were still pictured vacuuming in high heels in immaculate homes with perfect children. Erma Bombeck cracked open the feminine mystique her own way: with a sidesplitting laugh.

Her crack was a thousand wisecracks. Over the years, she wrote the truth about domestic life in all its madness and frustration, its car pools and appliances. She wrote with the uncanny accuracy of a fellow traveler and a born reporter. She wrote to and about women who were, in the name of her column, "At Wit's End."

This mother never signed on to the infamous mommy wars that pitted women at home against those in the workplace. How could she? She had done it all, and so she wrote for us all.

In the late 1970s, she went on the road to sell the Equal Rights Amendment in tandem with the redoubtable Liz Carpenter. "We did the razorback hog call in Arkansas. We sang Baptist hymns in a mobile home cruising through Iowa," she reminisced, "and Liz auctioned off my husband's underwear in Phoenix."

Later, this woman turned her heart and pen to children with cancer. She also shared those parts of her life that were not a laugh riot: her experience with infertility, her miscarriage, her breast cancer, the last fatal deterioration of her kidneys.

And whenever "family values" returned with grim serious-ness, Erma Bombeck, wife of one, mother of three, was around to remind us about "Family, the Ties That Bind and Gag."

A lot of columnists write words to end up in the Congressional Record or on the president's desk or at the Pulitzer Committee's door. But Erma Bombeck went us all one better. Her words won her the permanent place of honor in American life: the refrigerator door. Now we are again at wit's end.

Helen Gurley Brown, Editor, Cosmopolitan, *from a letter to the family*

. . . . She interested me in one way because of being such a cele-brated and successful journalist, the best there ever was and she had lots of dealings with other famous journalists. Art Buchwald, etc. At the same time she was wife, mother, human creature who never took it all very big. She took it *seriously* but never big. . . .

Pat McMahon, talk show host, KTAR-radio, Phoenix;
from his tribute at the memorial service.

I've been very fortunate that I've had very few regrets in my life, but I remember when I was a kid I would think with a certain amount of anxiety that it would have been nice to be able to sit by the Mississippi with Mark Twain. I later thought, wow, what it would have been like to be back during Will Rogers's time and to be able to appreciate that level of humor! And then Erma became my friend, and I didn't think about that so much anymore.

Tom Cecil, Dayton, from his book, I Want My Turn in the Shower

Bombeck fans are somewhat addicted and maybe even a little fanatical. Loving Erma is somewhat like admiring motherhood, the American flag and apple pie. We let our hero go with great reluctance.

But her legacy of humor will live on and be enjoyed by readers not yet born. Her style of writing will be taught in journalism and writing classes in colleges across the country. And we, her fans, will read and reread her books and columns, and they'll delight us as much as when they were first published.

This, indeed, is the end of an era. We'll miss you, Erma.

Marilyn Potts, from a letter to the family

I *have* lost one of my best friends!

I've never cried over the deaths of any celebrity in my 71 years (with the exception of JFK).

But I *am* crying tonight.

I have laughed until I cried over hundreds of her columns—they have been about *me*, my husband and my children! The first time I ever read her—it was about her husband's idea of a great night out, going to the grand opening of a K-Mart. I think I almost died laughing, and so did my husband—he recognized himself!

One column she wrote—I didn't laugh. I cried my eyes out. It was about the mothers of handicapped children, whom she felt were God's saints on earth. Well, I'm no saint, but I wrote her about this subject, as I had two, who have both since died. She answered my letter and said if I didn't mind, she would include parts of my letter in a follow-up column, and she did! I still have that letter and the two columns tucked away among my mementos.

What a wonderful mind. I stand in awe of the joy and laughter she has brought into so many lives—especially mine!

Aaron Priest, Erma's agent, from his tribute at the memorial service

Over the years I watched Erma. I watched Erma with number-one bestsellers. I watched Erma with literally crowds of people. I watched the adoration in people's faces. And I noticed certain things. Erma didn't change. People used to say to me, "Is Erma really as nice as she appears in her books, on television?" And I said, "Well, actually she's nicer."

Erma is the only person I have ever met who literally you couldn't buy. If Erma didn't want to do something, there was not enough money in the world to make her do it. And Lord knows, enough times people wanted her.

They wanted her to endorse products. They wanted her to do this; they wanted her to do that. I remember telling someone one day, if you filled a room with gold bars it wouldn't make any difference.

On the other hand, there were things Erma wanted to do and money had nothing to do with them. Erma wanted to do something for children with cancer. And she went to the camps and she made these kids laugh and she wrote a book and with the proceeds of the book she started a foundation for research for children with cancer and it was set up in Atlanta with the American Cancer Society.

And during the last four or five years, when she had more than her share of adversity, she exhibited more courage than any person I have ever seen. I remember all of the things that I saw her do in the kitchen—and she whipped up some great meals over the years—six weeks ago we sat there and talked, and she said she wanted a lemon. A few weeks before that Erma had fallen and dislocated her shoulder. Her arm was in a sling and she couldn't raise it. I watched her take her hand out, put the knife in her hand, move back and forth against the counter. I knew enough not to offer to help. She turned to me, made a remark about cutting the lemon, and sat down to eat it.

By D.L. Stewart, Dayton Daily News, *April 23, 1996*

The phone keeps ringing.

Every few minutes there's another call from another news organization wanting to know about Erma Bombeck. A network looking for a few seconds of reaction to her death. A local TV station looking for a two-line insight about the life of a woman who brought smiles and wisdom to millions of readers for as long as most of us can remember.

"What kind of a person was she?" they keep asking.

How do you detail a person's life in a sound bite? How do you do justice to a woman who became America's mom? Will they understand if I tell them about American Airlines Flight 311 from Dayton to Dallas?

In February 1977, Erma Bombeck already was a celebrity. Syndicated in 601 newspapers. A best-selling author. Nationally known. I was in my second year as a local columnist. Barely known in Beavercreek.

We had met just once before, five months earlier, when I interviewed her for a profile about the hometown columnist who had made good. There was no reason to believe she would remember me when we happened to wind up on the same flight to Dallas. She did, though, and we boarded the plane together. But she was first class, while I was not.

"C'mon back and join me after we take off," I joked.

"Are you kidding?" She laughed. "I'm not going back there with the little people."

So I said good-bye and found my seat in coach and the plane took off. Eventually the captain turned off the seat belt sign. A few seconds later, Erma Bombeck gave up her first-class seat and slid into the coach seat next to me. We laughed all the way to Dallas.

Maybe that's not enough to sum up a person's life. But perhaps it is. . . .

Now the phones keep ringing and the news organizations are asking about the real Erma Bombeck, and I keep feeling that I should find something more significant to talk about than a flight from Dayton to Dallas. That maybe I should talk about the tragedy and the sorrow of her death. Or about how, when I get this column finished, I am going to walk out of this office and, sometime before this day is over, I am going to break down and cry over the loss of an inspiration and a friend. But I think Erma would have hated that. So, for now at least, I'll just hold onto the memory of American Airlines Flight 311. And about what it was like to fly with a first-class lady.

———————————

By Mary McCarty, Dayton Daily News, *April 25, 1996*

My mother raised a glass Monday night to her old college classmate, Erma Fiste: "May she find all those mismatched socks in heaven." It's easy to imagine similar toasts being made all over America, all over the world. But especially, all over Dayton. Never mind that she was one of the most famous Daytonians ever, one of the most well-known women in the world. She was one of us, and she steadfastly refused to be anything else.

Erma Bombeck was, for Daytonians, quite literally the mom next door. So many of us knew her, knew people who knew her, encountered her unflagging good cheer at a book signing or a public appearance. Everyone else *felt* as if they knew her.

My mother studied journalism with Erma at the University of Dayton; studied her ABCs with her husband, Bill, at St. Anthony Grade School. Even then, Erma was more than just another eager face in Lou Riepenhoff's journalism class. Erma's wit was already famous in her circle; her stories entertained the other girls in the women's lounge at UD.

I met her just once, at a book signing at the old Town and Country shopping center. I was a timid ninth-grader, determined to get my book signed in time for Mother's Day. At last it was my turn. I had never met a famous person before, and I was scared. "I think you know my mother," I stammered. "Vera Seiler."

She laughed heartily, exchanged knowing glances with another former classmate farther back in line. "Of course, we remember Vera!"

She signed Mom's book, *Vera, I met your daughter. You done good. But I think I expected greatness from you!* I puzzled over that inscription a bit. Did she mean literary greatness, or did she somehow divine my inherent mediocrity? Still, I was pleased with my first celebrity encounter. She was kind, like my mother. Old, like my mother. Not scary at all.

My mother never expressed one whit of jealousy over her old classmate's success. "I just always enjoyed her so much," she says. "She related to the American housewife. In every column, we could see ourselves."

There were days when only Erma could make my mother laugh. Days when she might have made good her threat to move to the funny farm were it not for Erma's redeeming humor. Her columns made light of a mother's frustrations and failures at the same time they elevated her role.

Over the years, my mother kept tabs on Erma through mutual friends. The refrain was always the same: She never changed. Success never changed her.

She was, in fact, continually surprised by her success, humbled when she read the work of other columnists. She often told her close friend Marianna Cochran of Beavercreek, "I was just in the right place at the right time."

When Cochran asked how she could continue to work when she was so sick, Erma simply said, "It's what I do."

Friends say she never tried to use her wealth or fame to hasten her kidney transplant. She didn't become one of those celebrities whose names mysteriously float to the head of the donor list. She waited her turn.

She was kind to stammering children, true blue to her early friends, gracious with even the most mutton-headed fans. Cochran recalls the book signings for *Motherhood: The Second-Oldest Profession.* "Believe it or not, people asked her, 'What was the oldest profession?'"

She found poetry in pantyhose, humor in mismatched socks, and friends all over the globe.

Doesn't it just figure she's from our hometown?

Father Tom Walsh, from a letter to the family

I saw Erma visiting the celestial library, checking out the religion section. There next to the Koran, the Bible, the Analects of Confucius, the Tao Te Ching of Lao-tzu, the Bhagavad Gita of Hinduism, there next to all those classics are all of Erma's books. . . . I will be waiting for her next book on the Internet, *Having a Helluva Good Time in Heaven.*

Betsy Bombeck, Erma's daughter

I have often been asked what it's like to have Erma Bombeck for a mother. I'd always tell people, "She is my mother—and we all know how mothers can be," Now the question is what it's like to live without her, although in many ways she surrounds me.

Many of my friends lived with her clippings on their refrigerators, and I'd joke that my refrigerator was the only Bombeck-free zone in America. But her pictures are in my home and office, pictures with that big smile and our family all around. You couldn't miss how she brightened up a room. I will miss her energy. That presence that drew you toward her, that emanated from her and out to everyone. It was in her eyes, her hands, her laugh, her touch. It was infectious.

Her presence was so much greater than the five-foot-two she stood. I loved to put my hand in her small hands, the hands that could make those typewriter keys fly. From my mom I learned to laugh at myself and give much to others. Live each day to its fullest, so that when you go to bed you know you've done it all.

She challenges me to carry on her spirit of dignity, grace, courage, humor, love for others and most especially for family and God. In that way she never really dies—she continues to live.

Andy Bombeck, from his remarks at the memorial service

One thing that my mom was so adamant about was not to take yourself too seriously. Now people are telling me, "You don't take *anything* seriously," so I have to find the happy medium.

But I can tell you one story. I'm a fourth grade teacher. Last year I was trying to teach the kids how to write, and I told them I have two writers in my family so maybe I know something about it. (I'm not sure I agree with that.) I said there is a process to writing, and my mom would back that up.

Now I don't know whether she used the writing process, but I went home and talked to my mom and said, "This is what you have to tell them. Go in there and tell them that you use the writing process even if you don't."

The morning she came to visit, I told my class, "Don't ask any embarrassing questions. Don't ask about me. Don't embarrass me and don't embarrass her." When she showed up, the first thing she said was, "What do you want to know about your teacher?" She didn't tell them anything about writing. It was all about my childhood and what I did in school. . . .

I feel so lucky about having the greatest mom and dad that anyone could ever have.

Matt Bombeck, from his remarks at the memorial service

What I loved and respected most about my mother was that she was a doer. She didn't contemplate, analyze, think about it; she just did it. There wasn't a room in the house she didn't want to paint, a trip she wasn't planning, an idea for a column she didn't have in her head. I was constantly amazed by her discipline and originality. You had to have respect for a writer who could get a column out of my answering machine.

My brother and sister and I were lucky. Both my mother and father gave us so much: stability, always a place to come home to. Whatever path we chose, that was OK. And if it turned out to be the wrong one, that was OK, too. They are my example. They are my anchor. And for that I am eternally grateful.

I will always hear my mother's voice. My mother's laugh will always be with us.

Erma Harris, Erma's mother

Since Erma loved to sing and dance, I would show her off every chance I got. Her feet were never still and her mouth never shut. I couldn't lay claim to fame at this time, but I thought to myself,

"Move over, Shirley Temple. My daughter is on her way to take your place."

When Erma was in the seventh or eighth grade, she started to write little jingles and poems. In 1939 she wrote one called, "We're in God's Country." It was in *Stars and Stripes*, a publication for the service boys of World War II.

In high school she wrote part-time for the *Dayton Herald*. She wrote obituaries and a column, "Operation Dust Rag." She told housewives how to clean house in fifteen minutes with a ten-minute coffee break. At this time I knew that Erma was going to be a writer. Our dream of another Shirley Temple was gone . . . or was that just my dream?

Although I'm the proudest mother in all the universe, I don't love my daughter for being famous. I'm proud of her for being the most generous, warm and caring person I know. She used her God-given talents to help others. Erma is the kind of daughter every mother would be proud to have.

What was my proudest moment? The day God gave me this priceless and special person . . . Erma Louise.

Dear Readers:

In 1989 Erma began to experience a series of painful medical problems, but she disdained letting her readers know most of the details. She usually brushed aside rumors and inquiries with a joke and a plea that her purpose was to write humor and make people smile. Health reports are not funny. Her greatest fear was to become a "poster child" and have people feel sorry for her.

Throughout these assaults she remained unbelievably optimistic. Erma always knew that there was a pony in there someplace. Not only did the research and writing of her book *I Want to Grow Hair, I Want to Grow Up, I Want to Go to Boise* provide a nation with the heroics of kids surviving cancer, but it also helped give Erma the courage to face her many trials, including her last one.

I have met astronauts, war heroes, firefighters and police officers, but I have never known anyone with more courage than Erma. Courage has been called grace under fire. I would propose we call it Erma under fire.

Erma would not have approved of my words. But for this one time I will do what Erma admonished all who challenged her words, and that was to "go out and get your own column."

I have searched for a way to show my family's gratitude to the thousands of fans and friends who have shown so much love and compassion toward her. I'd like to share with you a personal recollection I read at the family services that were held before the funeral.

Bill Bombeck

In 1947, three or four couples were outside the Lakeside Ballroom in Dayton, Ohio. We were too early to be admitted for the big-band dance, so we all wandered over to the adjoining amusement park.

Not far from the ballroom was the roller coaster. All of the boys began cajoling their dates to ride with them. The girls giggled and said no. It was too frightening, and it would mess up their hair and dresses.

I looked at my date and asked her if she wanted to go. She

didn't hesitate. She said, "Sure, I'll go." I was surprised and looked at her again. She was slight, narrow-shouldered, with tiny hands and feet. But she had the greatest smile and laugh. Her smile had a charming space between her two front teeth. I thought, this is some kind of girl!

The Lakeside roller coaster was a rickety old leftover from the Depression. The frame was mostly made of unpainted 2-by-4s. No modern inspection by OSHA would have ever approved this for man's use.

The cars were linked together with what looked like modified train couplers. They were mostly red-painted wood with metal wheels and a coglike device that clicked loudly. The seats had worn black leather padding. There were no belts, but there were worn steel bars that had to be raised and lowered by the attendant.

The attendant was an old man in oil-stained bib overalls. He said little, but raised the bar and she entered the seat first, and I followed by her side. The bar clicked in place just above our waistlines.

There were two tapered 2-by-4s on the platform, each angled away from the other. He moved the one closer to the car to an upright position. The car moved forward, slowly picking up speed. The metal wheels on the metal track made so much noise you had to yell to your partner to be heard.

The car left the level starting track and began a slow ascent. In about 20 or 30 seconds, when the track became steeper, the cog device engaged the car. You could feel it grab. Then there was a distinct rhythmic clacking sound as the cog device labored to overcome the near-perpendicular angle of the track. You felt like it wouldn't make it, but just when it reached a point that forced the passengers to stare, not at the car ahead or the track, but only at the night sky, it plunged downward, a wild, almost free, fall. Maybe whatever controlled the speed was now broken.

She made her first sound since she had said, "Sure, I'll go." She screamed and clenched my arm. I said, "Hang on to the bar." She kept hanging on to my arm. Suddenly we were at the bottom, and we both were so relieved that we laughed, and I saw that smile again.

The ride continued, with bone-jarring twists and turns, dizzy heights and abrupt plunges. Sometimes we would enter a dark tunnel, so dark the sparks from the wheels and tracks made it look like it was on fire.

She kept hanging on to my arm. I was gripping the metal bar so tightly I thought I would bend it. This was some ride. We were thrilled and exhilarated, scared and breathless.

We had been in and out of many tunnels. Each time they ended with almost blinding light in our eyes, and then on to another straight-up climb.

We started into a tunnel that seemed to plunge deeper than all the others. It kept dropping. We both sensed this one was really different. Finally, instead of the bright lights, we were back at the platform.

We looked at each other. We didn't speak, but we sensed the ride had changed. The man in the bib overalls was standing by the tapered 2-by-4s. He started to push one from its angle to a straight-up position. The car stopped. I told him the ride was great, but it was too short; we wanted to go on. He raised the bar. She smiled again. I looked at the attendant again. He said, "This is April 22, 1996—your ride is over." I looked over at her seat. She was gone.